Giving
to Movement

Giving Life to Movement

The Silvestre Dance Technique

TAMARA LaDONNA WILLIAMS
(IFÁKẸMI ṢÀNGÓBÁMKẸ MOṢEBỌLÁTÁN)

Foreword by Lela Aisha Jones

McFarland & Company, Inc., Publishers
Jefferson, North Carolina

This book has undergone peer review.

Frontispiece: Element Fire position in the mud
of Morro de São Paulo, Bahia, Brazil.

LIBRARY OF CONGRESS CATALOGUING-IN-PUBLICATION DATA

Names: Williams, Tamara LaDonna, 1984– author.
Title: Giving life to movement : the Silvestre dance technique / Tamara
LaDonna Williams ; foreword by Lela Aisha Jones.
Description: Jefferson, North Carolina : McFarland & Company, Inc.,
Publishers, 2021 | Includes bibliographical references and index.
Identifiers: LCCN 2020058695 | ISBN 9781476674322 (paperback : acid free paper) ∞
ISBN 9781476641379 (eBook)
Subjects: LCSH: Dance, Black—Brazil. | Silvestre, Rosangela. |
Dance—Study and teaching—Brazil. | Folk dancing—Brazil. |
Dance—Brazil. | Self-actualization (Psychology) | Ethnology. |
Silvestre Dance Technique.
Classification: LCC GV1637 .W55 2021 | DDC 792.8/0981—dc23
LC record available at https://lccn.loc.gov/2020058695

BRITISH LIBRARY CATALOGUING DATA ARE AVAILABLE

ISBN (print) 978-1-4766-7432-2
ISBN (ebook) 978-1-4766-4137-9

Front cover photograph by Carla Grosso Fioramonti

Printed in the United States of America

*McFarland & Company, Inc., Publishers
Box 611, Jefferson, North Carolina 28640
www.mcfarlandpub.com*

To Rosangela Silvestre,
Vera Passos and
the Silvestre Family

The Triangles of the *Body Universe* in Silvestre Technique (photo by Rodrigo Chakra and Jahlyn Karuna).

Table of Contents

Acknowledgments

I am dissecting the influences of the Orixás (specifically of Brazilian Candomblé spirituality) in the practice of Silvestre Technique, envisioned by Rosangela Silvestre. While committed to discovering the connection to my higher being through this technique, I want to offer my sincere appreciation to Rosangela Silvestre for being the inspiration and catalyst for my writing. She has influenced me tremendously in my visions and insight; Rosangela, even today, continues pushing me to develop my own interpretations and discoveries for myself in dance technique and life.

I am very gracious to Vera Passos, for her spirit in teaching and dedication to her students. Vera's energy, stamina and creative influences are rare to find amongst technique instructors and I am truly grateful to have her as my *professora*. She has given me the tools to see the strength and power of my own moving body and the strength in others as well.

My heart pours out tremendous appreciation to the former Musical Director of the Silvestre Dance Technique Intensive in Bahia, Nei Sacramento. I am immensely grateful for the entire musical ensemble each summer including Luciano da Silva, Paulinho Dos Santos, Luciano Xavier and many others. Luciano Xavwier, I appreciate the long days and nights you committed to helping me review this text.

I offer much gratitude to my family including my father, Daniel Williams; my mother, Ira Williams; my sister, Tijwanna Ketter; and my grandmother, Ida Shannon. I thank my Olowu, Baba Chief Awósanmí Òṣuntógùn Sékou Alájé for your mentorship in Òrìṣà and Yorùbá culture. Your teachings have provided me a deeper understanding of the relationship of the elements of nature to life and this technique. Baba encouraged me to embrace my admiration for the Òrìṣàs and to not be afraid to have it manifest in my work.

Kendra Ross, Alysha Ali-Higgs, Stephanie Engel, Samantha Goodman, Kaley Isabella, Adrianna Yanuziello, Helio Oliveira, Safira Sacramento, Marcos Vinicio, Kamilah Turner, Ani Taj, and countless others, thank you for allowing me to realize how influential and powerful this technique can be in my daily life. Your friendships and motivation have been enormous contributions to my growth.

Sandra Orellana Sears, thank you for being my second eye in proof-reading, and your devoted support of my writing, dancing and spiritual growth. Maxine Montilus, I am honored to have you as a friend and I appreciate your encouragement throughout the process of writing this text. I offer tremendous thanks to Deko Alves and Jenifer Ferraro for your dedication to Silvestre Technique and this text as well.

Jacson Santos and Brooks Anderson, your photography documentation of Silvestre Technique catches the essence of the movement in stillness with power. Ace Murray, I am forever grateful for your documentation of Rosangela with Moving Spirits, Inc. in New York City. Diego Carrizo, thank you for sharing your artistry throughout this book. You have captured delightful moments that will continue to resonate for years to come. To the twins, Sonitra MacRall and Nikita MacRall-Angus, and Suzanne Achieng, thank you for all of your encouragement, support and creative suggestions.

Glenna Batson, Hilde Cannoodt, Jonathan Lassiter, Leila D. Lewis, Dandha da Hora, Marko Nektan, Yuko Tamura and Mariana Rose Thorn thank you for your invaluable feedback and suggestions for edits to this text. I offer tremendous thanks to the Learning Resource Center at Penn State University, Altoona. Anne Maucieri and Lee Peterson your assistance has been invaluable. I am thankful for the guidance of Dr. Ann Dils and Dr. Takiyah Amin in the publishing of this text.

The program at Hollins University prompted me to take my research of Silvestre Technique to an elevated level. To my Hollins University family, Jeffrey Bullock and Gina Kohler, thank you for your encouraging words and thoughtful ideas pushing me to dive deeper into the content of this text. Dr. Brent Stevens, thank you for offering your time and energy in the meticulous review of my work. To Dr. Thomas F. DeFrantz, thank you for motivating me to write this manuscript and being the impetus to create.

Foreword
by Lela Aisha Jones

As a dedicated embodied practitioner, movement artist, and researcher of Black and African diasporic movement cultures for more than 20 years, it is quite thrilling to see the work of author Tamara Williams come to fruition. *Giving Life to Movement* is a heartfelt and overarching read through the physical, socio-cultural, and spiritual technique of Williams' body in synchronization with Rosangela Silvestre's body of work. Williams research combines theoretical foundations and practice in a textual love of self and moves us to a collective consciousness or wokeness about how dance asks us who we are being in the world and who we will choose to be. This book is a *story journey* on what we will take on in our lives, maybe unexpectedly and unconsciously, as legacy making.

Resources such as this are often a long time coming for all us folks who identify as diasporic beings—teachers, artists, embodiers, lovers of self and collective, philosophers, theorists, environmental enthusiasts, history makers, writers, researchers, archivists, and activists. It captures the stories of the epic nomadic wanderings one does as they choose paths of conjuring ancestral knowledge through dance and the body. In this diasporic work folks rebuild, re-spirit, re-access, and re-soul through what Dr. Ananya Chatterjea, author of *Butting Out: Reading Resistive Choreographies through Works by Jawole Jo Willa Zollar and Chandralekha*, calls the *practice of imagination* or the art of what being alive is. There is no better place to do that work than in efforts to *mine, witness,* and *archive* beings (bodies) in relationship to spirit and the natural environment. For any person ever wondering because of oppression where they belong, I say to you what Rosangela Silvestre said to Tamara Williams: "Take the things that bother you and make them into magic."

The diasporic is calculated, recalibrated, conjured, intensive, and meticulous magic or work. Magic is a type of work. This is a sentiment of

1

Dr. Nzinga Metzger, the fully embodied Scholar and Cultural Anthropologist at Florida A & M University. Much of her work is focused on ancient and contemporary spiritual and cultural traditions of Black and African descent and this has led her to theoretical orientations on the *sacred grove*. Silvestre Dance Technique creates space for an embodied experience, moment, or revelation in alignment with the description of the sacred grove by Metzger. These attributes include:

> a natural environment … a hallowed ground … a place where humans can experience and commune with the divine … a place where permanent and spiritual transformation takes place … a place where ritual is enacted … a space where time is altered … an ancestrally designated space.

Afro-Brazilian and global diasporic folks and cultures have called upon so much nuanced socio-cultural and spiritual lived experience to transform what is bothersome and traumatic into essential restoration and revitalization. This book is a peek into *diasporic thriving* through the art of embodiment. Silvestre Dance Technique, as described by Williams, is deep bodily articulation and physicalization that intertwines the multi-narrative arts of Orixás, Bharatanatyam, and the wholeness of a body in the natural world. It is an open-ended story of these three ways of life as researched and honed by Rosangela Silvestre, then recalibrated, re-storied in the human (being) body of Tamara Williams. And now it is here for all of us diasporic beings to be **in the know** of courage—to feel just one more time, that there is *axé* in everything we are and all the things we make.

> The diasporic body is a human being, a reservoir, and a rebuilt body. It is the body that has done the breadth and made choices about the depth. It is not the body that dabbles. It lives in diasporic citizenship. It is the body that is **in the know** because of time in. It is the body that is **in the know** because of time done … time sitting … time moving … time flying by … time resting … time going hard … ancestral time … time honing the body of the person and the body of work, the muscles, the cells, the blood that becomes memoir/memory/nostalgia that is now. It is the body that is Earth wata … e no get enemy—in one moment solid, moldable and the next smooth … slipping through your fingers … fleeting. Take me to that righteous water. It is the body that sees the labor of it all as essentially reflexive … requiring resurfacing … landing … floating on undercurrents … meditating in the time provided … productively recalibrating with communities and collectives.

The reservoir of any dance technique is hard to capture in a textual form. However, Tamara Williams has tenderly and precisely placed the technique within the story of her life, given clear examples of the theoretical orientations, and chronicled specific sequences in the physical practice of Silvestre Dance Technique. *Giving Life to Movement* is on a continuum of archiving African, Africanist, and Black diasporic dance philosophies and techniques in literature, such as *Umfundalai* by Dr. Kariamu Welsh and *Danse Africaine, Afrikanischier Tanz, African Dance* by Germaine Acogny. This book joins epic *translineages* and legacies—reminding all diasporic beings that we are embodied, contemporary, triumphant, resourceful, and exquisite revitalizers.

Lela Aisha Jones (Okunlola Okikiola) is an artist, scholar and organizer. She is an assistant professor of dance at Bryn Mawr College and a Consortium for Faculty Diversity fellow. She is also the founder and director of Lela Aisha Jones | FlyGround, which is dedicated to building collective consciousness and creating contemporary cultural memories through movement performance.

Preface

Giving Life to Movement offers people interested in movement practices and spiritual enlightenment a detailed account of the Silvestre Dance Technique pedagogy. There are thousands of Silvestre Technique practitioners and limited amounts of published materials or resources regarding the dance technique, its philosophy and its impact on communities worldwide. This book is a manual to practice the technique and also explains the influences that culture has on the technique in various locations.

This book project started after studying Silvestre Dance Technique with its creator, Rosangela Silvestre, in Brazil for over a decade. My training with Rosangela inspired me to begin journaling and documenting my personal growth from the technique. I have been a professional dancer for years and I have never encountered a dance technique that incorporates spirituality, self-awareness and body conditioning simultaneously. For these reasons, I created this project to share the knowledge of Silvestre Technique with others in various fields. My initial questioning that molded the foundation of this text included:

- How does African-Brazilian culture, the spiritual practice of Candomblé, and the elements of nature influence the movements found in Silvestre Dance Technique?
- Can self-actualization be obtained through a dance practice that is founded upon the principles of traditional spiritual practices and cultural resistance?
- How does practicing dance technique lead (a person) to higher self-awareness or self-actualization?
- What are the connections between dance and spiritual enlightenment?
- How are international communities and/or connections formed through the practice of Silvestre Dance Technique?

Giving Life to Movement translates the theoretical practice of Orixá principles via the codified movements of Silvestre Technique. This book explains how Silvestre Technique can alter the dancers' performance and interpretation of movement, through utilizing the essences of the elements of nature as tools for learning and performing. My research has uncovered that there are no Western-based modern dance techniques that explicitly use the elements of nature (earth, air, water and fire) as its founding principles in movement. *Giving Life to Movement* provides a deeper look into the rich African-Brazilian culture that has birthed this dance technique providing new philosophies about dance practice and the synthesis of dance training into daily life. The elements of nature are a natural part of the human body, which inspire movement and therefore affect actions that occur outside of the dance studio, since the elements of nature are continuously present in life.

Laban Movement Analysis (LMA), created by Rudolf Labon of Hungary, examines movement by categories of body, effort, shape and space. Mobility, stability, expression, inner and outer connection, and physical exertion are key principles recorded in the LMA process of analyzing movement. Silvestre Technique's foundation relies on similar principles through investigating body, effort, shape and space as well as dividing the body into three parts, known as the Triangles of the Body. In Silvestre training, the three sections are identified as *Inspiration, Expression, and Balance*, which function together to create the *Body Universe*. The new knowledge that Silvestre Technique brings to the almost century old Labon Movement Analysis is the inclusion of spiritual elevation, ancestral memories, and personal growth in the practice and study of the technique. Silvestre Technique connects the physical body, metaphysical practices, internal dialogue and assessment, space and environment, and the Universal forces together as one, creating the *Body Universe.*

Cultural influences impact the structure and performance of the technique. Silvestre Technique practiced in Brazil is slightly different from the Silvestre training in London or Trinidad; each place has its own influences. In this text, I explain the cultural differences through my perspectives, offering reasons for change and adaptation in certain environments and spaces. This book contributes new information to the dance field by offering information regarding Silvestre Technique's philosophy, dance pedagogy, and a style rooted in African-Brazilian culture. The incorporation of the Orixás, and the elements of nature as contemporary principles, are new practices in the field of concert dance; these theories can transform the manner in which dance technique is taught and performed in contemporary dance forums.

Giving Life to Movement considers the controversial topic of the separation of dance and religion as an art form or dances originating from religious ceremonies as a form of entertainment. The Silvestre Dance

Technique has its roots in the African-Brazilian spiritual practice of Candomblé, which honors the elements of nature. This book analyzes the possibilities of dance being used as a catalyst for higher spiritual ascension and self-actualization. *Giving Life to Movement* presents dance vocabulary terms, imagery and images for its audience as well as theoretical, cultural and societal ideologies. There is currently no written text that specifically analyzes Silvestre Technique in regard to its connection to the elements of nature or the possibility of higher self-ascension through dance. Silvestre Technique merges aspects of modernism and Brazilian traditions, a topic which is often discussed orally, but has yet to be represented in writing.

Throughout this text, I provide information regarding Silvestre Technique's foundation and my personal reflections. This book is Tamara's story of Silvestre; I call it this because there are many stories, and this is mine at this time during my journey and my personal understanding as interpreted here. Silvestre training *is* dance; training for the body and mind and spirit. It provides me tools to use in life situations whether they are in dance, or my relation to space, time, and people. In regard to self, Rosangela affirms, "*I am Dance.*" There is plenty that can be learned from this statement alone.

I began my investigation of Silvestre Technique by exploring the following ideas: the Triangles of the Body, movement symbology, the role of the Orixás, and the philosophical foundation of the technique provided by Rosangela. Later, through my personal inquiries, I was able to articulate my findings of how environments for Silvestre training are created; understand the specific language used; how training affects the body and mind as well as the community in the space/environment; the preparation of the teachers of Silvestre Technique; the masculine and feminine energy of the technique; my process of self-actualization; and how training Silvestre Technique and life have become inseparable in my existence.

Throughout the years, I have experienced tremendous growth in my spirituality as I journeyed through my discoveries in Silvestre Technique. In 2014, after studying Silvestre Technique for over half of the year in Salvador, Bahia, my Babaláwo (priest of Ifá), Chief Awósanmí Ọ̀suntógùn Sékou Alájé, of the Ogundáse Ifá Temple took me on a cultural investigation in Osogbo, Nigeria. While in Osogbo, I grasped a deeper understanding of my ancestral roots as I became an initiate of Ifá and Ṣàngó. My Olúwos Agbongbon Fakayode Faniyi and Ṣàngódélé Ṣàngómáyòwá Ibuowo assisted me through a profound and meaningful life transition in which I was given the name *Ifákẹmi Ṣàngóbámke Moṣebọ́látán.* I oftentimes compare my experience in Silvestre Dance Technique to my paths in African traditional religion. It is a rebirth, influencing my entire life cycle. Names in Yorùbá culture are guides; Silvestre Technique guides me in a similar way that my Yorùbá name guides and influences my life.

Introduction

I define Silvestre Technique as a codified dance technique that incorporates the attributions of water, fire, air and earth, which are symbolized through the concepts and movements of the training. Silvestre Technique incorporates rudiments of several modern dance techniques, as well as yoga, capoeira, meditation, sacred geometry, Bharatanatyam, and awareness of the chakras. In classical Indian dancing, Bharatanatyam is comprised of five components: text, acting, movement, rhythm and music. These rudiments are also found in Silvestre Technique in the practice, symbology and performance of the technique. One of the most obvious influences of Bharatanatyam found in Silvestre technique is of the *mudra*, or hand and feet gestures. For example: In the *Messages* sequence in Silvestre Technique, there are distinct hand gestures that symbolize past, present and future. In other aspects of the technique, the symbols for the elements of nature provide meaning for the movement. The lotus flower represents higher consciousness; the four directions correlate to space and directions. Each symbol and gesture in Silvestre Technique, as in Bharatanatyam, have meanings that oftentimes tell a story. Bharatanatyam and Silvestre Technique are expressive dance styles that have foundations rooted in sacred spirituality. Both techniques also demonstrate appreciation of space, elements of nature, spiritual influences, rhythm, music and dancers. Silvestre Technique is a living and developing system that continues to evolve throughout the years.

Silvestre Technique incorporates symbols of the Orixás, divine forces in the Brazilian spiritual practice of Candomblé. Through the expression of earth, water, air and fire, the technique relates the body to the elements. Silvestre Technique embodies the Orixás given that the divine forces correspond to the energy of distinct natural elements. The conceptualizations used to convey the four elements of nature to the dancer can be deepened to understand the connection that the Orixás have to the movement and dancer. Silvestre training links the skillful techniques of dance (the elements of nature and interpretation the Orixás) and is used to further empower the dancer. Throughout this text, I will refer to Rosangela Silvestre by her first name in my efforts to eliminate confusion and repetitiveness regarding Silvestre Technique and her as the creator.

In Western society, there has been an obvious separation of dance and spirituality, yet there is an inherent humanistic need to connect to the divine or a higher self through dance. For example, Jean Barbot, a renown enslaver and author, published travel narratives in 1688 highlighting his account of traditional West African dance customs. In her book entitled, *Ring Shout, Wheel About,* Katrina Dyonne Thompson analyzes Barbot's descriptions:

> The slaver richly detailed a scene of music, dance and debauchery in his narrative, describing men and women "leaping and stamping their feet" while continually "running against each other, breast to breast, knocking bellies together very indecently ... and uttering some dirty mysterious words." The Frenchman described the participants as "more like devils than men" who danced in "strange posture ... as if they were possessed" [Thompson, 2014, p. 13].

Early journalists and owners of enslaved people represented negative perceptions of the dances and movements of West Africans in their religious and spiritual gatherings. Dance scholar, author and professor Dr. Katrina Hazzard-Donald explains,

> The dance movements in the sacred circle were initially more vigorous and elaborate, retaining much of the African ceremonial character. Spirit possession was true to its name as a particular divinity or spirit spoke through a possesee in the language of dance. In this instance, the possessing spirit gave council and advice to individuals and the community [Hazzard-Donald, 2011, p. 202].

This was the scenario for numerous spiritual traditions that migrated to the Americas during the Transatlantic Slave Trade and the Triangle Trade. The movement meditations are prayers that are often referred to as dance. They were demonized and negatively documented by missionaries and early researchers; these dances still remain a stigma in present day society. In fear of revolts and rebellions led by the enslaved people, the eradication of African cultural traditions developed into a primary focus throughout the Americas. Owners of the enslaved and their associates pressed the advancement of the assimilation of the enslaved into white culture, including the separation of dance and spirituality. These changes, which were widespread from the eighteenth into the twentieth century, remains acutely comparable in today's Western culture.

Silvestre Technique dismisses this separation, mending the physical body to a connection to the Universe through dance training. The aforementioned universe exists within the body and is termed the *"Body Universe"* by Rosangela.

The *Body Universe* is symbolized by three triangles present throughout the body. The triangles bridge the *Body Universe* to the Divine Universe through the embodiment of Earth, Water, Air, and Fire. The first triangle is the *Triangle of Inspiration*: Intuition, Visualization and Perception: located from the top of the head and flows down to the shoulders. The second triangle is the *Triangle of Expression*: Starting at the shoulders down to the belly button. The last triangle is the *Triangle of Balance*: Located from the hips down to the feet. Each triangle through its universal connection to the elements of nature unites the individual with the elements of nature and the Divine Universe. This method of dance practice allows for a deeper substance in the embodiment of technique. Dance and spirituality enlighten people and offers a means to self-actualization through discipline. Rosangela has formulated a system and philosophy for dance and spirituality to coexist through a codified movement structure.

Illustration of the *Body Universe in Silvestre Dance Technique.*

Who Is Rosangela?

"Who is she?," one might ask. Writing a list of her accomplishments or acclamations does not begin to describe who she is. Rosangela has to be *experienced*. To know her, enter the room with her. Imagine a soft hum, that is a force from the belly, radiating throughout the entire body; Rosangela may be that sensation of peace. Or perhaps a thought in the mind when one realizes that they have sold themselves short; when we have not given our everything or maybe we gave, and it was not enough. The mental check that happens afterwards is like entering a room with Rosangela. She is the calm before the storm. Yet, she can simultaneously be described as the storm that stirs things up physically, mentally, emotionally and spiritually. Afterwards, the person may learn to take hold of the reign to guide themselves in the right direction. Rosangela has been all of that for me. That is why I say she is the catalyst for this writing, this journey and this venture.

At first glance of Rosangela I always see light. I see a free spirit and a powerhouse. She draws me in with her presence alone, and I wait patiently and anxiously to hear everything she has to say. I know it derives from the enlightened seed within her. She is a native of Bahia, Brazil. I recall several of the stories she has shared with me about being a young girl heavily influenced by the spiritual practices of her family. Rosangela once shared a reflection with me of observing the movements of her grandmother doing her daily housework. She remembers the nature surrounding her. The trees, the streams, the earth below. I listened and felt a sense of freedom. She went on to explain her first encounters with Candomblé. She would often walk over to the *terreiro* (spiritual house) in the countryside. She would stand at the window and witness the women and men dancing around in circles for hours. She was captivated by the rhythms and the feet, the bodies swaying and turning, the drums calling on spirits to arrive, and moments of stillness.

When I witness Rosangela move through space, dancing or even walking, it is evident that she has been trained in classical dance techniques. Her form is impeccable, and her physical strength, unwavering. Rosangela's first studio training primarily consisted of ballet and modern forms. Sometime during high school, she began studying movements inspired by the Orixá with Mestre King. Rosangela was highly knowledgeable of these movement forms since she grew up around Candomblé; however, Mestre King's approach involved an interpretation of the Orixá movements through dance. It became an artistic practice to train the body while honoring the culture and history from which these movements emerged.

Rosangela shared with me the very first people that influenced her artistry and dance:

> I don't know where they are right now. I never asked them their names. They influenced me through their vibrations. One day, when I was very young and I saw a Candomblé ceremony and I saw these people dance, sing and play the traditional instruments. I saw these people get into trance and bring many things that would not allow me to take my eyes off of the situation. I had no idea that I would become a messenger of dance; I had no idea in that moment. But, now, anything that I do in dance, those people influence me [Silvestre].

It is incredibly significant that Rosangela still remembers those people in that moment. Their intentions of movements influenced much of the foundation of Silvestre Dance Technique. Even though she does not remember their names, Rosangela remembers these people through the basis of her movement—in silence and her messages of dance.

Rosangela studied dance at the Federal University of Bahia (UFBA) in Salvador, Bahia. She studied several forms of dance, including but not limited to Graham, Horton, and ballet. She traveled internationally studying and presenting dance in India, Egypt, Cuba, Japan, Australia, Argentina, Chile, Senegal, throughout Europe and more. Today, Rosangela continues to travel the continents teaching Silvestre Technique (including Symbology and theory of the technique) and movements inspired by the Orixás. I yearn to touch my feet down in a fraction of the places she has landed to immerse myself in dance, rhythms, customs and dialogues. I am honored to have shared a few experiences in the United Kingdom, Canada, Brazil, Trinidad and the United States studying with Rosangela.

Meeting Rosangela

I was aware of Silvestre Dance Technique and Rosangela's summer program for many years, yet I never understood exactly all that it entailed. I was living in New York City and learned that Rosangela would be performing at the Brooklyn Arts Exchange one December evening. This instance was my opportunity to see her perform and I seized it.

It was a unique dance presentation. She danced as a soloist with a drummer accompanying her movement. As I watched her dance, she moved about—*with* the space, as opposed to *in* the space. She carefully articulated each movement from the tips of her fingers to the direction and manner in which she moved her head and hair. The expression of her movement resonated in her face and her hair danced as an extension of her body. At one point during the performance Rosangela distributed cards to audience members. The cards were read aloud at random by spectators, sparking my interests. We became better informed about the meaning of her movements through their narratives; this interaction between her and the audience kept us especially engaged. She concluded by inviting the viewers to join her in her movement escapades on stage. It was a warm and encouraging signal. After we all danced, I made a point to stay behind and speak to Rosangela. I told her how moved I was by her vision in dance—the multiplicity of the dancer, space and environment. I also told her that I would attend the next Silvestre Dance Intensive in Salvador, Bahia, to train in her technique. It was in that moment that I experienced her innate ability to give of herself, offering to help me in my travel plans if needed and to keep in touch … and she did.

In working with Rosangela I continue to understand that dance can exist in any environment: a stage the size of City Center, an enclosed space, in ritual, or the ocean shore. Silvestre Technique has brought great amounts of transformation and awareness into my life and dancing. My connection to the elements of nature as they are represented in Silvestre Training resonates in my expression and relationship to dance more than any other techniques that I have studied. The ever-evolving structure of Silvestre Technique keeps me interested and focused on my continuous training. I continue to deepen my knowledge about the technique, the Orixás, explore my personal expression and how the elements of nature affect my living and my own self-awareness.

Spirituality

Many people are curious about the influences of Candomblé in Silvestre Technique. Through years of study and practice, I have realized that Candomblé is a spiritual practice that provides individuals and communities with tools of enrichment. Silvestre Dance Technique is influenced by numerous cultures of people; many who have been historically marginalized and/or displaced in some form. In African-Brazilian traditions, movement and music became tools of resistance. Candomblé was a method of communication, empowerment, and a means to preserve African-Brazilian culture; it is a spiritual practice that was created as a means of survival. The Orixás represent the tools utilized to achieve this perseverance.

Candomblé is a spiritual practice that was created by the enslaved Africans in Brazil. It was developed from belief systems of the Yorùbá, Fon, Igbo and Bantu people in various regions of Africa. Today, Candomblé houses or *Ilês* belong to one of the corresponding nations: Ketu, Jeje, Nago or Angola. The faith was practiced during the period of Transatlantic Slave Trade in Bahia, Brazil. The enslaved people were forced to practice Catholicism enforced by the owners of the enslaved population in order to create "property" that was obedient. However, some of the enslaved people continued practicing the religion of their ancestors in secrecy from those who held people in enslavement. Although the enslaved were practicing Candomblé centuries prior, the first official temple (Ilê) was not established until the early nineteenth century in Salvador, Bahia. The enslaved people of Salvador blended the culture and language of the First Nations Indigenous people and the Portuguese together with the wisdom of the enslaved African priests' culture and mythology, in the formation of Candomblé. Written texts of tradition did not exist. It was the priests and elders of the enslaved community that would share and pass down information in the ancient oral traditions. Practitioners believe in the one almighty, Olodumaré, and spirit archetypes called Orixás (spirit guides) that provide sacred tools for one's existence while here on Earth. There is also a high tribute reverenced to one's individual ancestors. Each Orixá is associated with a specific element(s) of nature and has correlating aspects of character based on the mythology of the Orixá. The mythology exists in the form of parables and riddles. In Candomblé, music and dance are central elements as they are both used to call upon, honor, and pray to the Orixás.

Since the practice of Candomblé was widely condemned by the Catholic Church, many practiced Christianity outwardly, but prayed to Olodumaré, the Orixás and their ancestors in private. The Catholic enslavers persecuted anyone found practicing Candomblé through violence, death, and in the nineteenth and twentieth century by brutal police action. In his book, *The Formation of Candomblé: Vodun History and Ritual in Brazil*, author Luis Nicolau Parés points out:

> And in fact, according to ordinance number 59, from February 27, 1857, "The batuques, dances and meeting of slaves, are prohibited in any place and at any time, under penalty of eight days in prison for each one found in violation" [Parés, 2013, p. 101].
>
> Some of the Brazilian elite considered Candomblé as "a haven for runaway slaves" (Parés, 2013, p. 103). In 1866, the popular journal of Bahia called the O Alabama published requests for "the police take measures to repress candomblés" (Parés, 2013, p.103). In his book, Parés highlights several accounts of police persecution amongst Candomblé practitioners forcing them to flee their terreiros. In 1869, following an initiation during a Candomblé ceremony, the group, or barco, were "immediately taken to a house in São Miguel, where they now find themselves, this precaution being taken for fear that, if the police had known of what happened, they would go there and find them." Two days later ... once again escaping police persecution ... all of the accessories of the candomblé arrived [Parés, 2013, p. 130].

In the 1970s the laws enforced to try to dismantle Candomblé were exonerated by the government. Nonetheless, practitioners and spiritual houses still encounter persecution by the government and society for their practices presently.

The first time that I stepped into a Candomblé house, it was with Rosangela. We went to experience a ceremony for Oxalá; the Orixá that represents wisdom, purity and enlightenment. I was captivated by the energy in the terreiro (spiritual temple). My spirit and mind were fortified in a new and familiar manner. The repetition of the movements in space, the vitality created through the songs, the intense rhythms of the drumming, and the intricately designed attire brought me instant stimulation. That experience influenced my understanding and appreciation for African-Brazilian spiritual practices and cultural resistance.

Why I Continue to Train in Silvestre Technique

Over the years I have continued training in Silvestre Technique as it endlessly affects my life in a positive manner. Through the technique's philosophy, structure and methodology I continue learning. Rosangela has taught me to always seek to find more in myself; ask questions and listen. Silvestre Technique has given me great physical and mental strength, flexibility, musicality and nuance in my dance performance. In studying Silvestre Technique and the movements inspired by the Orixás, I have gained a great respect for nature and the differences in which we all have. In gaining respect, I am more conscious of my effect on nature; everything from attentiveness to recycling so that there is less waste on the Earth, to turning off the faucet when I am not using water. In speaking of nature, I am referring to the elements represented in the Earth that are symbolized through the Orixás, for example: Xangô and Fire, Ogum and the forest, Oxum and fresh water, Ossain and plants. These energies exist in nature and within myself, as I am of nature. Through being exposed to the movement representation of these archetypes, it gives me a greater understanding of their relationship to nature and the functioning of the elements of nature. When a person completes an undulation, they are dancing Iemanjá or Olokun. It is the same water in the body that surges in the Atlantic Ocean each day. Using this perspective, my dance has greater value to me and as a result, my reverence of nature and all that it provides has grown. I have learned to honor myself. Rosangela once told me, *"When you harm nature, you are harming the Orixás."* (Silvestre Summer Intensive) I have become more conscious about the environment and my connection to my surroundings as a result.

Differences Have Taught Me Respect

I would be remiss if I did not mention how the culture of Silvestre Technique has empowered me as an African American woman in the dance field. Feelings of inferiority and anxiety often imposed by structures of society and studies of codified modern dance technique are dismantled by the value of the individual's agency in this training. Silvestre Technique provides me with the tools needed to push further with patience in understanding that "it will come to the degree that it will come" as my inspiration, Renee Robinson said in the highly celebrated dance series *A Hymn for Alvin Ailey* (Bagwell, 1999). In my twenty-plus years of dancing ballet, modern and various traditional movements, I have never encountered a dance form that combines the essence of nature within a structured dance form that awakens my consciousness inside and outside of the studio.

Giving Life to Movement investigates the following points:

- African-Brazilian history and culture that has influenced Silvestre Technique
- The potential of finding freedom in Silvestre Technique
- Communities created through the technique
- The foundation and philosophies of Silvestre Dance Technique
- Selected terms and Silvestre Technique positions
- Introductory sequences for a Silvestre Dance Technique class
- Methodology and Pedagogy: The structure of teaching the technique

These themes are highlighted throughout the following chapters:

Chapter I. African-Brazilian Culture in the 1970s and the History of Silvestre Technique

An explanation of how the socio-economic conditions of Brazil influenced the creation of the technique.

Chapter II. Creating Possibilities: An Approach to Silvestre Technique

An investigation of how joining the elements of nature (earth, water, air and fire) with higher consciousness can positively affect dance training. Readers learn how African-Brazilian culture is honored through the practice of Silvestre Technique and how dancers can gain freedom of expression through dancing the technique.

Chapter III. Practicing the Technique

A description of the context of studying Silvestre Dance Technique in Brazil, international study, and the communities that are created through the multi-continental reach.

The last section describes the overall shape of the Silvestre organization. It is an examination of some of the structures in place in the model of the technique and its unconventional functionality; rooted in Brazil with global reach and adaptation.

Chapter IV. Conceptualizations of Silvestre Technique

Includes detailed information regarding the foundation, philosophies and practice of Silvestre Technique.

Chapter V. Definition of Silvestre Terms and Positions

This chapter utilizes photos and diagrams to define specific Silvestre Technique terms and positions.

Chapter VI. Introductory Sequences for Silvestre Dance Technique Class

Chapter VI provides detailed instructions for composing and

completing a Silvestre Technique class. The instructions include counts, movement descriptions, sequencing and photos to accompany each exercise provided.

Chapter VII. Methodology and Pedagogy
This chapter describes and explains specific vocabulary and tools used for instructing a Silvestre Technique class.

Chapter VIII. Self-Actualization
The final chapter defines self-actualization as it relates to movement. Theories formed by psychologist, Abraham Maslow, and psychotherapist, Everett L. Shostrom, are used to support the argument that Silvestre Dance Technique leads to self-empowerment. Chapter VII also includes quotes from student practitioners of Silvestre Dance Technique discussing capabilities they have gained through dancing this technique.

Tamara's Story

In 2011, I decided that I no longer wanted to dance professionally for other companies full-time and started my own dance company, Moving Spirits, Inc. The decision to take this drastic step was made in Brazil during one of my trips of study with Rosangela and Vera Passos. Passos is Rosangela's longtime protégé of Silvestre Dance Technique. The strength and determination of these women greatly influenced me. Each time that I travel to Bahia, Brazil the energy and experiences I encounter push me to make life changes. Moving Spirits, Inc. has been one manifestation from my journeys to Salvador to study Silvestre Technique. The company has been quite fortunate and successful in our accomplishments. We have performed at numerous venues nationally and internationally including Mexico, Jamaica, and Trinidad & Tobago. Through the company I have produced three evening length concerts: *The Makings of You* in 2012 and *Epic Narratives: an Evening of Dance, Visual Arts, Theater and Social Commentary* in 2013. In 2015, the company produced *Moving Spirits to Enlightenment* in response to police brutality in the United States. In the spring of 2015, *Dancing in the Parks* was brought to Brooklyn parks near public city housing bringing awareness and opportunities for engagement with concert dance in these communities. The philosophies, the training, and the overall groundwork of Silvestre Technique continues to influence the work of Moving Spirits, Inc. In 2016, Rosangela engaged in a residency with the company in which she taught company and community classes. She also set a work on the dancers. The choreographic piece was performed at the Brooklyn Arts Exchange with live music accompaniment by Luciano Xavier, Fernando Saci and

Rosangela demonstrating movement while in residency with Moving Spirits, Inc. (photo by Ace Murray).

Eddie Martin. Mentorship from Rosangela revealed the possibilities and my desires to travel and study internationally; this led to me performing and teaching internationally with Moving Spirits, Inc.

Now, several decades after my first dance class, I am focused on writing again; combining two of my passions. I have traveled for several years around the world to study with Rosangela Silvestre. Her technique and philosophies have changed the way I dance and my perception of dance and life. They are no longer separate for me; they are one—Dancing is my *Spiritual Breath*. This text is my account of this remarkable woman's vision.

Dance has led me many places in life. I have been able to travel across continents, gain new friends with whom I have lasting relationships, and develop a strong sense of self. I never would have thought that dancing in a room full of adults, under gleaming lights would lead me here, but then again, that is what I am doing each time I share my movements with others. That is my story, and now we begin.

I

African-Brazilian Culture in the 1970s and the History of Silvestre Technique

"The quality of expression is enriched with an understanding of learning, discovering, and developing who you are as a human being."—Rosangela Silvestre, 2011 (Williams, 2011–2014)

History/Condition/Technique as Reform

Salvador, Bahia, Brazil was a major port for enslaved Africans entering Brazil. West Africans and Central Africans from the Congo/Bantu, Akan, Yorùbá and Nago nations were traded into Brazil to produce sugar, coffee and cacao (Kraay, 1998). Brazil has the largest population of African descendants outside of Africa, which considerably influences Brazilian culture. It is important to note that Brazil had the largest population of enslaved African descendants working in the world. As a result, African-Brazilians have powerfully demonstrated socio-political movements since the uprisings that first occurred during chattel slavery during the 1600s (Reiter, 2009). Slavery ended at various times throughout the Americas. For instance, the enslavement of people in Haiti halted after the end of the Haitian Revolution in 1804. Haiti was the first and only place in the Americas where the enslaved people revolted and became free countrywide. Despite several rebellion acts, slavery in Brazil ended more than 80 years after the Haitian revolt, and more than two decades after it ended in the United States. African-Brazilians were not freed until 1888.

From 1889 through the early 1900s, there were movements to educate and provide resources for the former enslaved people and their descendants. For example,

in the state of Bahia, schools were created "which offered day and night classes to freedpersons and their children" [Graden, 2006, p. 200]. During the same period,

21

"supporters of abolition and numerous freedpersons became active in the emerging labor movement in Bahia" [Graden, 2006, p. 201]. Despite these advancements, there was confusion in "the definition of property rights and individual freedoms" of the freed people [Graden, 2006, p. 206].

As a result, many African-Brazilians remained in the lowest caste of citizens after the period of enslavement ended. Years later, the African-Brazilian citizens' rights were stripped further under a military dictatorship led by Humberto de Alencar Castelo Branco. Branco's authoritarian military regime starting in 1964 and lasted until 1985 (Skidmore, 2010). From 1966 until around 1975 using armed force, the militia terrorized, tortured and killed citizens who were in opposition to their control (Hudson, 1998). According to the World Bank from the United States Census Bureau, the population of Brazil in 1965 was approximately 83.5 million people in which the majority of population lived in poverty. Brazil was experiencing an oil crisis during the late 1970s and 80s. The crisis was initially brought on by a severe power outage, increasing a demand for petroleum products. High interest rates (Ito, 1999) lead to inflation in the economy, resulting in widespread unemployment, particularly affecting poorer communities (Kraay, 1998). The oil shock of the 1970s caused overexploitation of the environment, leading to the practice of self-sustainability amongst many communities. Disparities in land ownership, also created by social and economic status, safeguarded the gap between lower- and upper-class citizens. The *favelas*, or heavily populated urban areas in Brazil, started to increase during the 1970s. It's important to note that *favelas* are largely inhabited by marginalized and underserved communities of people. The government implemented a favela eradication policy, which created more favelas because displaced families had nowhere to live after being removed. As a result, violence perpetrated with small arms and drugs flourished throughout the country (Skidmore, 2010).

White Brazilians dominated every facet of life including land, upper tiered job opportunities, and politics, creating an ongoing cycle of poverty for not only the African-Brazilian population but other marginalized populations. While there were never laws written to uphold segregation in Brazil, lower class citizens were often Black Brazilians. During the 1970s and 1980s many African-Brazilians did not pass elementary education, causing a higher illiteracy rate among the population (Ito, 1999). Consequently, African-Brazilians were not given the same opportunities in society. These systems amplified racism and injustices for Black Brazilian communities. African-Brazilians encountered traumatic social economic conditions in the late 1970s and 1980s, which influenced several aspects of Silvestre Technique's movement philosophies. The African-Brazilian population was underserved and marginalized in forums that related to politics, culture, religion, education, and wellness. The restrictions invited a host of racism and inequality for African-Brazilians and did not allow any forms of social elevation (Reiter, 2009).

Brazil's economy began to flourish with tourism on the rise; however, the government used the new wave of tourism to exploit African-Brazilian culture. *Capoeira* (a Brazilian martial arts form) and *Baianas* (women dressed in traditional garb symbolic of the African-Brazilian women of Bahia, Brazil) were displayed to represent Brazilian culture. Replicas of religious beads and tools were sold, capoeira paraphernalia became available for purchase without education about the history and culture that is associated. The culture and spirituality of the African-Brazilian people became largely commercialized. People that honored capoeira as a daily practice disagreed with the government that presented capoeira as a sport for entertainment. Capoeira Angola was considered "dirty." The *Confederação Brasileira de Pugilismo,* which is the Brazilian Boxing Confederation, viewed capoeira as an amateur sport. The confederation was controlled by the regime, who then trained the police in a "cleaner" capoeira form which is recognized today as Capoeira Regional (Kraay, 1998, p. 126–127). In short, people's daily lives were demoralized to make a profit. After the death of Mestre Pastinha in 1981, capoeiristas began to reclaim capoeira as more than a sport or glamorous folkloric practice as the government portrayed. The economic conditions begin to change, and the military dictatorship ended by due to democratic pressure in the 1980s.

Socio-Political Movements

Environmental activists formed organizations to counter the government's volatile actions of the 1960s and 70s. The Movimentos dos Trabalhadores Rurais Sem Terra—MST (Workers Party and the Landless Workers Movement) was created in the 1980s to advocate for land for poorer populations. Biased socioeconomic conditions made land ownership almost impossible for poorer communities caused by unequal income dispersal, sexism, racism and land control. The majority of the workers had no ownership or control of the land that they were working on and oftentimes living on. The organization fought for land reform as well as better education, housing, employment and healthcare that families without land struggled to attain (Mier, 2015). The MST organized to squat and farm on unproductive land—occupying, resisting and producing in the restricted space. The group protested through collective hunger strikes, demonstrations and marches (MST, 2003).

In spite of the government's harsh oppressive conditions, the

African-Brazilian communities organized themselves as a political tool for social reform in the late 1970s. One of the first nation-wide organizations for Black resistance was the Movimento Negro Unificado Contra a Discriminação Racial (Unified Black Movement) created in 1978 (Reiter, 2009). The founding activists of the movement, Thereza Santos and Eduardo Oliveira de Oliveira, were inspired by the Civil Rights Movement and Black Pride Movement that occurred in the United States of America. The organization was formed to oppose racial and class discrimination. They demanded equal treatment for African-Brazilians and pursued the advancement of African-Brazilian culture.

The Brazilian people had enough of the mistreatment and misrepresentation of their culture and lives by the government and they began to respond with the arts movements as well. The Tropicalia Movement brought attention to the political oppression of the military regime. The Movimento Negro Unificado was influenced by the Grupo *Evolução* (Evolution Group). *Grupo Evolução* embraced the arts: dance, plays, and poetry, to raise awareness regarding the inequalities that plagued African-Brazilians (Cabiao, 2011). As many of these sociopolitical movements started to emerge, the Black Women's Movement, or BWM, also formed. Many women laid the foundation for this movement prior to being acknowledged, calling for racial and sexual equality. During the 1970s, the Theater of the Oppressed was founded by Augusto Boal. The organization encouraged social and political awareness through theatrical engagements. Art is often persuaded by society in reaction to socioeconomic conditions. In Oscar Wilde's essay entitled, *The Decay of Lying: An Observation*, two fictional characters discuss the role of art in society. In the essay, Cyril states to Vivian that: "Art expresses the temper of its age, the spirit of its time, the moral and social conditions that surround it, and under whose influence it is produced" (Wilde and Pearson, 1950, p. 63). Art is a reflection of the times and is ever changing as society transforms.

Ilê Aiyê is a prestigious African-Brazilian *bloco* or organized community cultural group. Ilê Aiyê was created in 1974 by Antônio Carlo, most commonly known as Vovô, to raise awareness and consciousness of the Black communities in Salvador, Bahia. During the 1970s, having any association to African roots or African-Brazilian culture was negatively stigmatized. The African-Brazilian community was largely ignored. Ilê Aiyê uplifted the African roots of Black Brazilians, emphasizing respect and reverence through their colors: red, black, white and yellow. The red represents the blood that the ancestors bled while enslaved, black for their skin, white to symbolize peace and yellow signifies wisdom and power. Blocos such as Ilê Aiyê became a safe haven for Blacks in Brazil to discuss and learn about social, economic, historic, and cultural themes that affected their communities. In his book, *Black Consciousness, Samba Reggae, and the Re-Africanization of Bahian Carnival Music in Brazil,* author Laryy N. Crook enlightens readers about the re-Africanization of Brazilian culture that "involved the reinvention of Africa and the construction of a socially engaged image of Brazilian identity that celebrated African heritage and black distinctiveness but … was rooted in the social, cultural, and economic realities of blacks in contemporary Brazil" (Crook, 1993, p. 95).

In the 1970s, the Black blocos could not widely participate in the Carnival parades in the southern regions of Brazil. The African-Brazilian blocos were the meeting place to strategize on socio-economic issues that affected Black identity. Ilê Aiyê was the Bloco Afro that traveled to Rio de Janeiro and desegregated the Rio Carnival parade. Blocos Afros such as Ilê Aiyê (from the Yorùbá meaning spiritual house on Earth) and Olodum (name taken from the Yorùbá term Olódùmarè, meaning supreme God) were established to bring awareness to the African-Brazilians. The Blocos Afros became a place "where black identity (*negritude*) is privileged with a valorization reversing the stigma of racism." (Armstrong, 1999, p. 2). Blocos Afros were significant community centers for the Black Brazilians teaching African-Brazilian culture, history, and arts. They became a place of refuge for African-Brazilians during tumultuous times.

The centers taught music and dance as a political tool demanding rights from the government. The Blocos such as Ilê Aiyê suffered from intimidation and discrimination for years; however, Ilê Aiyê continues to flourish and their work is dedicated to the promotion of African-Brazilian culture and the socio-economic empowerment of these communities. The Oxford Handbook of Dance and Politics explains the impact of the arts as a political process further:

> … mobilization as both an energy to move and as a basis for collective action traverse diverse social, artistic and political practices, shaping and connecting bodies and prompting agency and coordination, divergence, and difference along the way. Likewise, dancing has the capacity of making the expressive efficacious, galvanizing the agency of individuals and groups in the work of constitutive action that works on the levels of signification and the social simultaneously [Kowal, Siegmund and Martin, 2017, p. 5].

Community projects, teachings of African-Brazilian history, music and dance became a way for the Blocos Afros to express African-Brazilian pride and heritage in the country. The dances themselves came from the descendants of enslaved Africans in Brazil. The dances were used as a means of survival by several cultures that were displaced and intertwined together. The people used dance as a form of resistance from their owners and as spiritual catalysts. The influences of these practices and cultures were so impactful that they are still emphasized in African-Brazilian society over one hundred and thirty years later.

While these socioeconomic, sociocultural and sociopolitical events were occurring, Rosangela Silvestre was studying with influential artists such as the late Mestre King (Raimundo Bispo Dos Santos), who she calls her *father of dance*. She started training with Mestre King at the end of her time in high school. Mestre King, born in 1943, was responsible for merging western dance techniques with African-Brazilian dance forms and implementing the *Movements Inspired by the Orixás* dance classes for the general public as a form of artistry and understanding heritage. Mestre King has an impressive lineage of dancers that trained with him to learn and understand the artistic approach to representing Orixá symbols through movement. Along with Rosangela Silvestre, some of his influential students in the dance field include Paco Gomes, Amilton Lino, Ze Ricardo, Nildinha Fonseca, Dudé Conceição, Clodo Santana, Jackson Pinto, Tatiana Campêlo, and the late Augusto Omolú to name a few. Rosangela also studied with African Dance Specialist, Professor Clyde Alafiju Morgan. Rosangela recognizes her first dance teacher, Marlene; her first ballet teacher, Rosita; Carlos (Carlinhos) Morais; and many others along her journey including her students, have greatly influenced her artistry. Rosangela is adamant in acknowledging that any dance practice that she has studied or witnessed has influenced her. Everything in the universe and nature also stimulates her teachings. (Silvestre, 2018)

Rosangela started traveling from Brazil to India, Egypt, and Cuba performing, teaching and studying various dance forms. Around 1982, Rosangela created a series of exercises and noted them as *conversations with the body*. The stimulus for the movement in Silvestre Technique is pursued through these conversations. In 1984, two years after Rosangela Silvestre created a series of exercises known as "conversations with the body," the people of Brazil participated in direct presidential elections and a candidate was chosen through democratic vote. Four years later a new constitution was generated. The new constitution highlights the concept of socio-environmentalism. In the "Social Conflict and Participation" section of *Brazil: A Country Study*, it states that socio-environmentalism "reflects a Brazilian belief that concerns with the environment are inseparable from concerns with development, social equity, and justice" (Hudson, 1998, p. 152). The above-mentioned concept is apparent in Silvestre Dance Technique as respect for the environment is represented through the elements of nature. Martha Graham, a modern dance pioneer, stated "a dance reveals the spirit of the country in which it takes root" (Stewart, Graham, Weidman, & Wigman, 1935, p. 101). Reform to these socioeconomic injustices are present in the foundation, formation and practice of Silvestre Dance Technique.

The technique was created during a period of oppression in Brazil; however, the technique paralleled various transformative social movements occurring during this era. Rosangela created a technique practice that utilizes the body as a point of expression. The technique honors each dancer's individuality while nurturing African-Brazilian influences in Brazilian culture. Silvestre Technique became a safe space for participants to practice a dance form and be proud of their identity. Silvestre Technique dance training fosters an environment of learning without discrimination as participants learn to appreciate the space, instructors, elements of nature, music, their own dancing body and the community of people in the space. The technique receives all people regardless of their race, age, gender, body type, or experience. The changes implemented by the various political and social groups as well as the transformation of oppressive energy to expressive energy by Rosangela Silvestre was vital to the well-being of innumerous people.

Technique as Reform

In her work entitled, "Researching Performance—The Black Dancing Body as a Measure of Culture," Dr. Brenda Dixon Gottschild states:

The body remembers. The body remembers. The body speaks. The body tells us what is valued in a culture. Bodies are mirrors that absorb, remember, and reflect society's politics, art, religion, aesthetics, hopes, fears, strengths, failings—both the officially sanctioned versions and the sub-rosa, closeted taboos. Bodies are barometers measuring the pulse of society. Let me begin by giving you a context. Now, all of us in this room may be aware that dance is as old as humankind, and that there are many kinds and forms of dance, and dance has served many functions in different societies and different eras [Gottschild, 2018].

Just as political movements are formed out of a need, Silvestre Dance Technique was also formed out of the need for freedom, harmony, and personal empowerment in Brazilian society. Motivation turned into thoughts, that became plans, which developed into strategy and goals, and became actions. Driven by inspiration, Rosangela's fertile thoughts became symbology and methodology, which developed into action to transform a community of people. Randy Martin explains in his book, *Critical Moves* that "the agency of performance is distinct from the one that transforms state or civil society as such, but in either case, such an agency elicits a desire for further participation" (Martin, 1998, p. 47). Over the years, dancing bodies have engaged in expression of collective values through the practice of Silvestre Technique.

Silvestre Dance Technique is a movement technique that can be used as a means of expression. The *Body Universe* is a resource of multiple ide-alizations. The actions of reform occurred during the 1970s in Brazil when Rosangela Silvestre developed the Triangles of the Body, perhaps as a needed reaction to uplift the communities of people surrounding her. The technique not only provides physical conditioning of the body but provides reassurance of the mind. I recall from my journaling about Silvestre Tech-nique that "the body functions as receptors and transmitters of energy and light, generating and maintaining the state of harmony" (Williams, 2011–2014). This state of harmony is synonymous to the balance and harmony that many of the underserved Brazilians were seeking during the 1970s and even today.

Inspiration

The *Triangle of Inspiration* allowed participants to clear their minds of the unjust conditions around them and allow for moments of inner and deep personal thought connecting to one's own personal power. Racism and prejudice existed against several Brazilian communities. However, the *Triangle of Inspiration* allowed people to contemplate all of humanity, those things that make people more alike than different, and personalize each person's experience.

Silvestre Technique holds the potential to awaken the participants' consciousness to listen to the inner guide that exists beyond social con-ditioning. The principles of Silvestre's *Triangle of Inspiration* allow danc-ers to focus, listen to their higher self, trust themselves, which may not always be led by conscious reasoning. The *Triangle of Inspiration* is used to visualize and perceive change and action. When the *Triangle of Inspi-ration* is activated, the person is motivated and ready for action. Action in the *Triangle of Inspiration* is symbolized through the element fire, which is represented through determination. The fire is activated in the *Trian-gle of Inspiration* through the throat, third eye (lower forehead between the eyes) and crown chakras (the center portion of the top of the head), pro-viding courage and purpose. The energy may be considered the divine fire, activating determination, and being our guiding light. In the same way that social change was ignited in Brazilian society during the 1970s, dance participants can ignite change in their movement in training the tech-nique. The wisdom that guides the intuition is part of the blood memory within each individual. Motivation and focus also influence the *Triangle of Inspiration*.

Expression

The *Triangle of Expression* was created allowing people to recognize freedom in their movement choices and sensations. Dancers are encouraged to convey what they are feeling within by listening to their intuition and expressing through the symbology within the technique. The breath of the body emphasized in the chest permits the freedom of the body and liberation of thoughts. The pelvis supports the water elements with the "sensation of fluidity" and "softness" allowing for a calmness throughout the mind-body when desired (The Training, 2015). Dancers have the freedom and autonomy to express their culture without fear of being marginalized. Expression also holds space to show appreciate for positive influences in life and other influences that create growth through transformation. Through expression, Silvestre Technique participants have the humanity to connect with others.

Balance

The *Triangle of Balance* helped communities to become stabilized in their emotions against the unjust conditions and judgments against them including racism, sexism, ageism, religious discrimination, etc. Occurrences in society can have impactful influences within a movement technique and can concurrently influence how a person enters into society. Silvestre Technique is a platform to enter society with a stronger sense of self. The *Triangle of Balance* connects the individual with the earth element, centering the individual in reality. The aforementioned positioning allows the person to connect with ancestral memories and symbols as a form of strengthening. The sense of Orixá Ogum (element earth) can be used to remove the obstacles, which may prevent one from attaining their endeavors. In mythology, Ogum is a blacksmith that makes tools from iron, including his machete and shield to accomplish tasks. One's focus on the symbology of Ogum's iron tools and power to remove hardships from life, connects to the *Triangle of Balance*. Likewise, understanding the essence of Orixá Omolú (element earth) and connecting to the wisdom of the Earth can be a valuable guiding tool to influence choices moving through difficult circumstances. In Brazilian Candomblé, Omolú represents ancient earth. He is responsible for sicknesses and cures of illnesses (physical and mental); the restoration of balance. Balance brings forth understanding, awareness and grounding.

Silvestre Technique strengthens communities of people due to its symbology rooted in empowering themes. It is an all-inclusive practice.

The technique, turning no one away, allows participants to bring a sense of community and harmony into their practice, focus on all of humanity and inclusivity, freedom of thoughts, and movement. Silvestre Technique offered vision, balance, and freedom of expression during a time of imbalance and persecution. Silvestre Dance Technique allowed different people to appreciate their communities and themselves as the government installed harsh political rule. Symbolism was implemented to represent aspects of daily life that was ignored and at times destroyed by powerful figures. Element earth was taken away from many Brazilians by the government through the removal of land; however, this technique empowered people by giving an inward appreciation for Earth and those that share it. Symbology of the elements of nature and the Orixás represented throughout the technique, granted its participants self-empowerment. This work occurred during a time in which the practice of Candomblé and honoring of the Orixás was frowned upon by the government. Through the practice of the technique, violent energies were removed from people's lives, even if temporarily.

Voice

Oftentimes, Rosangela may sing or Vera Passos will give verbal cues during a Silvestre Technique class. The use of voice is another method of transforming the silence imposed on Brazilians throughout history. Through the technique, one's personal voice is uplifted and empowered. The technique has become a catalyst for giving voice to marginalized communities, breaking barriers amongst people with different languages, educating about African-Brazilian culture, and offering expression of self. It guides dancers to understand an appreciation for oneself, one's body, the community that supports us, and the natural resources that we need to live. "Art is an effort to create, beside the real world, a more humane world, Andre Maurois" (Sharma, 2013, p. 67). Silvestre Technique connects participants to the universe around them through exploration of physical movements in the body. This connection is sought in an effort to explore the more humane world.

Many participants and spectators of Silvestre Technique have been curious about the formation and preservation of the form. The following passages contain Rosangela's brief explanations regarding the foundation of Silvestre Technique and how the technique is maintained.

2018 Interviews with Rosangela

THE CREATION AND SUSTAINABILITY OF THE TECHNIQUE

When I was a young girl, I saw the people that practice Candomblé in their ceremonies with their eyes closed—this fascinated me. I remember seeing those people as if they were almost sleeping, but at the same time very active. I always admired this. During the times in which I was taking dance class and not teaching, I would go into the studio with this kind of placement of presence ... even when the teacher would say, "Let's go! Let's go!," I kept this reflective manner within myself. I liked this moment because when I was young, I had a very interesting life—that was difficult at the same time. When I was a bit older and I went to dance class, I didn't want to bring so many negative experiences with me. So, I explored this quiet, reflective place. Years later, one day that I was teaching, the Triangles of the Body Universe appeared to me. The triangles appeared to me on the body of the dancers and revealed, "I am the Body Universe." This moment was so significant that the triangles became the foundation of Silvestre Technique.

Afterwards, I began to diligently research sacred geometry and I studied the arrangement of various triangles pointing upwards and downwards. I understood that influences of spirituality and inspirations come from the high place above, and reality (real-life situations) comes from below. With this information, I decided to research further and connect my finding with the Orixás. I discovered that the messages from the ancestors (ancestral messages) materialize from the earth below. In this case, the messages come from the earth and flow in a circular motion to the air [motions hand a circle from the floor going up towards the sky and back down towards the earth again]. My investigations provided a clear thorough line of how the Elements of Nature can be used to activate an expressive movement quality which is cultural, universal, memorial, with infinite possibilities of discovery.

Sometimes, we need a lot of support from the Triangle of Inspiration, and other times, we need the Triangle of Balance. Since one Triangle points up and the other points down, we need to find the most harmonious way of managing each day within ourselves, as it relates to our triangles. All of the discoveries happened naturally. The triangles connect with everything [Silvestre, 2018].

The Triangles of Silvestre Technique provide the dancer with the information needed to place their body in its true verticality within this circular pattern. The triangles also simultaneously move throughout and around the body. The Triangles of the Body gives the person permission to be the *Body Universe*, providing an open door of constant Sacred Science interaction in connection with the expression of the elements of nature.

Silvestre Technique brings all of these Sacred Sciences together. It is the intersection of the Sacred Sciences; for this reason, it is necessary to investigate further to understand personal connections, connections to the senses, and to nature that link to the technique. Each person is capable of creating their own foundation. The continuation of investigations creates the very structure of Silvestre Technique. Through practice, it is possible to connect with the symbols found in astrology, numerology, ancestral memory codes of traditional and sacred movement, chakras, etc.; all of these things exist within the technique [Silvestre, 2018].

One of the effects of being in tune with hidden, sacred messages of the universe is that it brings forth mystical presences. Rosangela explains:

> The wisdom [of Silvestre Technique] is of the universe. You have to go back there (to the past) to get your channels open to receive; the messages do not come from anyone. They come from your own intuition. You have to be open to receive the messages.
>
> There is much more to experience in the future, and some information that I have missed along the way, and even more that lives in my ancestral memories. For example, in observing the arrow of the Orixá Oxóssi; when the arrow is pulled back, and pulled back even further, it symbolizes the connection to the forces that I have missed. But, there is a chance to experience these missed connections in the present day when permission is given. This is apparent in the way that—I, you, we, decide ... then when you let the arrow go, it goes far. So far, that I have to continue dancing to experience that immense infinity [Silvestre, 2018].

Silvestre Technique started as Rosangela's response to her circumstances through artistic expression. Her life situations were a catalyst for continuous discovery. She created the technique before it was labeled as a technique, and the methodology continuously develops. What has been created is an open gate to show others the possibilities that can be cultivated within. This is a technique to express one's personal memory and help define oneself. Silvestre Technique continues to progress as Rosangela explains:

> ...this process hasn't ended for me, I have to make decisions in that very moment of what I want to express. If I allow things to be open, the possibilities are infinite. I am still developing and creating Silvestre Dance Technique—we ... everyone is creating and developing this technique. When I see people walking; they are the technique because I am gathering information and discovering from them ... in every situation.
>
> The mechanism of the body is to be engaged in training every day and every possible moment. Some people decide to practice training as a repetition of yesterday. I decide to train the body, seeking and discovering what new thing is going to happen tomorrow [Silvestre, 2018].

During the early 1980s in Brazil, Rosangela began the training of three students (Luanda Mori, Fabiana Guirar, and Noemia Reis) in Silvestre Technique. After taking several classes with Rosangela, these three dancers asked Rosangela to formally train them. They were the first students of the Silvestre Dance Intensive and they began to bring others to study with Rosangela during the summer program. The seeds of Rosangela's choreographic voice were created through a piece that she created on these three ladies. The dance was called, *Linguagem* (Language). This piece contained many dynamics and aspects that influenced the movements of Silvestre Technique.

Luanda Mori, one of the original dancers of the work and now Rehearsal Director of the piece reflects upon her experience with *Linguagem*:

For me, *Linguagem* is a master piece in the sense that it contains the essence of Silvestre Technique as a spiritual artistic proposal. In this work the sacred gesture, preserved and kept in the religious context seeks the universal, which can be communicated through the body. This for me is the Universe Body; the one that decodes and encodes to communicate, seeking the commonalities in us all. *Linguagem* for me represents the search to enter this temple that is common to all, the body. The choreography begins with this preparation and the salutation to the sacred and reveals at the end the stage of purity that maintains life [including]—the gesture of cleansing and water that washes, which represents life itself. *Linguagem* was danced for the first time in 1999 in Salvador. Several versions of the work have been created, including *Temple in Motion* danced by Cleo Parker Robinson Company in Colorado.

    Linguagem started as a unit of a workshop. At that time there weren't many of us in the process. Rosangela had many dance engagements abroad, so we, Noemia Reis, Fabiana Guirar, Kênia Sampaio and I, rehearsed and prepared ourselves together. Rosangela came to watch the work directly on stage. The process was intense, at that moment without much thought, but with an intuition; the message was profound. *Linguagem,* containing the essential, can always be revisited and recreated because the message is intrinsic to the inspiring motivation. Every time we recreate it, it provides us with more knowledge of this body symbol of sacred energy [Mori, 2020].[1]

In 2020, I had the honor of dancing sections of *Linguagem* taught by Luanda and Carla Grosso. Rosangela invited them to share the choreography with some participants during the twenty-fifth year celebration of the Silvestre Technique Intensive in Salvador, Bahia. Twenty-one years later after its first performance, the dance still thrives. The learning process was intense, just as Mori described above. We arrived every morning at eight to dive deep into the physicality, messages, and spirit of the work. It is truly the seed of Silvestre Technique connecting the rich symbology found in the training to the roots of African-Brazilian culture, virtuosity, and contemporary movement.

    Rosangela started to travel internationally and teach what is now known as Silvestre Technique in 1981. Dancers came to study with her in Salvador and began to invite her abroad to various countries to share her pedagogy. Since then, the technique, the training and the program have continued to evolve.

How has the technique changed, evolved and developed over time?

For me, it's like life. I do not have the answers that I seek until I experience for myself and everything that I share is what I have experienced so far. When people ask me, "what is this technique about?," it is very difficult for me to explain. It is about one's own discovery within the technique; the experience. That question can only be answered through the experience. I do not have one solid answer to this question because the

---

1. See Appendix for original response in Portuguese

discoveries never stop, the technique doesn't stop. It doesn't stop flowing, it doesn't stop growing, it doesn't stop creating. Every time that I am in the studio, I am in a process of discovery and each person there is in a process of their own [Silvestre, 2018].

If there are one hundred people in the room, there would be one hundred different processes connecting to Rosangela's process in which she is sharing. When they leave the room, each person will leave with something different from the day. That particular day will never return. It is the experience of training on that unique day.

What makes me sustainable in the training? What is the consistent tool? My body. The body will return the next day, or the next hour. However, the purpose of returning is to continue discovering, not to repeat. I don't know what's going to happen tomorrow. How can I define tomorrow, today? The most beautiful thing is to see how this technique has affected all of these people and how these connections brings us together to meet and continue working. I thank all of the ancestors, all of nature, all aspects of life that provide me with the strength to keep this Silvestre story alive. It is infinite. I decided to be this Infinitation [infinite expression] [Silvestre, 2018].

Vera Passos was asked the same question. How has Silvestre Technique evolved over time? Her response was in alignment with Rosangela's standpoint as she details below.

2018 Interview with Vera Passos

For me, Silvestre Technique is like a butterfly, it is always changing and shifting. It is moving in different spaces, has different colors, and appears in special places. It is important for the individual to recognize this place—where they are not restrained. Where individuality is respected. Maybe that is one of the reasons that [Silvestre Technique] has stuck with me [Passos, 2018].[2]

---

2. See Appendix for original response in Portuguese

II

Creating Possibilities

An Approach to Silvestre Technique

*"Dance is everything. Take the things that bother you, turn
them into magic and keep going."—Rosangela Silvestre, 2013*
(Williams, 2011–2014)

Culture

I consider Silvestre Technique to be an investigation and discovery
tool. An exploration of familiar elements of nature (earth, water, air and
fire), joined with higher consciousness, and how they can positively affect
one's training technique and dance. Silvestre Technique is not only offered
to take as a class but is an opportunity to experience. The structure of the
classes in the Silvestre Technique Intensive, occurring every January and
August in Salvador, Bahia in Brazil, offers classes ranging from theology to
symbology to technique. Participants immersing themselves in the intensive can find the link to nature's influences in understanding movement.

In the following passage, Rosangela explains to scholar and cultural
critic, Barbara Browning, that Silvestre Technique, like Brazilian culture,
has the ability to adapt to changing circumstances and society:

> My dancers are always ready, at any moment. At the bus stop, waiting for the subway.
> The philosophy of the technique isn't just for the studio—it's a way of always being pre-
> pared. And this comes from our culture.... We live from moment to moment. You have
> to be ready for anything [Browning, 2007, p.182].

Silvestre Technique prepares dancers for life. It is not strictly a modern
or contemporary dance form. It can also be practiced by all moving bodies
and has no limits or labeling. The technique can be taught in modern dance
class or a ballet class setting if it offers what is needed for the participants.
Movement is universal—contractions, release, rises, flatbacks, and bending
of the knees were not movements created by modern dance pioneers; they

35

have been practiced for centuries in movement. These types of movement are performed in West African dances, traditional dances of India, and traditional dance practices of Candomblé, Brazilian Indigenous peoples and others. Again, the technique is inspired by the traditional forms practiced by the Indigenous people of Brazil and the enslaved people brought to Brazil during the Transatlantic Slave Trade. Silvestre Technique is also informed by modern dance forms such as Graham and Horton technique, classical ballet and classical Indian dance forms.

Rosangela explains to Browning why she does *not* call Silvestre Technique a technique of Brazilian dance:

> I don't say that I teach "a technique of Brazilian dance." I say that I teach "a Brazilian technique of dance." Because the former would indicate—what?—samba? A Brazilian genre of dance? I say my technique is Brazilian, because it draws on a number of Brazilian cultural elements, but it's not limited to a particular style of Brazilian dance [Browning, 2007, p. 172].

Rosangela's point to Browning is significant. I have witnessed incidents in which people have suggested that Silvestre Technique is a folkloric or vernacular form of the Brazilian people. Although it does incorporate roots of African-Brazilian culture, the technique itself integrates artistic and theoretical practices of a global span. Occasionally, there is also an assumption that Silvestre Dance Technique is a study of dances of the Orixás. While I was studying with Rosangela in Trinidad in 2013, she said to me: "I am not teaching religion, I teach the art of the religion…" she continued, "movements of the Orixá are an interpretation, and this interpretation can be used to strengthen your dance" (Williams, 2011–2014). Rosangela speaks passionately about this interpretation. The art of the religion can give our movement substance, power. She says, "when we know Ogum, we can embody Ogum" (Williams, 2011–2014). The essences of Orixás give useful information for the body to use. When we know the fundamental nature of Xangô this can be used to make our jumps soar with fire, or our turns revolve effortlessly with the qualities and interpretation of Oyá in mind. In Silvestre Technique participants do not learn the dances of the Orixás; one would have to go to the Candomblé terreiro to study that. People may come to Silvestre Technique to understand the symbols that have been artistically developed through inspiration by the Orixás which have been formulated to represent specific qualities of movement.

In "Researching Performance—The Black Dancing Body as a Measure of Culture," Dr. Brenda Dixon Gottschild eloquently details the existing movement embodiment in Africanistic cultures as a means of self-empowerment:

> For example, in African and African American cultures—I use the term "Africanist" to embrace these two—so, in Africanist cultures dance is an integral part of religious

practice, and the deities present themselves to the community through the dancing body of the religious devotee who dances when and as the spirit moves her. On the other hand, in many traditional Europeanist Christian sects the dancing body is a "no-no" and regarded as the vehicle that leads to evil, rather than enlightenment. This is one example of what it means for us to think about the dancing body as a measure of culture that points out what is valued or repressed in a given society [Reclamations! Lectures on Black Feminist Performance, 2017].

These traditional Africanistic practices are fundamental to the movement foundation and symbology in Silvestre Dance Technique, and movements inspired by the Orixás. The vitality present in the movements of Silvestre Technique empower not only the dancing body, but the messages communicated through the dancing body.

Honoring Orixás

In Rosangela's success of capturing the nobility of the Orixás, my first observation is that she invites curiosity through this technique by educating students about the Orixás in a non-invasive manner. During my studies with Rosangela, only after the four elements have been closely studied as actions through the body does she introduce the Orixás into the technique class. During the intensives in Salvador, as well as several other workshops that Rosangela conducts, *Symbology of the Orixás* is a complementary class to Silvestre Technique to inform students about the movement archetypes of various Orixás and to empower the technique. The education of Silvestre Technique is extended through Symbology classes, which teach the symbols of the different Orixás in the expression and composition of Silvestre Technique movements.

Rosangela started exploring the gestures of the Orixás, taking inspiration from the African-Brazilian practice of Candomblé before the technique was formalized. She was a choreographer and professional trainer for the Balé Folclórico da Bahia and she invited some of the dancers to explore the gestures of the Orixá symbols with her mother, a Mãe-de-Santo (Candomblé priestess). The first gesture was with the front of the hands behind the back, over the sacrum with elbows extending side. This gesture became the connection to the *Triangle of Balance*, connecting with the root chakra of the body, the earth and the ancestors. From the sacred gestures, Rosangela explored how they could be activated to inform the body training including working the muscles, posture and flexibility. Through this exploration, Rosangela found that dancers can express any movement with the mindfulness of the *Body Universe*. People who train Silvestre Technique are not empty beings—neither in their movement experiences or spirituality. However, many train Silvestre Technique to discover more, about themselves and others.

Silvestre Technique honors the Orixás through acknowledging their potentiality and the study of their essences in the technique. Rosangela has created a system that provides, through dance, tools for people to understand the roles of the Orixás. Consequently, this opens the possibilities for a personal understanding of not only Orixás, but the universe. I have witnessed negative perspectives and conceptions debunked and removed from participants' minds from practicing this technique. The exposure to and the awareness of these energies can open one's consciousness.

Silvestre Dance Technique values African Òrìṣà culture, as practiced in Brazil (as Orixá culture), through the gestures, structures and sequences of the dance form. The movements highlight the essence of Orixás through the elements of nature. The fire that lights Earth from the sun, is the same fire running through our nerves, connecting sensors throughout the body. Xangô is one Orixá that helps manifest willpower; the power to manifest and act. Determination comes from a spark within. Just as a fire is ignited, or light is conjured by the force of positive and negative charges, the will to do has to be charged from a thought; a force and that ignites the action. In Silvestre Technique this can be represented with the determination to complete a difficult combination or overcome a physical challenge in movement. The igniting could also represent the preparation that is required to achieve a large leap or a quick movement of the feet.

The Orixá Oxum symbolizes fresh waters and is celebrated as one who unites and offers good fortune. Silvestre Technique honors Oxum by acknowledging the water within our body via corporeal performances of movement that embody water's aesthetics. Water runs through our bodies and according to scientists, the human body's anatomy is made up of fifty to sixty-five percent water. As a result, we can relate to the fresh waters of the rivers or the salty waves of the ocean. Blood flows through the veins of the body as rivers flow throughout nature. We undulate our torso as the waves undulate coming from the sea. Water brings together several forms of life including vegetation, insect and animal species, etc.

People are in constant dialogue with nature as our bodies make contact with the Earth through daily activities. Our connection to Earth is embraced by gravity and demonstrated through stability. The minerals of the Earth; iron, calcium, magnesium, sodium, etc., nourish our bodies. People feel the sand of the Earth as they walk along the beach and encounter salt of the Earth in ocean waters. Similarly, people taste, smell and feel the salt of our bodies when we expel water and perspire. Much that is eaten comes directly from the Earth; this is why scientists and physicians, such as Jack Gilbert, claim that "we are what we eat." An article in

the *Chicago Tribune* expands upon Gilbert's and states that the body is "…
like an ecosystem, like a rainforest that lives inside you—a living, breathing environment—which we can affect by the things we eat" (Chu, 2018).
Rosangela takes this thought even further and suggests that dancing is
also a reflection of what you eat. Dancers may choose to either properly
or improperly nourish their bodies to perform the movements required to
dance.

In Silvestre Technique we honor one of the ancient Orixá energies
energies, Omolú; the Orixá associated with the Earth and contracting and
alleviating the body of disease. At the start of the technique class, we honor
our bodies, that which is nourished by earth. We find our balance and harmony, internally through our thoughts, and kinesthetically within our
body. Participants recognize the balance within the *Body Universe*. Next,
dancers clear their minds of all unnecessary chatter or challenges that they
may dwell upon. It is one task of Orixá Ogum (earth energy) to remove
obstacles. Afterwards, dancers set an intention for movement. Tradition-
ally, Orixá Oxóssi assists in achieving goals. Oxóssi aims a bow and arrow
on the desired targets and helps find direction to achieve. Aside from the
theoretical practice, in Silvestre Technique, we dance with continuous connection to the earth. There is tactile experience with feeling the feet and
parts of the body supported by the earth. Dancers acknowledge the earth
each time they plié or bend their knees, each time they transfer weight,
when they relevé and seek balance, and so forth. We have constant kines-
thetic connects with the four elements since they are ever present within
and around us. Silvestre Technique creates the body's ability and physicality, making the dancer explore the development of the language used in the
body's expression. The technique reveals not only the body's ability, but the
body's infinite possibility of artistic communication.

The foundation of this work connects with the ancestral messages providing us with the expression of the symbols. The sacred messages and the
symbology that has emerged are connected. Rosangela explains in the passage below.

2018 Interview with Rosangela

Ancestral Memories and Symbols

I think that we are connected with many people because they bring this ancient memory inside of them. When you go to the Silvestre Dance Intensive in Bahia or when I go
around [the world] teaching, we encounter people from everywhere, and all walks of
life. They do not feel disconnected—because the ancestral messages and the symbols
work together for everyone. Everyone starts to exchange their ancestral memories, that
for us, speak in a manner of symbolical vibrations. From there, we start to exchange

how the symbols make connections within ourselves and with the others around us [Silvestre, 2018].

The ancestral messages that Rosangela speaks of, also consists of the symbols found in the movements of the Orixás. It is making the connection between the essence of the ancient energies with contemporary movement while using that information to transform the dance through space.

Freedom

> *"Dance is everything to me. Everything I do is because of dance. When we feel we can't speak what we want … [if] we aren't heard or justified, we dance. We share our life through dance."*—Rosangela Silvestre, 2011 (Williams, 2011–2014)

In 1934, Lucien Price described the movements of a United States' dance pioneer's company: "I think the combination of high intellectual content and genuine spiritual feeling in the dances … are letting people feel, if not see, for the first time that there need be no conflict between flesh and spirit" (Price, 1962). Although these words reference the work of Ted Shawn, this quote reflects my experience watching and practicing Silvestre Technique. I have come to learn through the practice of this technique that dance is spirituality; spirituality helps me to have confidence. Dance is my confidence.

Rosangela says "I am teaching the **art** of the Orixás" (Williams, 2011–2014) and this art is naturally present in each of us. Inspiration. Expression. Freedom. Rosangela teaches movements of the Orixás, not Orixás dance class. An interpretation of the Orixás, symbology used to inspire our movements. This practice gives knowledge and a deeper understanding of the universe to gain stimulation for movement. Symbology introduces students to the culture from which Silvestre training seeds have grown. I would not suggest continuously dancing Silvestre Technique without studying African-Brazilian culture; it is a part of the learning process and knowledge.

The knowledge of the Orixá archetypes gives dancers of Silvestre Technique personal tools to pull from that informs the dancing. The information provides freedom of expression and interpretation of the movement. Say for example, the dancer would like to be more grounded in the movement. Therefore, the dancer could use the archetype Ogum to influence their dancing by bending the knees and reaching lower towards the Earth. In Orixá mythology, Ogum lives and works in the forest. His tools come from the Earth, and the movements of Ogum reflect these conditions. If the dancer wants to use the imagery of cutting through the space, Ogum could also be used to inspire this movement, since Ogum uses a machete to cut through obstacles along pathways. The mover may become more confident in their dancing using the aspects of Ogum to empower the quality and message of their movement.

The study of Silvestre Technique may be rewarding in various aspects. However, the training of the technique does not exist without challenges. In 2014, participant Yuko Tamura shared some of her challenges in practicing Silvestre Technique with me:

> I personally always have great difficulty in the choreographic part of the class. I am not a trained dancer and so my choreographic memories and my abilities to absorb choreography are underdeveloped. I usually need much more time to get the choreography than most other students. Meanwhile, I feel much more comfortable in the sequence part of the Technique, even though I still face a lot of technical difficulties [Tamura, 2014].

Tamura expresses her frustration; performing choreography that is inspired by this technique can be complicated. However, growth rarely manifests without challenges. With the tools of Symbology in this training, the body and mind are stimulated to reveal one's *Greater Self.* Four years later, after continued practice of Silvestre Technique, Tamura shared:

> Over the past several years, I've been discovering how Silvestre training helps me in the aspects of life outside of dance as well. The sense of connection with self and belief in one's intuition make me feel grounded when I am faced with challenges at my workplace. In the continuation of dance studies, the same sense of connection and belief in my capacity have helped to clear my mind and focus better in the moment, contributing to greater calmness in my learning process. This means that I feel less intimidated and more open to absorbing when learning new sequences of movements, even when they become long and complicated. The mental aspect of the training continues and can grow internally [Tamura, Scheduled Interview Via Email, 2018].

This was a development for Tamura after years of training and synthesizing Silvestre Technique practices into everyday life. The technique has expanded from the training in the studio, into practices for day to day life situations. One thing that I have realized throughout the years of training Silvestre Technique is that the principles, symbols, and the inspiration found within the training can be applied throughout my existence.

"There is no separation between physicality and embodiment. When we go from first position to second position you don't need to look, you must feel because it is you" (Williams, 2011–2014). These are ideas that Rosangela would like students to retain throughout dance training. Silvestre Technique explores how to use the mechanisms of the body through its training. The principles of physically training the body through practice and the ideas of the *Body Universe* create the essence of the technique. Everything that is needed is already inside us. The training is a tool of discovery to help identify what is already there. A living part of the memory.

> When you come into this world your head is first, you are initiated. Babies are born [into the world] with energy. They observe people and are connected to the energy of people. This starts to change when we tell babies "no." In Silvestre Technique we discover what this first phase of life is like again through our dancing. In life, we believe what the systems tell us. Systems say, you are African-American, you are a minority, and you are the image of what people make you. What they want you to be. With Silvestre Technique we have freedom [Williams, 2011–2014].

Through this freedom that Rosangela speaks participants have agency to discover, challenge themselves, connect with their ancestry, express and continue to find their artistic voice.

The Body's Agency

"The 'body' is an agent, not a resource" (Williams, 2011–2014) and in Silvestre Technique it is the body that enters the space, physically interpreting the symbology of nature and the Orixás. It is the "Universal Body" that expresses the movement and maintains corporeal balance and harmony in the codified sequencing. The eyes and mind of the body visualize and implement the perception of the environment. The body in Silvestre Technique has self-determined power. The theoretical concepts of the Orixás and nature are integrated to the agency that the body initially possesses within the technique.

III

Practicing the Technique

"When you dance, you bring your life to the stage.
When you dance, you dance your life.
You bring your own"
—*Rosangela Silvestre, 2011* (Williams, 2011–2014)

A dear friend of mine, Lilka Mimbella, urged me to study in Bahia with a woman that created a contemporary dance technique that somehow incorporates Orixás. For years and years, Mimbella mentioned this to me until one day, as I was researching international dance intensives I came across Silvestre Technique training. Undoubtedly, this was it: a codified technique, movements that express the essences of the Orixás, and symbology through the use of the triangles. I looked at the website every day for weeks before deciding that I would take a giant leap of faith and study in Salvador, Bahia for one month with Rosangela Silvestre.

It was an experience that I never could have imagined. My initial thought of the program was that it was a force of artistry. Rosangela was the commander and Vera Passos was second in command. The musicians came with just as much force as the instructors. The strength, poise, knowledge, and integrity of these women were what I found most fascinating. Seeing them in this light made me more eager to study. The movement vocabulary was quite demanding; I took the highest-level class offered during the summer intensive. After completing the course, I was probably in the best physical shape that I have ever been in my life—after only four weeks of dancing. This is my personal testimony; someone that makes a living as a professional dancer.

So why did I choose to study Silvestre Technique? After my initial curiosity, it was the connection to nature and the Orixás, self-consciousness, community (which I now consider family), and the class structure that has kept me invested. I am empowered through this technique—physically, mentally and spiritually. Each year, I continue my growth and discovery. There is a widespread Silvestre Technique Family that share these commonalities and support of each other in this work. Each year, Rosangela spends her time traveling throughout the Americas and to Asia, Europe, Australia and Africa to introduce and share this technique. In January and August of each year, those that she has met abroad arrive to Salvador, Bahia to receive more of what Silvestre Technique has to offer. The training in Salvador, Bahia is a unique experience. Everyone travels to the *Escola de Dança* (dance school) at the Fundação Cultural do Estado da Bahia (Cultural Foundation of the State of Bahia) also referred to as FUNCEB. In one of the seven studios found in FUNCEB, participants study with local Brazilians, as well as others that have come from all across the country and the globe. The technique is investigated in its native language of Portuguese, allowing for a deeper understanding of the movement through metaphors and symbols. Discussion and analysis of the Silvestre Technique occurs throughout the intensive. The music of the technique resonates throughout the entire building into the historic streets of Pelourinho. Silvestre Technique in Salvador, Bahia is framed by the building, the school's location, the language, the music and the people. These factors impact each person's individual experience of practicing the technique. In her email exchange with me, Yuko Tamura (from Japan) writes about the technique:

> I like the fact that Silvestre Technique makes me aware of the importance of physical, technical abilities in such training. I started learning dance regularly at the age of twenty-eight, and when I started to learn Silvestre Technique at the age of thirty, it was my first and only dance technique training. With my background, the concept of three triangles was a big eye-opener for me at the time. I felt that I had the first Triangle open to receive *Inspiration*, while I perceived my *Triangle of Balance* and technique was underdeveloped, and so was my *Triangle of Expression*. While Technique introduced me to the importance of physicality, I also discovered the feeling of internalization and spiritual connection with the unknown universe and the elements of nature. I guess for me, this harmony and strong union between two polar concepts (physicality and spirituality, Internalization and *Expression*, fire and water, and so forth) was something so unique that has attracted me to the technique to this day. Maybe verticality is a great visualization and manifestation of all this polarity of things that are opposite, but which work in harmony [Tamura, 2014].

This is Tamura's journey, complex yet fulfilling. Even though she had limited experience when she began her training in Silvestre Technique, Tamura was able to apply the concepts of the *Body Universe* to deepen her understanding of dance movement. The theories presented in Silvestre Technique training are accessible in this manner. "It is possible for everyone to come and discover. The decision is yours … to come and risk—dive deep" (Silvestre, 2018). Tamura, like myself, continuously travels to Salvador year after year to continue training, practicing and reshaping.

Everyone's journey and connection to Silvestre Technique is different.

Instructors Vera Passos and Deko Alves reflect upon their passion of the technique and how it has influenced life.

2018 Interview with Vera Passos

During my interview with her, Vera Passos speaks of her passion of Silvestre Technique:

In the past, many people asked me "why don't you do something that is your own? With your name?" Some people thought it was absurd that I have worked for a long time under the name Silvestre Technique. Mainly because I had a job that was distinguished. I was also already a teacher before working with Silvestre. I had a group of people following me—for my talent as a dancer and also as a teacher. But the technique, it ended up captivating me. Not hiding me but silencing this place … to focus solely on something that was mine [Passos, 2018].[3]

2018 Interview with Deko Alves

HOW DOES SILVESTRE TECHNIQUE INFLUENCE YOUR LIFE?

I started my modern dance training with Mestre King; it was the first technique I did. But, I could not find myself in one place [in dance]. So, from the moment that I encountered Silvestre Technique I realized—that was the place that respected where I was. This has been influencing me in such a way that today—I see Silvestre Technique as a philosophy of life. It is a moment that I seek to balance myself as a person, as a dancer. It is the place that inspires me. I always tell Rosangela and Vera that I need to attend the intensive in January and August. It is the moment that I renew myself. It is the moment that I seek within myself; something that the day-to-day will not allow. I receive tools to think—this influences every day in the studio … with a question, with an exchange with them [Rosangela and Vera], exchanging with a student, exchanging with someone at the door, or exchanging with the children of the preparatory school that attend the classes. The children become enchanted with you, with the lesson, and afterwards come and give you a hug. This completely changed my life. It influences my essence as a person, as a professional, as a teacher, as a child, with my relationship with people. My way of seeing the world, is completely different. Understanding myself as part of a whole. I am not alone. What I am depends on who you are, what everyone is. That makes all the difference [Alves, 2018].[4]

I remember sitting in theory class with Rosangela one year and she asked, *"why do people come here?"* (Williams, 2011–2014) There were several distinct responses throughout the room. Many people commented on the energy of the environment and spirit of the technique. Several others stated that they felt welcomed because the technique accepts everyone. I remember an overarching theme of the conversation being that this is not only a

---

3. See Appendix for original response in Portuguese
4. See Appendix for original response in Portuguese

Rosangela demonstrating floor sequence while in residency with Moving Spirits, Inc. (photo by Ace Murray).

technique; it is a philosophy. One student stated why she comes, "it is the energy in this space that's created." Another stated, "dance is spiritual; there is no need to separate the physical and the spiritual." Later during the same theory class, Sandra Sears, a dear friend and student of Rosangela, stated, "symbology allows transformation through being present." Personally, I have learned that, through practicing Silvestre technique, we are embracing the symbols present in the body and spirit. Rosangela elaborated on this subject stating, "I think people come to discover their freedom" (Williams, 2011–2014). Whether through energy, the essence of spirit, or a sense of awareness, Silvestre Technique provides freedom for discovery. For some, the process of exploring this technique and its movement theories allows for self-understanding.

Connections

Whose history are the participants embedding? This question can be answered in countless ways and each response would be just as valuable as the next. However, I strongly believe that practitioners of Silvestre Technique are embedding the history of their ancestors. Vera Passos shares her understanding of her ancestral connections through dancing Silvestre Technique.

2018 Interview with Vera Passos

ANCESTRAL CONNECTIONS

> I am very reflective—I try to understand why dancing did not occur for me this way [with ancestral connections] before Silvestre Technique. I always had great concern when I was dancing … of expressing myself. So much so that I carry this as a strong discourse within my classes as a teacher. I always maintained this thought even before working with Silvestre. Two of my teachers were Jorge Silva—he really was fantastic in his training process, and Gal Mascarenhas, also my dance mother who was my first contact with dance. However, I met many teachers who asked me to have this dedication of expressiveness, but they did not tell me how. They did not tell me that I could find this path within my culture. That this [expression] was in me, which was a part of my essence, of my origin. No one had ever told me about my ancestry that surrounds me. I never even heard that word, ancestry, when I started dancing. If I had heard this, it would have been easier to know that my ancestors were dancing with me. That they were my kings, my queens. That they were there guiding me. The path would have been more interesting to me because I would be conveying something more substantial. The path is much easier when you understand who you are—and the strength that you seek, are those that have represented you in the past. You know that this star, that this princess, these queens, these warriors—you have their [same] blood. They fought for you, they did for you, they suffered for you. Now you bring them through the symbols [Passos, 2018].[5]

Each person that comes into contact with this technique has a reason for the journey, whether it is known our unknown. There is no doubt in my mind that the hundreds of students that travel to Brazil each year to train with Rosangela and Passos have a calling to study with them. The amazing stories each person shares demonstrates that, and for the ones that continue to return, the technique is feeding a vital part of their life existence. For this reason, those that are exposed to this technique and continue training have a deeper connection than just taking a dance class. There is an instinct that exists to constantly connect them to Silvestre training; as Tamura and Alves previously explained. All who participate make the Silvestre Technique Family what it is today, embedding something from within connecting us. We are sharing the works and spirits of our ancestors. During an interview with Rosangela in 2019, she states "it is possible for everyone to come and discover." Silvestre Technique is a training that is open and accepting regardless of each individuals' background.

Through studying the symbology of Silvestre Technique, we learn that

---

5. See Appendix for original response in Portuguese

Rosangela demonstrating the placement of Element Fire arms—January Intensive in Salvador (photo by Diego Carrizo).

Rosangela demonstrating the placement of *Triangle of Balance* arms—January Intensive in Salvador (photo by Diego Carrizo).

we are diversity of the same (more alike than not). We as people are the same seed planted here in Earth; however, each of us blossoms as a different tree, plant, flower, and so forth, all while maintaining the same roots and fundamental characteristics.

Community

> *"The energy of what occurs in a space stays; in a building the bodies have left, but the energy remains. When you have something—be careful not to lose it. Be careful and preserve energy and the symbology. The sacred energy comes from preservation."*—Rosangela Silvestre, 2011 (Williams, 2011–2014)

One of the beautiful aspects of Silvestre Technique is that it is rooted in Brazilian traditions but global in appeal and reach. Through saluting their bodies, acknowledging the elements of nature and ancient symbols, participants are granted opportunities to find their own self agency. The unconventional structure of Silvestre Technique training allows students to learn from their instructors in various ways. The teachers constantly navigate through the space. Circular formations are common as well as facing various directions. Teachers lead; students lead.

For many Silvestre Technique practitioners, the dance itself is spirituality. Oftentimes, participants say they are meditating or praying when dancing. There is the higher association that attracts hundreds of new investigators each year. Solana Hoffmann-Carter expresses her encounters with Silvestre Technique:

> I found Silvestre Technique at Brazil Camp in California. I went there and I fell in love with it automatically because I come from a mostly ballet background, and I feel like I've had trouble with expressing myself. With all of the symbology and the ideas that are shown to you [in Silvestre Technique] I have been able to manifest them within myself and it helps, it feels good moving and it makes sense. I feel like I know the intention behind why I am doing things [Hoffmann-Carter, 2014].

The above quote highlights the purpose embedded in Silvestre Technique. Dancing that is more significant than a story line, or beautiful crisp lines, shapes and choreographed movement. Silvestre Technique is purposeful dancing, built upon the philosophy of the *Body Universe* containing the elements of nature. In giving purpose to movement, purpose is reflected in life because life is movement.

In 2012, I found myself in Pelourinho at the Escola de Dança–FUNCEB again to train in Silvestre Technique. After entering the school and walking up two sets of stairs, I brushed the sweat running down my

neck and shoulders as I turned the corner to the left. I found several dancers sitting in a row on the floor, stretching gently and talking about last
night's outings. I stepped over a few legs and ran into two familiar smil-
ing faces—arms stretched wide offering hugs, and *beijos* (kisses). I turned
around and see other friends stretching while standing near the open win-
dows; they were showing off their insanely flexible legs, foot in hand reaching towards to skies, bending forward, bending back, and to the side.

I peeked inside the open double-doors into the studio with the sounds
of Nei Sacramento on the trumpet and Luciano Da Silva on the drums
beaming from within. The dancers were dripping wet with sweat as they
briskly dart across the floor; turning like the wind and jumping with the
power of horses. Passos' cues, "YAAAHH!" and "HEE-BAH!" could be
heard over the music. "My GOD!" I thought to myself. "Is that what we're
doing today? No, it can't be. That's level two, who knows what's in store for
level three today." I turned around leaving the doorway without speaking
a word. One of the dancers on the floor grabs my leg, looks in my eyes and
says "EXACTLY! You better get to stretching, Tamara." And so, I did.

This is the normal atmosphere before starting Silvestre Technique class
during the intensive in Salvador. We greet each other, giving our warmth.
Sometimes sharing without speaking, only feeling, and this is the community that this technique creates and builds. Once we enter the space everyone claims their starting position on the floor. Stretching and conversations
continue until everyone hears that admirable call from Passos, "Vamos!"
and then our journey begins. Starting class from the internal assessment
and dialogue (Internalization) allows participants to become more comfortable in their self-esteem and open themselves to others in the class.

The technique teaches its participants to *trust* themselves in all of their
development and to continuously *teach* themselves. Never give all responsibility to the teacher—he or she may not always be accessible. Instead, participants are encouraged to use what the teacher offers to teach self and
others. In the higher-level classes self-doubt oftentimes has to get thrown
out of the space as Passos and Rosangela regularly call on participants to
demonstrate combinations, unexpectedly, within the blink of an eye, as
solos or duets. This method of teaching empowers dancers to trust themselves as they do not have time to contemplate every reason in the world as
to why they *cannot* perform the solo—they just do it without giving thought
to doubts, only feeling themselves in the moment. When these moments
happen, the others show their support through words of encouragement
and applause. It is in these situations, heavy breathing across the floor, challenging self-doubt and accomplishments, that community is built.

Other attractive aspects of this technique include the movement lines
that travel across the floor, which are called "Famílias" (Families). Famílias

are organized lines to perform progressions across the floor. There are four people in each line with each person representing one of the four elements within the technique. The lines travel through space as the four elements moving simultaneously in unity. In addition, the lines move towards the musicians and split in the center. The lines circle back around to begin in the same starting position. The aforementioned structure includes the musicians in the circle of energy that is carried throughout the class. When moving across the floor dancers use the *Triangles of Inspiration, Expression,* and *Balance.* A significant concept of Silvestre Technique's methodology is practiced in this format: establishing relationships with others in the space. The Famílias provide space for acknowledging other dancers, acknowledging the musicians, and showing community appreciation for their presence. In addition, it opens the space so that all participants can view what is occurring in the space.

The locals are welcoming to the *estrangeiros* (foreigners) in the space. During my first-year practicing Silvestre Technique in Salvador, many of the locals spoke to me inside and outside of class. We talked about dancing and life in general, despite the fact that my Portuguese speaking skills were not developed. I have noticed the people that enter the studios to observe, enter with great curiosity. The people are full of eagerness and a willingness to learn.

Since Silvestre Technique cultivates an environment that oftentimes feels like family, there is a widespread community of practitioners including dancers, musicians, yoga practitioners, tribal dancers, nurses, world travelers, expectant mothers, and the list goes on…. In her article entitled "Conversations with Rosângela Silvestre and Steve Coleman," Browning points out that "Silvestre is convinced that putting her technique in global context is essential to its relevance" (Browning, 2007, p. 172). Silvestre Technique closes its doors to no one because it is intended for anyone and everyone to practice.

Expectations

What is expected from participants in Silvestre Technique? My experience has taught me that discovery and freedom of expression are most essential. Expression of *who* we are as individuals, not what we may think Rosangela or Passos want to see expressed, is a part of developing expectations within ourselves. In her book, *Harnessing the Wind: The Art of Teaching Modern Dance,* Jan Erkert explains, "the teacher's demonstration provides a very powerful key to students' visual imaginations" (Erkert, 2003, p. 135). Oftentimes, students think they should imitate what an instructor demonstrates during class; Erkert provides one example, "students copy the teacher's tensions or bad habits…" (Erkert, 2003, p. 135). Unfortunately, students are not regularly taught to express movements for themselves. Erkert further explains that "dancers learn by watching other dancers. When students see a professional articulate a movement well, they incorporate it into their movement knowledge" (Erkert, 2003, p. 135). I am taught to understand the embodiment of movement instead of mimicking what the instructors present through Silvestre Technique. Erkert describes this phenomenon eloquently: "We dance to fully become ourselves, not our teachers" (Erkert, 2003, p. 135). This mindset encourages a continuous cycle of growth and learning. Silvestre training continues to help me develop physically and spiritually. In dance and life, I must think of myself circularly, not like a box or a square.

Through training, I have learned **teach me because I am capable.**
NOT
Teach me because I am incapable.

I believe Rosangela wants students to enter the space with this mindset. We are trained to have meaningful movement and to feel something inside through the dance training of Silvestre Technique. I oftentimes hear Rosangela say, *"give life to the movement"*; when this is done, the movement becomes dance. It has a history, a story, meaning and value. We can each feel something on a personal level regardless of what movement is executed.

Silvestre Technique is not a training to learn to dance either this way or that way. It is a technique to *dance* and then the person can decide *what* they are going to dance. In the interview that follows, Rosangela provides contextualization for training in Silvestre Technique as preparation for a professional career in the dance field.

2018 Interview with Rosangela

THE ESSENCE OF SILVESTRE TECHNIQUE

Silvestre Technique is a training. If someone enters into the world of dance without the essence of dance, this technique will empower the person to feel the dance as their own essence. Rosangela states:

> Silvestre Technique trains the dancer to enter the dance field. How? When dancers train in Silvestre Technique they will be able to go to auditions, residencies, etc. and will be able to get work. Like you, Tamara. You are an example of this. Look at how much work you have received through the years of training. When I met you, you only had the understandings of ballet with some African training and influences. When you got into this technique, you blended all of this. You started your dance company, entered into academia—you did all of these things because this training made you

delve deeper inside of this essence. Where you go, you decide. However, the essence of dance has nothing to do with the business of dance [Silvestre, 2018].

That is one fundamental philosophy of this technique. First, one must find their own essence, or voice, of their dance. When the dancer finds this, they can go anywhere. In order to go into the field, dancers need training. With training, the dancer can penetrate the business of dance. A dancer may be asked to leave an audition due to their physical aesthetic (the way they look). These types of decisions are made around the business of dance, not necessarily about the dance itself. Dancers have to be ready to face that, otherwise, what's the point? If you are training, you are training for the work. If a person only wants to dance a certain style, it is for them to decide, but they are ready.

Many people are an example of this process, you are an example of this…. Vera Passos, Agata Matos, Safira Sacramento. This technique made a difference for me because it reveals something about oneself that makes sense. The technique tries to remove the fakeness from dancing. It's to be realistic [Silvestre, 2018].

Silvestre Technique has allowed me to continue in the business of dance as Rosangela describes. Traveling to Brazil, studying the technique and being emerged in African-Brazilian culture, gave me the confidence to start my own dance company, Moving Spirits, Inc. Witnessing the strength of brown and Black women leading multitudes of people through Silvestre Technique, gave me the courage to make business and artistic decisions. I was in a place of realizing my own potential.

The Triangles of Silvestre Technique force participants to question their realness. For example, are you faking, or do you realize what you are doing? Is the movement generated from a place of intention or is it performed aimlessly, without reason? The practice of Silvestre Technique challenges the dancer to inquire about the purpose of the movement. For instance, the dancer may ask, which elements does the movement connect to? How might this information inform the dancer's interpretation and expression of the movement? The triangles can provide inspiration, but, we all live in this life and it is also necessary to remain grounded.

We must continuously ask questions and find our limitations. We then work with our limitations to go forward. The triangles work with us to help discover what comes from our own inspiration, and manifest into our reality to express. This is true in the classroom and outside of the classroom … in life. This is not a technique that only makes you function in the class or studio. You bring it to your life [Silvestre, 2018].

Rosangela explains that groundedness is vital in our movement practice and day to day lives. Remaining informed with mindfulness helps us to care for our bodies and our environment. Self-care is beneficial as we seek to ameliorate our limitations.

Dance is giving and receiving. Silvestre Technique training is influenced by several technique styles: ballet, modern, yoga, capoeira, Bharatanatyam (classical Indian dance) and dances influenced by the African Diaspora. Rosangela has made it a part of her life journey to explore these styles of dancing and various others. A careful study and fusion of these styles have helped to shape the Silvestre Technique.

Many people contemplate, "What is dance?" and "What is technique?." Can a person dance without technique? I answer, "Yes!"—imagine a night out on the late-night dance floor. However, technique gives freedom within the movement. Technique grows strength. Technique and dance are two different things. The technique is training; a tool. People practice *Balance, Expression* and *Inspiration*. This practice begins with technique. Anyone can dance having technique or not; though, Rosangela recommends never place technique before the dancing. A person with a lot of technique training is often grounded and needs to discover the intuitive-universal possibilities of their dancing voice; the dancing voice is the essence of *Expression*. A person lacking codified technique, for example, has intuitive strength and creativity. The person may need to become more grounded to know what possibilities are within the body, to eliminate limitations, and so forth. From my experiences in studying Silvestre Technique, I now define dance, training and technique as the following:

- Dance is the movement performance of the body. Dance may also be a phrase of movement that is performed by the moving body.
- Training is the repetition of practicing dance movement or dance technique.
- Technique is the training of the body to obtain or maintain movement aesthetics, including but not limited to flexibility, strength, musicality, coordination, balance, etc.

I remember Rosangela asking me one day before class, "What does technique do for you?" (Silvestre Summer Intensive, 2013) It took me a few moments to ponder this since I never thought of technique *doing* for me. I always thought of myself *doing* technique and what I do for technique. I answered simply that technique gives me tools that I need to strengthen my dancing body: flexibility, coordination, proper alignment, and so on. In reality, this list is ongoing since new discoveries are made each time I practice technique. Specifically, Silvestre Technique helps me in my structure to go beyond my limitations so that I have more freedom in my movements. Today, this is a thought that I often contemplate, which allows me to be a more conscious dancer. "What does technique do for me?" I ask this question in all forms of technique that I practice, whether it is ballet, modern or capoeira. If the answer is ever "nothing," I know it is time to leave that technique. Luckily, I can say that I have not needed to step away from any form; instead, I am open to a new awareness of receiving. During the 2012 Summer Intensive Rosangela stated, "when we are frustrated, sometimes we give up. Technique never gives up. If the voice in your head says, 'No you can't do it.' DO IT and the voice will go away" (Williams, 2011–2014).

Social Ideologies

Silvestre Technique, founded by a woman; Rosangela Silvestre, has post-structural feminism qualities in play. The training embraces the natural state of all identities. During Silvestre Technique class, the energy is directed toward the front of the class where the instructor initially stands to begin the sequences. The teacher guides and leads the participants, usually with the focus directed straight-forward while dancing with the students. Students that are new comers generally stand in the middle or towards the front of the space to follow the sequencing. Instructors moving with the students symbolize a balancing and sharing of power together. The aforementioned method of teaching is comparable to Muska Mosston's (physical education pioneer and scholar) *Command Style* of instruction. The dancers respond to and learn from the instructor's direction. The teacher provides feedback throughout this structure. Learning occurs through repetition and recalling the movement sequences (Mosston & Ashworth, 2001).

After the first few sequences, the teacher removes herself from the frontal position and weaves in and out of the students offering corrections and verbal cues. When the teacher moves from this frontal position, the students gain control of themselves and the movement. At times, the student in the front of the class may modify or slightly change a conversation by completing a different variation. Other students may choose to follow, or they may continue with the sequence as demonstrated to them previously. This process is similar to Mosston's *Practice Style* of teaching. As the dancers perform the Silvestre Technique movement conversations, the teacher circulates throughout the space to provide individual feedback. At times, dancers experience independence in determining rhythm, pace, and sequence modifications (Mosston & Ashworth, 2001).

After the phrases and combinations are completed, the teacher will provide individual corrections. Students may choose to watch, practice, or work on something else for their bodies. Again, this setting offers choices for students. For example, in most cases, I prefer to watch and apply correction to myself as well; I know the same information can be useful for my own body. I also observe corrections since the study of how corrections are given is valuable information as an instructor of the technique. The teacher may ask the class as a whole to repeat a conversation a conversation or ask a student to demonstrate a phrase if their movement has an emphasis or suggestions to offer the class.

As the class progresses, the teacher may call on a student to stand in front of the space for others to follow (if it is a lesser known conversation) or the student may lead a sequence. The teachers always orient themselves in various spaces throughout the class observing from all viewpoints and angles. When a student leads, the teacher watches without speaking and most often commends the student afterwards for their guidance. As explained in Mosston's *Reciprocal Style* of teaching, the teacher challenges students to demonstrate their own movement decisions. Participants share the roles of performer and observer in the space. Feedback may be provided by the instructor, and at times by the observers. This aspect of learning also involves Mosston's *Self-check Style.* Dancers assess their understanding of symbology and memory as they lead the sequences for the everyone (Mosston & Ashworth, 2001).

Class is usually positioned to face the musicians. There is a dialogue between their movement with the instruments and the dancers' movement with space. In an advanced level class, the codified movement conversation in Silvestre Technique can be performed as long as one hour without pausing. The instructor provides prompts, but generally without much involvement in these instances, allowing dancers to take charge of their experience. The structure of the Silvestre Technique class decentralizes the hierarchy present in many western dance technique forms.

Everyone is encouraged to dance a full spectrum of movement qualities. Sometimes participants are asked to embody the essence of a warrior. In Candomblé traditions, masculine *and* feminine warriors exist; each dancer is taught to embrace this duality within. In addition, dancers are asked to embody softer qualities that are also present in warriors. For example, Oyá is a feminine warrior and she cares for her children. The imagery and symbols help to remove gender roles for the beginner in this technique. Water, air, fire and earth tend not to have gender correlations for many. Water can flow gently as a stream or as powerful as a waterfall or tsunami. Wind can be a tender breeze or a tornado. The body symbolizes these characteristics in Silvestre Technique. Orixá archetypes personify male and female power within their creation. Each Orixá whether it is Ogum, Xangô, Oxum, Oyá or others have mythology explaining their existence as spirits connected to gender. Masculine and feminine energies are present through Silvestre Technique since they are expressed in the Orixás. There is an ongoing interchange and conversation of dynamics in this codified technique. Movements that are sharp, quick, and grand may be perceived as masculine energy while phrasing with curves, suspension, and minimalistic movements may be perceived as feminine energy for some.

A unique characteristic of this technique is that class is not always performed indoors in the conventional setting of a dance studio. It orients itself in new locations: the beach, park, forest, even a long-standing fortress. The atmosphere is ever-changing and due to this, Silvestre Technique is atypical in its own right. Rosangela has created a dance compound in Morro de São Paulo, Bahia, Brazil. In this space, the compound's dance studio is constructed partly outdoors. The front and sides of the studio have no walls, allowing the participant to experience the lush greenery of the trees, foliage, and plants. The structure of the space offers stimulation and inspiration for movement, expression, and instruction. The space in Morro de São Paulo will be discussed in more detail in Chapter VII.

Practicality

There is a distinct progression of the technique as Rosangela and Passos are continuously developing and expanding exercises and sequences. Teachers of Silvestre Technique are constantly learning from Rosangela, Passos, each other, and their students. A system of information exists within the technique that strengthens personal development. The training can be applied to and infused with all types of movement whether it is belly dance, yoga, or salsa dance.

As the creator of Silvestre Technique, Rosangela travels the world to share her vision and developments. Rosangela mentors the instructors of the technique and encourages teachers to deepen their individual voice within the training. Each year in January and August, the Silvestre Technique Intensive offers *Silvestre Technique, Theory, Symbology of the Orixás, Movement Analysis, Composition* and *Dance Capoeira*. In past years, *Methodology* (for Silvestre Dance Instructors) has also been offered.

When she is not travelling, Vera Passos teaches Silvestre Technique and Symbology of the Orixás at the Escola de Dança in Salvador. During the intensive, she often teaches Silvestre Technique Level II and Level III, Symbology, Floor Barre, and has previously taught Composition. Deko Alves teaches Silvestre Technique at the Escola de Dança in Passos and Rosangela's absence. All of these classes in combination with ballet and music, which are also taught during the intensive, are offered to empower the dancer's experience in Silvestre Technique.

Many Silvestre Technique followers and practitioners are interested in Vera Passos' history with the technique since she is a prominent figure in the training. Others that travel to Salvador, Bahia for the Silvestre

From left to right, Rosangela Silvestre with Vera Passos (photo by Diego Carrizo).

Technique Dance Intensive are eager to know Deko Alves' story. Passos and Alves describe their individual journeys to Silvestre Technique in the following interviews.

2018 Interview with Vera Passos

How did you become a teacher of Silvestre Dance Technique?

I was already studying technique for a long time. Long before I met Rosangela, when I understood that I wanted to work with dance, I really wanted to be a teacher. In reality, I did things the opposite way. First, I was a teacher, then I went to study dance. I had a dance group on my street where I danced; I already choreographed, without even knowing what a plié was.

FUNCEB was not my first dance school. It was actually a school in my neighborhood, Bar Balho, called Arte Viva. The school had three new graduates from the Federal University of Bahia (UFBA) as instructors. I went to study dance there in Bar Balho. It was Jorge Silva who took me to FUNCEB when it was in Campo Grande at Castro Alves Theater. There, I started to see Rosangela, and followed her. I started to take her classes. There was a contemporary dance conference that happened each year that Rosangela would come to and teach. As a student at FUNCEB, I had a scholarship, and I took classes with her; I became her follower. So, everywhere she went, I was there…. I was with her, all the time.

Ten years later, I danced in the Bale Folclórico da Bahia and when I left the company,

I was once again at Villa Velha taking her [Rosangela's] course. During the summers in January and in February, she came here to FUNCEB to continue the classes with some students who would stay in the city. I participated during these two months, January and February. And on the next to the last day of class, she told me that the students were asking her if I could continue the class since some would stay in town for another month. Oh, I did! I said, okay, well…. I'm going to teach. [At that time] I was not teaching because I had just left the company and Safira, my daughter, was very small. But then, I did; I invited Nei [Sacramento]—he was closest to me as a musician, and the classes were with live music. Nei called Felipe [Alexandro] and Luciano [da Silva], and we started like this, here at FUNCEB. At the time, my class had thirty students. The proposal was to have another month of classes, so I asked for a room for one month. After a month, no one wanted to leave, they asked me for another month. I renewed [the space] for a month, and I kept renewing, renewing, renewing—that lasting for years here in Salvador. People are going, people are coming back. There was something very interesting … for class having stayed at the same time for many years; we had people who participated in the first year and returned five years later—and at the same time, came here to FUNCEB and I was there—still teaching Silvestre Technique.

So, it was a class that marked the season. People came and went because they knew it was happening. All of Salvador knew what was happening. So, it was like that, I did not choose to teach Silvestre Technique class. I wanted to study the technique. I had no intention of being a teacher of Silvestre Technique. The technique chose me [Passos, 2018].[6]

2018 Interview with Deko Alves

How did you become a teacher of Silvestre Technique?

I never wanted to be a teacher, I always wanted to be a dancer. Being a teacher, it was a very distant thing—I would say, I'm going to be a teacher when I cannot dance anymore.

In the process [of Silvestre training] I was in the classroom, always giving assistance. I had a very good memory of the exercises [sequences] and had a facility to understand the physicality of the exercises. That was a positive aspect of mine, with no pretensions at all to teach it, because I thought it was far beyond me. When I saw Vera and Rosangela, I thought of something transcendent. One thing that was very difficult for me to achieve.

Within the Silvestre Technique process, I was very close to Vera and Rosangela. And since I was always close to them … they brought me. When we were in the intensive they put me and Lucimar Cerqueira together in the process. Sometimes I taught classes and other times it was Lucimar. I always thought it was a half-sacred place—that place I thought I was never prepared for. There was a moment when they decided, "This is the moment! If you wait for another moment, you will never be ready." The discovery, it happens every day as a student, you go in search for the discovery … always in this way.

During the intensive, I was responsible for Grupo I (Group One). I was only a supplier of information for Silvestre Technique during those times. Vera came to me and

---

6. See Appendix for original response in Portuguese

Deko Alves training Silvestre Technique (photo by Diego Carrizo).

said, "Deko, people come to Salvador and they do not have a reference. You are already here, you are discovering things, doing great things, and we have exchanged a lot of information. Why don't you multiply that?" It was at this moment that I understood the call.

I was a teacher in the dance technique intensive, and that was a comfortable place for me. I have the support of them [Rosangela and Vera]. If there is any problem, I have support. If there is any doubt, if there is anything that I discover, I am asking, and we are always in communication. They are here. And even from afar they are close … to understand the necessities of the universe [Alves, 2018].[7]

Alves became an instructor by way of his diligent studies of Silvestre Technique under the tutelage of Rosangela and Passos. There are a host of Silvestre Technique instructors in the United States including Samantha Goodman in Los Angeles, Stephanie Engel in Santa Cruz, Maria Isabel in Montreal, Adrianna Yanuziello in Toronto, Tika Morgan in San Francisco and numerous others. Other students of Rosangela infuse Silvestre Technique within other styles of movement, such as belly dancing and even fire dancing. The freedom of interdisciplinary practice allows students to train in their preferred form with influences from Silvestre training. Nonetheless, if Silvestre Technique is taught without infusion of other genres

---

7. See Appendix for original response in Portuguese

Passos teaching Silvestre Technique during the intensive in Salvador (photo by Diego Carrizo).

the foundation of the sequences remains the same. There may be modifications depending on each teacher's preference for class, but whether you train with Goodman, Engel, Passos, or Rosangela herself, the movement vocabulary and symbols always remain.

Music

Through my trainings in Silvestre Technique I have learned that the movement becomes musicality. The technique embraces music and musicians in a unique manner that Rosangela and Passos describe in their interviews.

2018 Interview with Rosangela

Music in Silvestre Technique

There is a marriage of the instrument that a person is playing, with the body of the dancer; transmitting the sound through movement. Movement manifests musically. This musical movement allows the musician to perceive the musicality. As a result, the musicians dance this musicality with their instrument. Essentially, the dance becomes the music and the music

Nei Sacramento playing the saxophone for Silvestre Dance Technique Intensive (photo by Diego Carrizo).

is the dance. Furthermore, the music compositions are also determined in that moment; each musician has a process of their own.

> I have worked for a few years at universities that have courses to prepare musicians for dance, and it is interesting that these musicians for dance do not play only one single instrument. They play various instruments and they also utilize their voice. One university that I worked for was in Boulder, Colorado, and there were musicians who were trained specifically for this. So, for the Silvestre Technique they understand what to bring in terms of musicality [Silvestre, 2018].
>
> We also have Nei Sacramento, and several musicians who go through this process. Each class is an improvisation, composition and performance of music.... A music that comes from the carriage of the movement, and the essence of the dancer with the movement. A long time ago, I remember that my brothers, Marivaldo and Paulo Cesar, created musical themes for the technique. Every time that we completed the conversation of the body, the movement sequences that we call conversations, it became a dialogue with the musicians. With the composition that Marivaldo and Paulo Cesar created, there existed a musicality at the beginning of class and it varied throughout the practice [Silvestre, 2018].
>
> The musicality in this work is allowed to be discovered. It embraces the various expressions of numerous instruments. It can be a saxophone, flute, berimbau, set of congas, violin ... the instrument that is present there, will be the instrument of musicality of that day—this is in addition to the musicality of silence itself.
>
> Since we do this kind of practice with the moving body, when everyone stops, and the musicians stop playing, the music is not gone. The music is still there. However,

it is the body that brings it—the impulse and the quality of the music with the movement. What fascinates me about this work is that everything is possible, we just need to be in tune to understand what the potential is in that moment. It's like poetry. You can start moving, and then another dancer or the musician, they start talking. This talking … poetically, will be the sound; the musicality of the movement. They can look at you move, and they can talk by saying what you express. The body is constantly in emotions [Silvestre, 2018].

2018 Interview with Vera Passos

Music in Silvestre Technique

I started the technique classes with Nei Sacramento. Nei already had a process with music before he met me. He comes from a family of artists; Paco [Gomes] is a choreographer, his uncle by blood, but, whom practically raised Nei. The Silvestre Technique in itself does not have a direct connection with a musical style; it is free to work with any style. Nei worked with me and we developed each dance sequence within a music—within a musical quality, that is differentiated. For many years, each movement sequence had a different song. When he started to recognize that song inside the exercise, he was already ahead of us. Nei was discovering other things and [the music] began to change every day; for each exercise sequence there was a different musicality. For me, this was the best place to live with music.

Nei specializes in dancing the movement with the music. In January 2018, a class occurred in which I left a cell phone filming. Nei decided to stand exactly in front of the cell phone. So, I captured a very beautiful image. Because, he stood in front, and the image was between Nei's legs. All of the dancing was there in the same place. Nei was dancing with us the entire time! The saxophone played "PAAAAN!," and Nei "PAAAAN!" with his body. He pliés, he jumps. He kept dancing.

I am bringing this principle of music to all my practices. I really like this place; it is a place that is not defined. I think it has nuances, rhythms, that are beautiful and necessary for the dancers to develop their artistry. This marriage of music and dance, where one pulls the other. It is not only for the music to stay on top of the dancer.

For me, today, it is very important to work with live music, because the body responds differently and gives us more possibilities within the process. I will always take a musician wherever I go. For classes of Movements of the Orixás, for technique, for composition, it is very important to have live music. Mainly, musicians of the land—who understands the music, dance, and culture. It is not the same to have someone who is still studying. Music is special, and you have to have confidence in the music [Passos, 2018].[8]

Through studying this technique, I have learned that all actions are used to condition the body and the mind. The body moves with meaning, not aimlessly. As humans, we condition our bodies to walk or to eat with one hand. The more we condition, the better we feel; comfort is essential for

---

8. See Appendix for original response in Portuguese

Vera Passos (center) demonstrating movement with live music provided by Nei Sacramento (left) and Miminho (right) (photo by Diego Carrizo).

many people. Technique is used to condition the body to move—to understand, to feel comfortable in the movement. Rosangela calls for participants to train their bodies so that the body executes movement the way it is desired.

IV

Conceptualizations
of Silvestre Technique

"My body is the Universe power, Open to Receive."—Rosangela Silvestre, 2011 (Williams, 2011–2014)

Philosophy

I have traveled to Salvador, Bahia for several years to immerse myself in African-Brazilian culture and to study Silvestre Technique intensely at the Escola de Dança in Pelourinho, the historic center of Salvador. In these years of studying Silvestre Technique, I have kept a journal of my daily encounters, lessons, and experiences. Throughout the remainder of this text, I will share some of my thoughts and reactions to the training and the impact that it has had in my life. So, as Vera Passos says while we anxiously wait for our training to begin, "VAMOS!!"

January 4, 2011 (Journal Entry)
Today was the first day of technique class this year. It kicked my ass. It is very powerful and demanding of the body, but I am definitely up for the challenge. There are so many layers of understanding.... I need to take time to process [Williams, 2011–2014].

In the following passages, the information from my journaling and notes have been dissected and restructured to describe the concepts and principles of Silvestre Technique.

January 7, 2011 (Notes)
Silvestre Technique is a technique to train the body, which is composed of the following ideas:

- Discovery
- Learning
- Development
- Dance

The technique contains symbols and vocabulary, which allows participants to better understand the movement theories. The imagery used in Silvestre training assist participants in supporting their growth [Williams, 2011–2014].

In Silvestre Technique the Body connects to the Universe, which is why the dancing body is conveniently named the *Body Universe*. The *Body Universe* is composed of three triangles.

Triangles

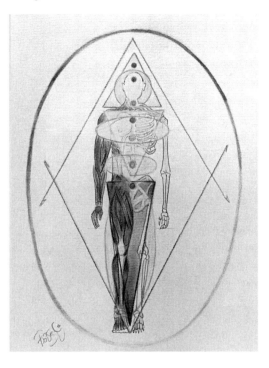

1st Triangle

Inspiration, *Visualization*, *Perception*
Location: From the (top) center of the head to the shoulders.

2nd Triangle

Expression, Freedom: speak to your Body
Location: From the shoulders to the navel.

3rd Triangle

Balance
Location: From the hips to the soles of the feet.

The Triangles of Silvestre Technique represent existence. The triangle pointing up points to the Sacred Force (Universe/

Photo by Maria de la Paz Ramos Reyes.

God) and the two triangles pointing down point to reality and stabilization. There is no separation between the three triangles (The Training, 2015).

1st Triangle Inspiration	Communication: reflection, meditation or prayer
2nd Triangle Expression	Community: unity
3rd Triangle Balance	Communion: spiritual union and empathy

I asked Rosangela about the significance of the number three since there are three distinct Triangles of the Body. Three symbolizes balance.

When one investigates religious practices, for example: Judaism, Hinduism, Islam, Buddhism, Christianity, Yorùbá traditions, Indigenous traditions and many others, the number three has great spiritual significance. Silvestre Technique provides tools to transmit information to and from the *Body Universe*. Discovering how the elements of nature, triangles, chakras, body, and Orixás work in relationship together is an essential part of understanding the *Body Universe*.

The Body Universe and the Body's Organs

The *Triangle of Inspiration*, extending from the top of the head to the shoulders, points upwards towards the universe. Within this triangle our senses are housed. The body's senses are activated through the mouth, nose, ears, eyes and touch. The brain sends signals to all of the body's organs via the nervous system. Several of the body's main organs are located in the next triangle. The *Triangle of Expression* is represented through the shoulders to the navel. Several of the body's major organs are found in this region including the heart, kidneys, liver, lungs, pancreas, and spleen. Some of the body's systems such as the circulatory, digestive, endocrine, lymphatic, muscular, and skeletal travel throughout the *Triangle of Inspiration* and/or the *Triangle of Expression* and into the *Triangle of Balance*. The *Triangle of Balance* extends from the hips to the feet. For example, the circulatory system pumps blood to and from the heart in the *Triangle of Expression* and supplies oxygen to the *Triangles of Inspiration and Balance*. Silvestre Technique provides its participants an opportunity to focus on the use of the body's senses, (sight, sound, smell, and taste), through the *Triangle of Inspiration* and the sense of touch through all three triangles.

Students demonstration the triangles of the arms in connection to the *Triangle of Balance* (photo by Jacson do Espirito Santo).

January 2011 (Notes)

The philosophies of Silvestre training can be found in any technique, because it is a part of our existence. You could take any class and only be concerned with physicality. But you can also bring in your inner self, core, relation to the Earth and universe. How do you process information? Inspiration is there. Jumps and turns are not a technique that anyone can do. You need technique to discover how to jump and turn. Share your ideas, share your discoveries. Symbols talk to us all the time. [Williams, 2011–2014]

Nature

In Silvestre Technique, each triangle has corresponding elements of nature that are used as symbology for the body.

1. **Fire**—Divine Power

Fire connects with the *Triangle of Inspiration*, Perception, and Visualization giving the dancer determination, courage and purpose.

2. **Air**—Freedom

Air connects to the *Triangle of Expression*, permitting liberty in movement and freedom.

3. **Water**—Birthing and nurturing

Water also complements the *Triangle of Expression*, allowing a greater sense of freedom.

4. **Earth**—Grounded, Balance, Reality

Earth, which correlates to the *Triangle of Balance* provides stability and keeps people grounded, giving assurance and confidence. Connecting the three triangles and their intentions opens dancers to greater possibilities. In Silvestre Technique the language of nature is used to interpret our dance, create dynamics, and give meaning to the movements. Silvestre Technique teaches people not to destroy their own nature. Nature is strength; it does not die, it only transforms.

Chakras

January 7, 2011 (Journal Entry)

Today is a great day of discovery. In class I came to realize that whenever my crown chakra is pointing towards the ground there is a strong connection from the root of groundedness to the crown of enlightenment. It is very strong, and I feel it charging through my body [Williams, 2011–2014].

In the text, *Wheels of Life: A User's Guide to the Chakra System,* author Anodea Judith uses comprehensive and concise terms to define the chakra system of the body. In summary, Judith describes the chakras as:

- a center for the reception, assimilation, and expression of life-force energies

- any of the seven energy centers of the body
- a disc-like vortex of energies made from the intersection of different planes
- the revolving wheel of the gods
- the wheel of time
- the wheel of law and celestial order
- a tantric ritual circle of people, alternating male and female (Judith, 2012, Glossary).

I define chakras as the energy centers of awareness and harmony in the body. There are thousands of chakra points throughout the body, and there are seven major chakra centers found along the spinal column in the body. Silvestre training teaches its participants to release tension by opening the chakras while dancing. I remember Rosangela telling me during one class, *"Open. Let the energy flow. Allow yourself to work calmly"* (Williams, 2011–2014). This opening is embedded as one of the first elements we unveil within a Silvestre Technique class.

Triangle of Inspiration

Crown Chakra = Fire
Third eye = Fire
Throat = Fire

Triangle of Expression

Heart = Air
Solar Plexus = Water
Sacrum = Water

Triangle of Balance

Root Chakra = Earth

The chakras in the body should develop vertically to open (Judith, 2012); this opening facilitates the projection of my personal illumination, or enlightenment. Chakras open the body, connecting energy and the universe to the body. Students can also generate energy in their bodies, through

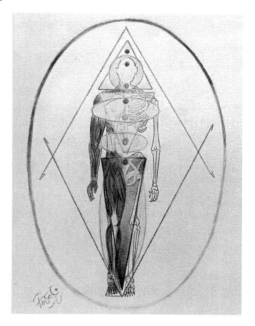

Photo by Maria de la Paz Ramos Reyes.

musicality. We can use these ideas to enliven and fortify ourselves. When we express physicality by incorporating the chakras and the elements of nature, we are in harmony. Rosangela urges participants to "Listen to your body. Talk to your body when you move." She explains that this dialogue promotes growth and unearthing from within. *"Give to your body"* she says, "Feel your body and do not imitate (what you see)" (Silvestre Summer Intensive, 2013).

In Anodea Judith's *Wheels of Life*, she describes the chakra systems of the body and their correlations to nature. She states that, "chakra is a Sanskrit word meaning 'wheel' or 'disk' and denotes a point of intersection where mind and body meet" (Judith, 2012, p. 16). The body contains thousands of chakra points throughout; however, there are major and minor chakras. I have described the seven major chakras below, informed by specified ideas from Judith's text. Along with the synthesis of my studies of Vedas (ancient texts) from the Hinduism traditions of India, I offer a summary of the connections between the elements of nature and the chakras (spelled cakra—in Veda texts) of the body.

The Root Chakra—Element Earth

The root chakra is located at the base of the spine. It fosters self-preservation. An open root chakra provides balance through sound decisions and choices; this brings forth stability. The root chakra is associated with survival as well as physical and mental support. A balanced root chakra has the potential to open one's life pathways and assists in making logical decisions. The root chakra informs how we navigate our time, space, and energy in connection with others and in connection to the world.

The Sacral Chakra—Element Water

This chakra is located in the pelvis region/lower abdomen and is associated with emotions and desires. Self-gratification is the result of an empowered sacral chakra. Life is formed from the sacral chakra. As a result, this chakra is affiliated with our ability to create. An unblocked sacral chakra initiates the creative process. Drawing from the unconscious mind and similar to the darkness of the womb, it is this chakra where thoughts and ideas are aligned to blossom creativity.

The Solar Plexus Chakra—Element Water

The solar plexus chakra is located in the upper abdomen and cultivates personal power and self-esteem. Self-determination is fortified through the solar plexus chakra. Harmony with oneself is manifested through a balanced third chakra. According to Judith, matter and movement together create energy, she explains in *Wheels of Life* that this stimulus "psychologically, relates to the spark of enthusiasm that ignites power and will" (Judith,

2012, p. 152). The solar plexus chakra is associated with transformation, change, inspiration and willpower.

The Heart Chakra—Element Air

This chakra is located in the chest, around the sternum. It nurtures acceptance of others, and relationships with others. A balanced heart chakra illuminates harmony with self and the world, love, freedom, and peace. Rejuvenation, liberty, and openness are associated with this chakra. The heart chakra makes connections throughout the body, as a result, this chakra is linked with unity—with others and within oneself. The heart chakra is responsible for connections with others, and the heart chakra is connected to our relationships with others.

The Throat Chakra—Element Fire

This chakra is located in the throat and is associated with self-expression, truth, communication and creativity. With a balanced throat chakra, a person is able to communicate efficiently and clearly. Truth is spoken. Listening abilities are enhanced. A well-balanced throat chakra will also improve one's confidence, without ego.

The Third Eye Chakra—Element Fire

This chakra is located between the eyes and is important for self-reflection, clairvoyance and wisdom without conscious reasoning. The sixth chakra is associated with intuition, imagination and transcendence. When this chakra is balanced, one listens to and understands the intuitive mind well. The unconscious and the conscious minds become one. The person reaches a higher level of enlightenment from the awareness of the unconscious and conscious minds.

The Crown Chakra—Element Fire

This chakra is located at the top (crown) of the head and is associated with self-knowledge, understanding and deep thought—connecting with clarity to the subconscious mind. The crown chakra is also associated with transcendence.

In the text, *A Beginner's Guide to Constructing the Universe,* Michael Schneider expounds upon viewpoints of the ancient philosophers. He summarizes the energies that bring the elements of nature, the chakras, and sacred sciences together.

The Ancient philosophers saw the natural world of Earth, water, air and fire within us as the quatrain of our soul. In this inner symbolism, the four elements are seen as four levels of motivation within ourselves, a human tetrachord upon which the forces of nature play. The ancients symbolized it many ways in architecture, religion, mythology, and arrangements of society. Since the whole Earth was symbolized by the human microcosm, it is we who are referred to as the "four corners of the globe" containing the "seven seas" (chakras), as well as the four stages of a spiritual journey... [Schneider, 1995, p. 91].

We cannot see the chakras of the body, but we can sense the chakras. We can use the energy of the chakras to inform the movement of the body and its intentions. In the same way, the essence of the Orixás can be embodied to transform movement.

Orixás

Rosangela suggests, "don't concentrate only on the Triangle of Balance. You will neglect Expression; your body won't speak, and you will not receive inspiration. The Orixás are your Inspiration" (Williams, 2011–2014).

In her interview with Barbara Browning, Silvestre states:

The naturalness of movement comes from the fact that it's also linked to the mythology of the Orixás. Because, when I studied in the terreiro, this is what I took—when I teach the movement of the Orixá dances, I draw on the traditional forms, but when I train my dancers in my technique, it's through these quotidian gestures which are transformed into technical movements [Browning, 2007, p. 177].

Learning about the Orixás is more than a lifetime's journey. However, I am offering a brief description of a few Orixá archetypes that are often explored in Silvestre training.

Ogum. Represented through Earth—iron: Fierce warrior that removes obstacles.

Oxóssi. Represented through Earth—forest: Hunter that provides direction.

Oxum. Represented through Water—fresh waters (rivers, streams, and lakes): Fertility, wealth, protection, creativity, and abundance.

Iemanjá. Represented through Water—ocean and salt waters: guardian and provider.

Omolú. Represented through Earth—herbs: Herbalist and healer.

Oyá. Represented through Wind—storms: Female Warrior creating transformations.

Xangô. Represented through Fire—lightening: King and overseer of justice and victory.

If interested, I strongly recommend readers to delve deeper into an investigation of the mythology and essences of the Orixás for more understanding. Pierre Verger, a French photographer and anthropologist, researched and documented the history and cultural mythology of the Orixás in Brazil over several decades. His ethnographic studies also took him to Nigeria, Mali, Togo, Benin and the West Indies. His work has been published in over 100 books and is a notable resource for examination. Nonetheless, the most advantageous information regarding Orixá traditions will come directly from the Candomblé terreiros with the Mãe or Pai de Santo.

During the 2012 summer intensive, Rosangela provided a simple breakdown of the placement of the Orixás throughout the chakras in the body as she interpreted them at that time:

Crown Chakra = Ori and Olódùmarè (in oneself)
Third Eye = Xangô
Throat = Exu
Heart = Oxalá, Oyá
Solar Plexus = Oxum, Iemanjá
Sacral = Oxum, Iemanjá

Root Chakra = Ogum, Omolú
(Williams, 2011–2014).

There are varying models regarding the strongest locality of Orixás throughout the body. In the book *Grasping the Root of Divine Power* HRU Yuya T. Assaan-ANU has a slightly different perspective regarding the position of Orixás (or Òrìsà in Isese l'agba—spiritual practices of the Yorùbá people) as they relate to the chakras. Assaan-ANU explains the existence of Òrìsà in the body according to his studies of the Yorùbá based Ifa tradition (Assaan-ANU, 2010):

Crown Chakra = Olódùmarè
Third Eye = Orunmila, Obatala (referred to as Oxalá in Brazilian Candomblé)
Throat = Obatala
Heart = Ògún (Ogum)
Solar Plexus = Sàngó, (Xangô), Oyá
Sacral = Osun (Oxum), Yemoja (Iemanjá)
Root Chakra = Èsù, Sàngó, (Xangô), Oyá

My sentiments are as follows: Orixás are divine spiritual forces that exist throughout the body. As the chakras are complex energies of the body, so are the Orixás. My Orixá chart incorporates aspects of both theories:

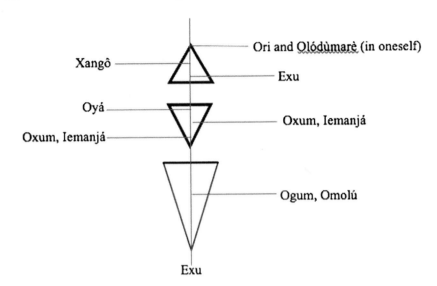

Xangô

Ori and Olódùmarè (in oneself)

Exu

Oyá

Oxum, Iemanjá

Oxum, Iemanjá

Ogum, Omolú

Exu

Orixá Archetypes in Relation to the Triangles of the Body Universe.

It is important to note that Rosangela suggests that in Silvestre Technique the Orixá Exu delivers messages throughout the entire body and to the universe. The best method to draw a personal philosophy regarding Orixás throughout the body temple is to explore and learn the chakras and understand the Orixás.

Why are these correlations throughout the body important? The knowledge of Orixá placement through the body allow a person to empower him- or herself in their movement. This information also provides substance for people to care for their bodies in a different manner since there is awareness of the Orixás residing inside. Rosangela further explains how the ordinary movements of the body in the terreiro are interpreted in Silvestre Technique:

> …in my technical training, other elements are added—the bending over movements of labor are translated to the parallel position with bent knees, which will read differently on the stage. Any technique for the stage, you'll find, will demand a certain awareness—of alignment, of the alignment of the posture, of the feet, of the arms. It becomes naturalized because of the quotidian movement. In the terreiro, people don't use the term "technique"—they speak of a "maneira," a manner of movement. We add the word technique because there are other elements, other things we're aware of [Browning, 2007, p. 178].

In the previous passage Rosangela speaks of the self-conscious awareness of the technique in Silvestre training. In other words, by adding the information of technique to the movements that the body already inherently knows and performs daily, the dancer becomes well-seasoned in the physical presentation of the art form.

Ori

Oftentimes, literature focuses strongly on the role of the Orixás in movement. However, the Ori is just as important. The Ori literally means "head" in Isese spirituality (from the Yorùbá people). Ori refers to one's spiritual intuition, destiny, and the conscious mind. Some people may refer to this as the will or drive to action. In Silvestre Technique, I begin connecting my Ori with the *Triangle of Inspiration*: Intuition (third eye), Perception (occipital, back of head) and Visualization (eyes). I always acknowledge my Ori, the universe, and the Earth to remain open to inspiration and grounded in physicality—this helps me to discover and listen to my intuition.

Through movement, my Ori shapes the reality of present and future circumstances. My Ori allows me to fully engage in each moment that I dance while visualizing future possibilities and honoring my past. Ori is considered the highest place of one's self-consciousness. One strong aspect of Ori in Silvestre Technique is embraced in our *Triangle of Inspiration*. Ori guides our self-awareness. When the body moves through space to dance it is often the conscious mind that is credited with movement. In reality, the unconscious mind is just as important. Our past experiences sheltered in our thoughts and our muscle memory influence our every move. We dance our histories. In Silvestre Technique we do not practice consciously focusing on our past, instead we use the symbols and representations of nature to discover in the present.

Ancestors

We are standing on the shoulders of our ancestors. Silvestre Technique is firmly planted in this belief. The ancestors are honored by saluting the earth below. In the photo displayed, my Ori is connecting with the ancestors by directing the crown of my head to the earth below. My fingertips are pointing to the earth and beyond towards the ancestors. The connections developed from the Ori to the ancestors through these sorts of gestures are powerful. This physical relationship to the ancestors is significant in each person's individual history. If welcomed, the ancestors can provide strength and support the dance. My ancestors are manifested through my art form. The memory of the ancestors is brought to the dance through symbology and the *Body Universe*.

Appreciation to the earth and Ancestors with the Ori directed towards the earth (photo by Brooks Anderson).

Rosangela says, "We are the creative being of ancestors. The ancestors are in our blood. The creativity and art is passed on through the ancestors. We allow our ancestors to come or we choose to close the door. The spiritual energy connects with the physical energy" (Williams, 2011–2014). The body remembers the ancestors. Silvestre Dance Technique could be used to apply ancestral messages through movement. The dancer should not kill the messages with the physical ability of the body. In other words, the technique itself should never have more importance than the message that the dancing body is delivering. The audience should see the message delivered, not the pose.

Everyone has an ancestral memory, which can be used to inform the dance. Ancestral memory is defined in a variety of ways. For instance, in 1896, the text *Atalanta* described ancestral memory in two ways. First, it notes that there is a suggestion that ancestral memory "refers to the memory of our ancestors, or to the unwritten history of tradition, or to the thrilling romances of family history...." The authors of the text argue that ancestral memory is that which "the same scene or incident, or something remarkably similar in whole or part, has been experienced by an ancestor, and the memory of it has descended from generation to generation ... and thus being perpetuated in the same family tree" (Meade, Symington, & Oliver, 1895–1896). I agree with both notions previously mentioned. Ancestral memories highlight the memory and experiences of our ancestors, which are passed down through generations. In *The Cauldron of Memory: Retrieving Ancestral Knowledge and Wisdom* Raven Grimassi describes ancestral memory as: "where the living memory of your lineage flows from the hidden messages residing in your DNA. This is where the ancestral spirit lives and breathes" (Grimassi, 2009, p. 3). For Grimassi, ancestral memories are not only recollections and occurrences fostered over time. Ancestral memories are embedded in the genetic codes of each individual. I find this to be the most fitting definition of ancestral memory as it refers to Silvestre Technique. The collective memory of the body impacts the ancestral memory of each individual. In Silvestre Technique, the ancestral memory can be discovered through the *Triangle of Balance* and *Triangle of Inspiration* allowing connections to one's past roots. Rosangela suggest that dancers seek and discover how to dance this ancestral memory; it is this memory that does not separate us by race, class, sexual orientation, religion or another caste system. The ancestral memories are thousands of years old and they remind us that we are all human.

Ancestral connections also exist in Silvestre Technique through the study of *Dança Capoeira*. *Dança Capoeira* is a class offered during the Silvestre Dance Intensive, making links between the contemporary movement of Silvestre training and capoeira. Capoeira is a technique that developed out of the same energy as Candomblé. People dance, sing, play music and train the martial arts form. Ancestral connections from capoeira can be illustrated through the *martelo* (kick), which is akin to an attitude leg in contemporary form or Silvestre Technique. A *bênção* is comparable to a *développé* (a gradual unfolding of the leg). The contemporary movement known as a *penché* (leaning position with the leg extended) relates to the *meia lua de compasso*. Within Silvestre Technique, all of these movements become a reflection of the work of the ancestors that came before—honoring their resilience, physical and spiritual wisdom and persistence.

Discovery

Internalization and Expression are emphasized in Silvestre training. Participants are asked to open themselves to the universe without limitations. I have found that each person is responsible to discover his or her own self and abilities. In the process of connecting the body to the universe, the guiding question is always "How can you discover?" I learn through my discoveries, feeling the vibrations of my body and through this knowledge I grow and continue to evolve. Before discovering, inspiration should come; it is through *Inspiration*, the connection of the first triangle, that we become wise. Wisdom is the seed of science; the seeds planted in the mind grow, producing knowledge and through studying, blossoms into understanding. It is this seed of science that is discovered in the body and creates wisdom.

Universe (open yourself to Inspiration)
Express. Expression
Balance

Everyone is capable of discovering themselves when they dance freely and also when dancing is difficult. It is during these challenging times that the universe supports the intention most. In Silvestre training I have learned to constantly connect to the universe. Through my connection with the universe I learn to use what has already been given to me naturally.

Silvestre training encourages expression through the technique. Every day is new; every tendu (pointed foot) is new. It is the obligation of the dancer to decide how he or she could perform these actions differently, each time. In my eyes, Silvestre Technique is not a series of exercises, but instead a conversation with Symbology and expression. The expression allows individuality. Rosangela urges us to "dance your training." How a person decides to express themselves is a personal decision. When people enter into the classroom they are dancing. Rosangela asks, "What are you doing to stop yourself from letting you reach your full potential for developing?" Rosangela advises students to see things from the universal perspective and incorporate it into life, *DANCE*. In reference to the questions that Rosangela poses to her students she says, "it is important to continuously ask ourselves these types of questions in order to gain more from ourselves and others in our dance community" (Williams, 2011–2014). During the January 2012 summer intensive, Rosangela affirmed the following to her Theory class:

> How do you perceive movement? You express because you visualize. Because you visualize, you express, not imitate. Work with your body. Legs go higher—always push your limits. Work your physicality proportionally. Listen to your body. When you feel your body can't do something or your mind can't do something—train more. See the beauty and discovery in all types of movement. Dance. Consider the people who work out— training, how important it is and how dedicated they are. You must be the same involving yourself in the same manner. Work to improve limitations. Have more patience. Always have responsibility. Dance technique will never say "STOP," only you can [Williams, 2011–2014].

It is during these vital moments in the intensive training with Rosangela that these concepts are investigated through trial and error using the body. It is the foundation of the training that provides participants with the messages to build the dance.

In Silvestre Technique class, we start with Internalization; a scan within oneself to connect to the source of the being. Visualization and Expression follow, where the participant envisions the potential of the body in movement. Here, the dancers bring awareness to their muscles, joints and body placement. Equilibrium is next—this is dedicated to exploring and discovering within the motions of the body. Expression is added to this these moments of seeking, learning and finding. To conclude, we return to Internalization at the end of class while giving appreciation for our journey.

Internalization in Silvestre Technique focuses on the presence of the four elements throughout the *Body Universe*. Internalization starts with element earth in the feet and legs reaching upwards to the pelvis, giving the body stability. Water in the lower abdominals (2nd chakra) and in the solar plexus (3rd chakra) providing the person with the will to do and the power of creation. The chest and lungs filter the air flowing within the center of the body, offering freedom and expression; the heart beating. Fire exists throughout the head in connection with the sky and the heat provided from the sun. The distinct correlation to the elements during Internalization makes the experience of Silvestre training different from others that I have studied.

Visualization is defined by what is embodied and absorbed. Visualization works together with perception and expression. The moment we see, we perceive. If we do not embody the movement, we are simply copying or imitating what is seen. Visualization in Silvestre Technique focuses on use of the four elements in assisting the body to soar and function in the work. Students are instructed to visualize how the use of air from within the body will help with turns, how the visualized element of fire will generate force and height in a battement (kick), or how the visualization of the wave formed in the second and third chakra will move the body through undulations.

Equilibrium connects participants to physicality, discovering within the body's faculties. Deriving from the earth, equilibrium helps to keep the moving body balanced, even during off-centered movement. In the Silvestre Technique context, equilibrium is concerning much more than the distribution of weight. It is being aware of the power contained by the element earth. The earth is the support system providing basic necessities for life. The connection to earth in this technique is reliant upon this idea of support as well as the support we gather from our ancestors; as we move upon the Earth in dance.

Combining the *Triangles of Inspiration, Expression and Balance* requires participants to investigate the concepts of Silvestre Technique interchangeably. I have learned to dance with the energy of the Earth and the energy of the universe. Silvestre Technique is about the participants' discovery of inspiration, visualization, expression, and physicality.

Class Structure

The Silvestre Dance Technique provides an opportunity for dancers, movers, and any person that is interested in body training to investigate the combination of symbols that express aspects of the universe through the body. The training occurs both cosmologically and physically. The study of Silvestre Technique occurs through the process of movement discovery that highlights the possibilities of movement by connecting to *Inspiration, Expression,* and *Balance.* In 2015, the Silvestre Technique website shared the following information:

> The Silvestre Technique is a continuously evolving codified modern dance technique with the objective of conditioning the dancer through physical and expressive training—regardless of level or previous experience. The training incorporates the attributions of water, fire, air and earth, which are symbolized through the concepts and movements of the training technique. The Orixás, divine forces in the Brazilian spiritual practice of Candomblé, are incorporated into this technique through the connection of these four elements. Silvestre Technique embodies the Orixás since the divine forces are linked to the energy of distinct natural elements. The conceptualizations used to convey the four elements of nature to the dancer can be deepened to understand the connection that the Orixás have to the movement and dancer. Silvestre training links the skillful technique to the Orixás of Candomblé and can be used to further empower the dancer.
>
> In 1982, Rosangela Silvestre began the early stages of developing the Silvestre Technique, which over time has progressed into a series of exercises—"conversations with the body"—working to prepare body, mind, and spirit for dance. The Silvestre Technique brings to dance training a connection with the physical body and its connection to the Universe, which Silvestre calls, "the Body Universe." The *Body Universe* is symbolized by three triangles formed on the body [The Training, 2015].

Within the *Body Universe,* the three triangles work together simultaneously in training the body, mind and spirit. In the Silvestre Technique, the triangles are connected with the four elements of nature: earth, water, air, and fire. In addition, the Silvestre Technique brings the foundation of the chakras, the central forces of the body, to enhance the internal connection with the dancers' verticality and alignment.

Training

"Dance your training, train while you dance."—Rosangela Silvestre (Williams, 2011–2014)

Training in Silvestre Technique begins with a series of breathing and movement phrases that help the individual to focus internally on their body. This creates an environment for participants to set their intention and connect their body to the four elements. After acknowledgment of the breath, body, and elements, a series of codified sequences or movement conversations are practiced. This series includes the use of the arms and torso to symbolize the illumination of the body, undulations, body rolls, contractions, arches, pliés, transfer of weight, balances, développés, pirouettes, as well as additional phrases that develop musicality, rotation, flexibility and fluidity. These movement conversations occur in center floor. The designed phrases have an infinite number of variations that are adjusted according to the individual dancers' ability; it is through each dancer's experience that they are challenged to discover. Through these series of exercises, Silvestre Technique works to strengthen both the core and body alignment of the dancer. Following the phrases at center floor, the class continues to movement progressions across the floor that are larger ideations of the development of the body at center floor. Dancers will focus largely on; spatial awareness, syncopation and rhythmic changes, and taking risks with their body. The Silvestre Technique class advances with participants learning a movement phrase that allows the students to incorporate the work of the class and further their opportunity to discover using the concepts of the Four Elements. In the physical study of the technique participants:

- Always starts in silence—eyes closed Internalization and putting ego aside
- Focus without concern of outside thoughts, things or occurrences
- Breath—Inhale, Exhale
- Find alignment—Verticality
- Focus on the physical body, initiated by having respect for the body
- Connect with personal physicality including groundedness— Trusting the body
- Be Secure

During the 2014 Intensive Rosangela spoke, "when you are dancing, and you try to hide, people don't see your dancing they see what you are hiding" (Williams, 2011–2014).

Class ends with acknowledgment through movement. The dancers remember their energy centers, personal light, reflection, strength, and possibilities. Each class ends with a gesture offering appreciation. Everyone salutes and appreciates what is discovered. Saluting:

- The *Body Universe*
- Musicians

- The entry way/exit—The energy that brought everyone into the dance space (or studio) and the energy that takes everyone out into the world
- Observers/Visitors
- Dancing Family
- Teachers—We salute our teachers, those in front of you, those who may not be in the studio, and those that have become ancestors

Through this training, I've learned to remember to always be ready. Rosangela says, "don't forget to listen to the universe and let your body be the instrument of the Universe Dance; your dance, your life. Be Alive!" (The Training, 2015) Silvestre Technique trains dancers to be present in the moment, equipped and prepared for all things to come, whether it be in dance or in life.

> Sometimes, we listen and understand, but don't process. We must embody. We must connect with the earth. We start every movement from the ground. Participants have to discover this for themselves. Visualize and embody [Williams, 2011–2014].

In the above passage, Rosangela clearly articulates the complex training of the body. When speaking of embodiment, I am referring to one's own physical representation and ownership of movement. Anyone can watch Vera Passos demonstrate a dance phrase and afterwards copy the movements that she has danced. However, embodiment encompasses the articulation and nuances of movement, dynamics and physical expression. This expression is important as it provides freedom to the dancer. It empowers, allowing self-discovery through movement. Embodiment is a form of analyzing. The analysis can be used as data in which the mind calculates and the body shares.

In "Of Meanings and Movements: Re-Languaging Embodiment in Dance Phenomenology and Cognition" Edward C. Warburton writes, "Merleau-Ponty's 'phenomenology of embodiment' makes the physical (somatic) being the site of the psyche" (Warburton, 2011, p. 66). In this instance, I am interpreting Warburton's reference of psyche as the soul. Essentially, being present in the moment to interpret and express through the body creates the situation for the person to speak from their soul. Warburton continues this thought by adding, "bodily movement is essential to an understanding of all aspects of life" (Warburton, 2011, p. 66). Warburton makes the point that the human spirit resides in the physical body and movements of the body in connection to the spirit affects one's outlook in life. This theory could also be applied to the relationship of body, spirit and world in Silvestre Technique. The physical body in movement connected to ancestral memories, the Ori and the *Body Universe* can influence how one perceives themselves in their daily life. This also influences how a person may identify others and their actions. As previously mentioned in Chapter I, connecting to the *Triangle of Inspiration* can be a catalyst for self-expression and balance in society and in life. Student Yuko Tamura stated:

> For me the biggest difference I feel is whether I feel the movement from inside the body; the sensation of physical internalization [feeling the body from inside] and mental internalization—focused on the connection with music, the self and the energy that surrounds, but less distracted by external happening [Tamura, 2014].

In *Embodiment and Experience* Thomas J. Csordas explains that embodiment "is a methodological standpoint in which bodily experience is understood to be the existential ground of culture and self" (Csordas, 1995, p. 269). In this regard, in order to truly understand Silvestre Technique, students must also understand the culture from which it comes. The technique allows space for students to challenge, learn from and trust the "self."

Choreography

Silvestre Technique provides various tools for choreography through its symbology. Movement can be generated through the embodiment of the qualities of the elements of nature. The symbology within Silvestre Technique can assist in creating choreography with purpose of movement and understanding. In other words, the significance of the elements and symbols used in the technique can be applied to the choreography of dance pieces. Silvestre Technique provides dancers with the skills to create movement through the exploration of musicality and the principles of the triangles. The training of the technique is deepened through the practice of choreography; the choreography prepares and strengthens the body to dance. Vera Passos explains the choreography aspect of Silvestre Technique further in the following interview.

2018 Interview with Vera Passos

SILVESTRE TECHNIQUE AND CHOREOGRAPHY

> Sometimes when I choreograph, people ask if they will see Silvestre Technique. I respond, "you will not find what is done in [technique] class." People should not think that I'm going to put [the symbology of] water, earth or fire element [in the choreography] … because they will not find it. The technique works as the medium of things. But, what I'm going to present in the show is *dance* [Passos, 2018].

Sometimes, the codified symbols from the technique do not show up in the choreography. Nonetheless, the technique is there guiding the choreographic process.

Symbology and Imagery

Rosangela taught me that as a dancer I have to understand where movement comes from. Movement is movement, but technique is speaking. No movement is ever wrong; however, some actions may not be desired. It is important for participants to understand the action of movement, not only shapes. If the distinction is not made, discomfort may take the essence from dancing. All movement is an expression of symbology. If students of Silvestre training speak internally, they will project from within the expression of movement; this expression should always be present.

Students must also invest in the curiosity of the research, thinking about and investigating the movement. Rosangela says, "do not train to say nothing. In Ballet-speak, in Modern-speak, and in African dance—speak" (Williams, 2011–2014). Essentially, dancers must use their own expression to translate the messages of dance. The dance itself is sufficient, regardless if it is a ballet adagio, contemporary dance combination, African diaspora sequence or another form. The interpretation of the dance is first executed by the dancers using the *Triangles of Inspiration, Expression and Balance.* Dancers must not only train for strength, flexibility and virtuosity, it is also necessary for the dancer to train in expression, so that when they move, the dance *speaks*—the narrative is told through the moving body.

Symbology and imagery play a prevalent role in Silvestre Technique. Earth, Water, Air and Fire all have related hand movements and gestures in correlating spaces of the body. The symbology vocabulary creates a system for participants to understand the codified technique. Other symbols of the body include the Four Directions, the Four Elements, Lotus Flower and many more. The symbology and imagery encourage participants to bring inspiration from the elements of nature and the universe. While turning, participants could imagine the essence of air moving; seek the fire energy of Xangô when jumping; or embody water when contracting the torso. A few complementing symbols and movements may include:

Earth = Transitions, bending of the knees, movements that take the
   pelvis towards the earth.
Water = Undulations, contractions
Air = Turns, jumps
Fire = Grand battement, jumps

Silvestre Technique is movement that tells a story. The Symbology of the Silvestre Technique focuses on the ancient symbols of the Orixás represented in the movements and gestures of the technique. Silvestre Symbology is influenced by the movements of the Orixás and greatly incorporates

Orixá dance movements, which are infused with Silvestre Technique movements. Rosangela says that the "symbols are brought to us by our ancestors" (Williams, 2011–2014). The past physical, hard work of our ancestors is important. We often speak of Ogum when we mention the machete cutting. We must also remember those that physically cut through soil, sharpened tools for hunting, those that built before us. We think of Oxóssi through the symbology of the bow and arrow, but we must also remember the ancestors that went into the forest to find the wood, molded it, and sharpened the arrow to hunt. The symbols of the Orixás are oftentimes the actions of our ancestors.

It is in Silvestre Symbology that the synthesis of the *Body Universe* and the concepts from each of the three Triangles of the Body are coalesced seamlessly. Artistry is emphasized through the symbolic movement. The symbols of the technique are there to remember. The elements of nature are represented through their embodiment in forms such as Bharatanatyam, hula (Polynesian dances), movements inspired by the Orixás, and other training styles. Silvestre Technique uses the vibrations of the elements of nature as symbology throughout the body. As a method of training the body, symbols are used as inspiration and information to implement movements. The elements are a source for understanding the movement intentions of the body. The symbols also relay the messages of the body to the audience.

Barbara Browning, states that Silvestre Technique is "a highly abstract understanding of movement comprehending physical gesture, historical migration and the cosmological negotiation of time through space" (Browning, 2007, p. 177). Silvestre Technique's foundation is rooted in the symbology of the movements of the Orixás brought to Brazil by African traditionalists. The displacement of African people from the western and central regions of the African continent led to the sacred traditions of Candomblé. The migration that Browning refers to also includes the intersection of the native indigenous people with the African descendants throughout Brazil. Silvestre Technique serves as a method of cultural preservation through the embodiment of these sacred gestures birthed from a mixture of these cultures. The technique negotiates the use of symbols as inspiration for movement expression as an artistic form. Through this process, Silvestre Technique creates a constant negotiation of the body through time and space, as this negotiation has been chronicled throughout Brazil's history.

Energy forces that often impact our lives including family, religion, political systems, and school can be profoundly connected in our dance. Silvestre Technique is a methodology in which dancers can investigate this connection more deeply through the body. The *Body Universe* allows participants to discover a conscious connection to the universe surrounding them. Silvestre Technique is the study of the *Body Universe*. I perceive the *Body Universe* as a connection to the cosmos through movement. This connection allows a deep understanding of each individual's natural capacity.

V

Definition of Silvestre
Terms and Positions

"I have no desire to be recognized as the owner of Silvestre Technique. It is much bigger than that kind of idea ... possession. For me, this work is about everyone's contribution; this is how I know the technique is working. That is much more significant."—Rosangela Silvestre, 2018 (Silvestre, 2018)

2018 Interview with Rosangela

Rosangela explains the use of terminology in Silvestre Technique

For me, I do not deny the [western] terminology, because you are training dancers for the dance world. For example, if you go to the audition, you are going to hear the western terms. When I apply this technique, it allows a lot of people to understand the capacity of the training ... and that matters, too. Being in this capacity does not mean that it eliminates you because you say plié. Plié for me does not come from a terminology that stops my flow. When I hear plié, I can sense that I can bend my knees, but if I only bend my knees I will not function with the same understanding as with plié. For example, Germaine Acogny says, "this is my plié," she did not say that is not plié. It is, that's my plié, because she added some things ... as Martha Graham did, as Katherine Dunham did, and it never took away the essence because they called it plié.

How can the plié manifest in this technique? Plié in this technique makes you feel the essence of the groundedness from the element earth. It's not only plié. You plié because it is a language that you are understanding, but the substance of that—besides bending the knees—has the connection with the element that provides you an understanding to express, and not only be in the formality of plié. As well as dégagé, and tondu, these always have a connection with the element to takes you outside of that box, that mentality.

Any technical movement in the body, came from the body. We have bent our knees sense we were born. But, ballet provided a codification the same way as the four elements. This is not the earth [Rosangela shows the symbol for element earth], this is not water [she shows the symbol for element water], but the intention is what makes me create the expression, even with the physicality. I can say, this is water ... how is it water? The gesture is only to remind you that the physical is included in that intention to be water. If I want to talk about a particular element—if I create a code of that, I can make everyone train the body without forgetting that you can flow as water. So everywhere you go, the four elements become a symbol for the technique:

> Verticality
> Point to the Universe
> Point to the Past

All of these are codes, when you hear them—if you study this technique, you understand. When you do it there's an understanding … the same as plié, that it is not only that.

Every time that I do a pirouette, I think about all of the strengths of Oyá and the speed of the tornado. It's not only a pirouette. That's the point. If I place my foot in passé to turn, it's not a turn, it's a pirouette. In this technique, this pirouette expresses your air your freedom [Silvestre, 2018].

In the following section, I have personally defined the terms as they specifically relate to Silvestre Technique movement sequences. Although, I understand the purpose of using western terminology in the description of the movement phrases of the technique, I also recognize the marginalization that may cause for some dancers of various technique styles. In effort to decolonize the vocabulary used to describe the movement in the technique, I have used common terminology in addition to western terms, that may be familiar to ballet or modern training in transcribing the technique.

Vocabulary

Ancestrality/Ancestral Memory: The cognitive, metaphysical, and physical practice of acknowledging ancestral connections through movement intention(s).

Appreciation: Acknowledgment and appreciation in the practice of Silvestre Technique. Appreciation is symbolized by the fingers extended towards the universe and slightly apart and palms facing outwards. Hands reach up towards the universe and slowly come down in front of the body.

Attitude (leg): With one leg as the support/base, the other leg is lifted (usually at 90-degrees from the hip), with the knee bent at a 145-degree angle. Attitude can be performed in turnout (outward rotation) or parallel.

Base: The support system of the feet and legs in the Triangle of Balance. The base refers to the standing leg or supporting leg(s) for movement.

Battement: A kick of the leg, usually performed with the knee fully extended.

Body Universe: The existence of the universe in the physical body. Acknowledgment and connection to the Body Universe is made through

Appreciation arms.

Attitude leg in parallel position (author photos).

Attitude leg in turn out position.

Battement leg in turn out position (author photos).

the dancing body using ancient traditional symbols and the elements of nature.

Contraction: Concave movement of the torso; creating a bowl shape with the front of the body, through the separation of vertebrae of the spine. Opposite of arch.

Discovery: Personal investigation of self-findings through dance and the analysis of Silvestre Technique concepts.

Duality: Harmonizing positive and negative energies as one.

Expression: The physical manifestation of the conversations of the body. One's unique personal demonstration of dancing the Body Universe.

Contraction in plié (photo by Suzanne Alila).

Extend: To elongate a part of the body. Reach further.

Famílias: Lines of four people formed to complete progressions across the floor.

Element Air: Element Air symbolizes freedom. The fingers on each hand are held together, the backs of the hands touching with fingertips touching the sternum; the elbows are lifted and reaching side.

Element Earth: Element Earth symbolizes balance and foundation. The palms are facing the body with the fingers held together, pointing diagonally down towards the Earth. The elbows reach towards the side. This position is placed in front of the second chakra.

Element Fire: Element Fire symbolizes determination. With the fingers together and the palms facing each other, the fingers point up towards the sky with the elbows reaching to the side. The heel of each hand should align with the ears, slightly above the head.

Element Air position of the arms (author photo).

Element Earth position of the arms (photo by Sontira MacRall).

Element Fire position of the arms (author photo).

Element Fire can also be symbolized with the fingers touching and reaching towards the sky, crossed at the wrist so that the palms are facing outwards. The elbows reaching to the side.

Element Water: Element Water symbolizes fluidity. The fingers are together and pointing towards each other at the fingertips. The palms are in front of sternum and the elbows reach to the side.

Element Water position of the arms (photo by Suzanne Alila).

5th position arms | Encircling Crown Chakra (author photo).

1st position arms | Encircling solar plexus (arms) (author photo).

5th position (arms)/Encircling Crown Chakra: In connection with the crown chakra, the hands directly above the crown of the head in alignment. Containing the energy of the crown chakra. Movement extends from the heart chakra.

1st Position (arms)/Encircling Solar Plexus (arms): In connection with the solar plexus chakra, the hands directly in front of the solar plexus in a circle of energy.

1st Base position of the feet.

1st Base (Primeira Base): Feet in parallel lines touching (6th position).

1st position (feet)/Open Triangle Feet: Heels of the feet touching due to outward rotation of the legs, starting from the hip socket.

1st position of the feet | Open triangle feet (author photos).

Flatback position of the body.

Flat Back: The back extended forward, perpendicular to the legs; parallel to the floor. Table top position.

Flex: To bend. Specifically, when flexing the foot, the toes reach back (as opposed to forward when pointing) towards the head of the body.

Forced Arch/Foot Arching: Lift the heels off the floor to their highest extension with the knees bent. The balls of the feet remain on floor.

Flexed right foot (author photos).

Forced arch feet with Lotus arms (author photo).

Four Directions: Four directions symbolize the four cardinal directions: north, east, south, and west. The arms extend side from the back and shoulders extending to the fingertips. Fingers are together, and palms are facing down.

Four Elements: Four elements symbolize the balance and harmonizing of the four main elements of nature. The arms extend side from the back and shoulders, slightly bent at the elbows (95-degree angle), fingers are together, with palms facing down.

Four Direction arms (photo by Suzanne Alila).

Four Element arms.

Projection/High Release/Arch: Creating a bowl or C-shape with the back side of the body. The sternum reaches up and forward, without breaking the line of the spine in the neck. Opposite of contraction.

Projection/High release/arch position of the spine (author photos).

High V position of the arms.

High V (arms): Arms placed above the head, in line with the ears, in a letter V position. The fingertips are pointing toward the universe with the palms facing out.

Internalization: Personal reflection and analysis of one's own Body Universe.

Inward Rotation: Rotation that begins at the joint that rotates parts of the body inward, towards the center or midline of the body.

Lotus: Full extension and separation of the fingers. The

Lotus position of the hands (author photos).

fingers spiral inwards around the palm of the hand representing a lotus flower.

Musicality: Musical connection (and quality) demonstrated and discovered through movement.

Outward rotation: Rotation that begins at the joint that rotates parts of the body outward, away from the center or midline of the body.

Parallel (feet): Feet and legs situated in parallel lines. For example, 1st base/ Primeira base or with feet hip width apart.

Parallel position with the feet hip width apart (author photo).

Passé: One leg remains the base (supporting leg). The other leg creates a triangle as it bends until the big toe reaches the knee of the base leg. Passé can be performed in parallel position or outward rotation and the big toe can be placed in front, on the side, or behind the knee of the standing leg.

Perception: One's awareness through the use of the senses of the body. An interpretation and understanding.

Piqué: Transfer of weight onto the ball of the foot onto an extended leg.

Pirouette: To spin or turn on one leg. The pirouette may be performed as an inward or outward turn.

Plié [bent knees]: To bend (or flex) at the knees. In plié, the knees

Passé in turnout position with arms in Element Air.

remain over the 1st and 2nd toes. Plié may be performed in parallel position or in outward rotation.

Point (feet): Extension down the leg, through the top of the foot, to the toes. The instep of the foot is dramatically arched as the toes extend and the top of the foot is stretched.

Possibilities: The potential for discovery.

Relevé [lift heels]: Maximum extension through the front of the foot with the toes on the

Plié position of the legs (author photos).

Grand plié position of the legs with arms in Four Elements (author photo).

ground. Heels are lifted to the highest point possible from the floor.

2nd Position (feet): Feet placed hip width apart. 2nd position feet can be in parallel position or rotated outwards, from the hips.

Symbology: Codes used in Silvestre Technique to represent ancient symbols with the body.

Tendu: An extension (or stretch) of the leg from the hip to the toes. The foot is pointed away from the body and the big toe remain on the floor. This action may be performed in parallel or outward rotation.

Relevé in turnout position (photo by Sontira MacRall).

2nd position turnout of the feet (author photo).

Triangle of Inspiration: The first triangle present in the Body Universe of Silvestre Technique focusing on determination, internalization, visualization and perception.

Triangle of Expression: The second triangle present in the Body Universe of Silvestre Technique focusing on fluidity, freedom and personal expression.

Triangle of Balance: The third triangle present in the Body Universe of Silvestre Technique focusing on stability, equilibrium and ancestral connections.

Tendu in turn out from 1st position (feet) | Open triangle feet (photo by Sontira MacRall).

Triangle of Inspiration **position of the arms.**

Triangle of Expression **position of the arms (author photos).**

Triangle of Balance **position of the arms (author photo).**

Verticality: Spine placed in vertical (upright) alignment with vertebrae stacked.

Visualization: One's personal view of the potential of the Body Universe.

Important to Note

- In Silvestre Technique the codified movement positions have specific placement of the elbows. When the body moves through any of the positions of the elements (Earth, Water, Air, Fire), salutes the triangles, salutes the body, or the Four Elements, the elbows point towards the side (laterally). This helps to activate the abdominals, open the space between the scapula, and engage several muscle groups in the back.
- As Silvestre Technique students become more advanced, sequences are lengthened and connected so that they are performed continuously without stopping. This helps to build stamina, strength, cognitive and physical memory. There are various transitions that exist for the sequences that may not be included in this text.

- All sequences in Silvestre Technique have an ending position. Dancers should continue to be present until the end of the sequence is complete with the final position defining that moment.

VI

Introductory Sequences for Silvestre Dance Technique Class

"Silvestre Technique is a cycle of continuation."—Rosangela Silvestre, 2018 (Silvestre, 2018)

This chapter provides detailed instructions for composing and completing a Silvestre Technique class. The instructions include counts, movement descriptions, and sequencing to accompany the conversation provided. The phrases described are written as they were taught to me and are developments of my Silvestre Technique pedagogy with my students within a community and university setting. This material is to be used as a reference for class and it is imperative that I stress that modifications to the sequences are natural. Rosangela Silvestre is continuously developing this technique as it is a living and growing method. This section should *not* be used to teach a Silvestre Technique class without the proper certification and permission granted by Rosangela Silvestre. In addition, this material is *not* intended for anyone to use that has not yet trained in Silvestre Technique in person with a certified instructor, for at least one full calendar year. This information is provided as a reference tool for those that have experienced the technique, to maintain and continue developing with their bodies. In order to better understand the terminology, I have notated the technique so that it can also be understood by those that may not have experience in studying western dance forms.

Tempo

For the purpose of this text, the counts written are only *suggestions* for foundational development of movement phrases. In a Silvestre Technique class, the counts are within the musicality of the body. There are no set counts. Every moment, every class and every phrase is different each time the movement is performed. The musicality of the phrases is influenced by each person in the room, the musicians and the sequences danced.

Note

Have consciousness of the triangles formed by the arms throughout the practice of these movement conversations. In addition, the triangles of Silvestre Technique are not static and move throughout and with the body, as the body moves.

Beginner/Level I

Opening Sequence

Begin:
Center floor, feet in first base position (feet touching). Spine is vertical, arms are along the side of the body with palms facing in towards thighs. Eyes are closed.

- Centering thoughts
- Connect the body to the triangles

Tempo: Described counts are suggested for foundational development of movement phrases.

Internalization

CONNECT THE ELEMENTS
Scanning the body starting from the soles of the feet connecting to the earth below. Feeling stabilization, security, and balance. In this position dancers should be aware of their weight distributed evenly through the feet. The energy of the earth in the feet is drawn up through the legs along the backs of the knees, elongated through the hip flexors, and arrives into the pelvis where elements water is recognized. The water is present in the core of the body where contractions are initiated. Visualize water flowing throughout the body in various forms, including through the blood vessels

and veins. The essence of water releases any tensions that may be present throughout the body. Energy from the core of the body continues up through the spine and diaphragm into the chest cavity where the heart and lungs are housed. Attention is given to the element air, which enters and leaves our lungs as we breathe, allowing our heart to beat continuously. The person should feel the air on their skin as they stand in space. The energy from the chest continues up through the back of the neck, releasing any tension in the jaw. The energy shoots out through the top of the head connecting to the sky, sun and universe above. Imagine the heat from the sun on the crown of the head connecting the body to element fire. Acknowledging the connection of the four elements throughout the body starts the illumination of the *Body Universe.*

Inhale through the nose, and exhale with plié [bent knees] in first base position. After the breath has fully exited the body, straighten both legs into verticality.

Body Universe | Three Triangles

From the top of your head to your shoulders imagine the *Triangle of Inspiration,* offering perception and visualizations for movement. Set the intention for the dance.

From the shoulders down to the navel, imagine the *Triangle of Expression* allowing freedom of movement and the dancer's creative voice to speak.

From the hips to the base of the feet imagine the *Triangle of Balance,* providing stability, harmony, and security. The reality of the physical realm manifests in this triangle.

Inhale through the nose, and exhale with plié [bent knees] in first base position. After the breath has fully exited the body, straighten both legs into verticality.

Open eyes (slowly).

Saluting the Body Universe

Begin:
Feet in first base position (feet touching). Spine is vertical, arms are along the side of the body with palms facing in towards thighs.

Saluting the Triangle of Inspiration

[4 COUNTS]:
Slowly bend elbows towards the side, allowing the hands to glide up the side of the thigh, until the wrist reaches the hip. Elbows continue pointing side.

[4 COUNTS]:
Reverse the action by gliding the palms back down the side of the thigh until elbows are no longer bent.

Saluting the Triangle of Expression

[4 COUNTS]:
Repeat arms with plié [bent knees].

[4 COUNTS]:
Straighten the legs and arms.

Saluting the Triangle of Balance

[4 COUNTS]:
Repeat arms without plié [bent knees].

[4 COUNTS]:
Straighten the arms.

Saluting the Body

[4 COUNTS]:
With elbows straight, the palms of the hands draw towards each other, wrapping around just under the gluteus. Fingertips pointing towards the Earth below.

[4 COUNTS]:
The elbows bend allowing the palms to glide over the gluteus until elbows are bent and are facing completely side. Palms are resting on hips and fingertips are pointing inwards, towards the spine. The thumb reaches forward in line with the hip socket, leaving the fingertips back (embracing the gluteus).

[4 COUNTS]:
Elbows remain in place, bent towards the side. The hand rotates downwards until fingertips point towards the Earth.

[4 COUNTS]:
Elbows straighten as the palms glide alongside the thigh.

Center Sequences

Stimulating the Body

Begin:
Feet in first base position (feet touching). Spine is vertical, arms are along the side of the body with palms facing in towards thighs.

[4 COUNTS]:
Roll down.

[4 COUNTS]:
Plié [bent knees], place the hands on the floor.

[4 COUNTS]:
Lower the knees to the floor.

[4 COUNTS]:
Stretch back into child's pose.

[4 COUNTS]:
Bring hands to the sides of the knees.

[4 COUNTS]:
Roll over to the right, onto the back—arms in triangle position while holding knees into the chest.

[4 COUNTS]:
Flex feet.

[4 COUNTS]:
Point feet.

[4 COUNTS]:
Extend the arms above the head along the floor, while simultaneously extend the legs on the floor, feet pointed, parallel.

[4 COUNTS]:
Flex feet.

[4 COUNTS]:
Point the feet and return to the knees to the chest, arms in triangle position while holding knees in the chest, with head off of the floor.
Repeat flex and point and extend.

[4 COUNTS]:
Roll back to the right, the belly on the floor, with arms and legs extended.

[4 COUNTS]:
Bring the hands to the shoulders, tuck the toes.

[4 COUNTS]:
Push back into downward dog.

[8 COUNTS]:
Walk the hands back on the floor, until the weight of the body is over the feet.

[8 COUNTS]:
Roll up.

Four Elements

Begin:
Feet in first base position (feet touching). Spine is vertical, arms are along the side of the body with palms facing in towards thighs.

[3 COUNTS]:
Plié [bent knees], arms in Element Earth.

[3 COUNTS]:
Extend legs, lift to Element Water.

[3 COUNTS]:
Arms to Element Air.

[3 COUNTS]:
Return arms to Element Water.

[3 COUNTS]:
Right hand crosses over left, flex wrist, fingertips are pointing forward and palms facing out, elbows side.

[3 COUNTS]:
Maintain shape, arms move overhead to Element Fire.

[3 COUNTS]:
Slightly extend elbows, rotate wrists so that both palms are flat, facing forward, (right palm touches backside of left hand) extend fingertips up towards the Universe, Duality.

[3 COUNTS]:
Plié [bent knees], feet flat and lower the shape of the arms in front of heart.

[3 COUNTS]:
Open arms to Four Elements while in plié [knees bent].

[3 COUNTS]:
Drop elbows towards the Earth, palms acknowledge space (palms facing forward towards space in Appreciation).

[3 COUNTS]:
Extend knees, extend and lengthen arms down, by the side of the body.

Contraction

Begin:
Feet in first base position (feet touching). Spine is vertical, arms are along the side of the body with palms facing in towards thighs.

[3 COUNTS]:
Plié [bent knees] bringing arms to Element Earth.

[3 COUNTS]:
Contraction, knees remain in plié [bent], arms parallel to the floor, extended front from shoulders.

[3 COUNTS]:
Retract position, Element Earth, vertical spine.

[3 COUNTS]:
Extend legs, hands to Element Water.

[3 COUNTS]:
High contraction, legs remain extended, arms parallel to the floor, extended front from shoulders.

[3 COUNTS]:
Retract position, vertical spine, Element Water.

[3 COUNTS]:
Flex wrist, fingers point towards the Earth, elbows side.

[3 COUNTS]:
Reach fingers towards the Earth, extend elbows.

[9 COUNTS]:
Three shoulder rolls (shoulders rolling front, upwards and back).

[3 COUNTS]:
Plié [bent knees], reach arms out in front of the heart extending from the shoulders.

[3 COUNTS]:
Arch chest, heart pouring forward towards the Earth until chest is over thighs and fingertips reach on the forward diagonal.

[3 COUNTS]:
Bring palms to the Earth, fingertips pointing towards each other.

[3 COUNTS]:
Plié, roll up.

Contraction with Four Elements

Begin:
Feet in first base position (feet touching). Spine is vertical, arms are along the side of the body with palms facing in towards thighs.

[4 COUNTS]:
Plié [bent knees] bringing arms to Element Earth.

[4 COUNTS]:
Contraction, knees remain in plié [bent], arms parallel to the floor, extended front from shoulders.

[4 COUNTS]:
Retract position, Element Earth, vertical spine.

[4 COUNTS]:
Extend legs, hands to Element Water.

[4 COUNTS]:
High contraction, legs remain extended, arms parallel to the floor, extended front from shoulders.

[4 COUNTS]:
Retract position, vertical spine, Element Water.

[4 COUNTS]:
Flex wrist, fingers point towards the Earth, elbows side.

[4 COUNTS]:
Reach fingers towards the Earth, extend elbows.

[12 COUNTS]:
Three shoulder rolls (shoulders rolling front, upwards and back).

[2 COUNTS]:
Plié [bent knees], reach arms out in front of the heart extending from the shoulders.

[3 COUNTS]:
Arch chest, heart pouring forward towards the Earth until chest is over thighs and fingertips reach on the forward diagonal.

[4 COUNTS]:
Touch palms of hands to the Earth, fingertips pointing towards each other.

[4 COUNTS]:
Plié, roll up to vertical spine.

[4 COUNTS]:
Plié [bent knees], arms in Element Earth.

[4 COUNTS]:
Extend legs, arms to Element Water.

[4 COUNTS]:
Arms to Element Air.

[4 COUNTS]:
Return arms to Element Water.

[4 COUNTS]:
Right hand crosses over left, flex wrist, fingertips are pointing forward with palms facing out, elbows side.

[4 COUNTS]:
Maintain shape, arms move overhead to Element Fire.

[4 COUNTS]:
Slightly extend elbows, rotate wrists so that both palms are flat, facing forward, (right palm touches backside of left hand) extend fingertips up towards the Universe.

[4 COUNTS]:
Plié [bent knees], maintain shape of arms and lower in front of heart.

[4 COUNTS]:
Open arms to Four Elements while in plié [knees bent].

[4 COUNTS]:
Drop elbows towards the Earth, palms acknowledge space (palms facing forward towards space in Appreciation).

[4 COUNTS]:
Extend knees, extend and lengthen arms down, by the side of the body.

Opening the Channels (Chakras) Part I

Begin:
Feet in first base position (feet touching). Spine is vertical, arms are along the side of the body with palms facing in towards thighs.

[4 COUNTS]:
Right foot steps forward, left foot steps forward into first base position, spine is reaching forward on the high diagonal. Arms are reaching in front of the body on the low diagonal with palms down.

[4 COUNTS]:
Extend the knees, continue to extend the arms forward and reaching up towards the universe, vertical spine.

[4 COUNTS]:
Right foot steps backwards, left foot steps backwards into first base position, vertical spine.

Arms open in a Low V position to the sides of the body, palms facing towards the body.

[4 COUNTS]:
Extend the knees, arms extend through Four Directions to a High V position.

[4 COUNTS]:
Lower arms.

Repeat, starting with the left side.

[4 COUNTS]:
Slowly bend elbows, palms facing the front of the thighs. Element Earth. Elbows continue to reach side as fingertips touch each other in front of the heart. Element Water. Shoulders are pressing down.

[4 COUNTS]:
Palms face the body as the elbows continue reaching up—elbows same level as the ears. Palms scan in front of the face and pass over the forehead, stopping over the crown of the head.

[4 COUNTS]:
Flex wrists until the palms face each other and fingertips reach up towards the Universe. Element Fire. There is space between the two palms.

[4 COUNTS]:
Extend the elbows completely, fingertips reach towards the Universe.

[4 COUNTS]:
Flex the wrists, arms open to the side of the body—stopping at shoulder level—fingertips reaching towards the Earth.

[4 COUNTS]:
Arms retrace movement until palms face the Universe above the head.

[4 COUNTS]:
Flip the palms over towards the crown of the head, fingertips touching.

[4 COUNTS]:
Bend the elbows.

[4 COUNTS]:
Flip the palms over towards the Universe.

[4 COUNTS]:
Extend the elbows.

[4 COUNTS]:
Arms extend over the top of the head into Four Directions and plié [bent knees].

[4 COUNTS]:
Remaining in plié [bent knees], rotate palms up, towards the Universe, bring extended arms in front of the heart.

[4 COUNTS]:
Relax the hands, lift the elbows up towards the Universe while extending the legs.

[4 COUNTS]:
Palms over the top of the head with elbows and legs extended in vertical spine.

Repeat 3 times.

[4 COUNTS]:
Relevé (lift heels off of the floor), with palms reaching towards the Universe.

[4 COUNTS]:
Lower relevé, arms extend to Four Directions.

[4 COUNTS]:
Lower arms .

Repeat sequence in:

1st position (feet) | Open triangle feet

Opening the Channels (Chakras) into Contractions

Begin:
Feet in first base position (feet touching). Spine is vertical, arms are along the side of the body with palms facing in towards thighs.

[4 COUNTS]:
Slowly bend elbows, palms facing the front of the thighs. Element Earth. Elbows continue to reach side as fingertips touch each other in front of the heart. Element Water. Shoulders are pressing down.

[4 COUNTS]:
Palms face the body as the elbows continue reaching up—elbows same level as the ears. Palms scan in front of the face and pass over the forehead, stopping over the crown of the head.

[4 COUNTS]:
Flex wrists until the palms face each other and fingertips reach up towards the Universe. Element Fire. There is space between the two palms.

[4 COUNTS]:
Extend the elbows completely, fingertips reach towards the Universe.

[4 COUNTS]:
Flex the wrists, arms open to the side of the body—stopping at shoulder level—fingertips reaching towards the Earth.

[4 COUNTS]:
Arms retrace movement until palms face the Universe above the head.

[4 COUNTS]:
Arms extend over the top of the head into Four Directions and plié [bent knees].

[4 COUNTS]:
Remaining in plié [bent knees], rotate palms up, towards the Universe, bring extended arms in front of the heart.

[4 COUNTS]:
Relax the hands, lift the elbows up towards the Universe while extending the legs.

[4 COUNTS]:
Palms over the top of the head with elbows and legs extended in vertical spine.

[4 COUNTS]:
Relevé (lift heels off of the floor), with palms reaching towards the Universe.

[4 COUNTS]:
Lower relevé, palms remain overhead.
Repeat relevé, 3 times.

[4 COUNTS]:
Extend arms to Four Directions in plié [bent knees].

[4 COUNTS]:
Lower arms to the side of the body and extend the knees.

[4 COUNTS]:
Plié [bent knees] bringing arms to Element Earth.

[4 COUNTS]:
Contraction, knees remain in plié [bent], arms parallel to the floor, extended front from shoulders.

[4 COUNTS]:
Retract position, Element Earth, vertical spine.

[4 COUNTS]:
Extend legs, hands to Element Water.

[4 COUNTS]:
High contraction, legs remain extended, arms parallel to the floor, extended front from shoulders.

[4 COUNTS]:
Retract position, vertical spine, Element Water.

[4 COUNTS]:
Flex wrist, fingers point towards the Earth, elbows side.

[4 COUNTS]:
Reach fingers towards the Earth, extend elbows.

[4 COUNTS]:
Three shoulder rolls (shoulders rolling front, upwards and back).

[4 COUNTS]:
Plié [bent knees], reach arms out in front of the heart extending from the shoulders, arch chest.

[4 COUNTS]:
Heart pouring forward towards the Earth until chest is over thighs and palms touch the floor with fingertips pointing towards each other.

[4 COUNTS]:
Extend the knees and roll up the spine.

[4 COUNTS]:
Vertical spine.

[4 COUNTS]:
Open arms to Four Directions.

[16 COUNTS]:
Plié [bent knees] and extend, 4 times .

[4 COUNTS]:
Lower arms and plié [bent knees].

[4 COUNTS]:
Extend knees.
Repeat sequence in:
1st position (feet) | Open triangle feet.

Opening the Channels (Chakras) Part II

Begin:
Feet in first base position (feet touching). Spine is vertical, arms are along the side of the body with palms facing in towards thighs.

[4 COUNTS]:
Roll down, palms on the floor, fingertips pointing towards each other.

[12 COUNTS]:
Three pliés.

[4 COUNTS]:
Plié, flatback, hands to Element Water.

[4 COUNTS]:
Remaining in plié, lift torso to vertical spine.

[4 COUNTS]:
Extend knees.

[4 COUNTS]:
Flatback over with legs extended.

[4 COUNTS]:
Plié [bent knees] and relax hands to the floor.

[4 COUNTS]:
Palms flat on the floor and fingertips pointing towards each other.

[12 COUNTS]:
Plié [bent knees] 3 times.

[2 COUNTS]:
Remain in plié [bent knees] and sharply open hands side—from the elbow—until the fingertips are touching the floor and palms are facing outwards.

[4 COUNTS]:
Remain in plié [bent knees], contract from the 2nd chakra and roll up to vertical spine.

[4 COUNTS]:
Extend knees while simultaneously rotating the arms from the shoulder socket so that arms are in a High V position.

[4 COUNTS]:
Relevé.

[4 COUNTS]:
Plié [bent knees].

[4 COUNTS]:
Extend arms to Four Directions.

[4 COUNTS]:
Lower arms and extend knees.
Repeat sequence in:
1st position (feet) | Open triangle feet
2nd position (feet) in parallel
2nd position (feet) in outward rotation

END SEQUENCE

[4 COUNTS]:
Plié [bent knees] in second position, arms in the Four Directions, rotate and walk feet in to parallel second, to 1st position, and first base position.

[4 COUNTS]:
Bend elbows and extend legs.

Direction Changes

Begin:

Feet in first base position (feet touching). Spine is vertical, arms are along the side of the body with palms facing in towards thighs.

[2 COUNTS]:

Traveling towards the left—step left, step right. Facing the left wall— arms reach down towards the Earth and extend up towards the Universe.

[2 COUNTS]:

Traveling back towards the right—step right, step left (half turn), arms extended side.

[4 COUNTS]:

Swing right leg around, lunge with left leg forward, right leg back (parallel), facing the left wall.

[4 COUNTS]:

Extend body into plank position.

[4 COUNTS]:

Bend the knees and elbows while twisting the body towards the right. Place the left side of the body onto the floor, facing front.

[4 COUNTS]:

Sit up (with extended spine), facing the right wall, with arms in Four Directions and legs in parallel 2nd position, feet pointed.

[4 COUNTS]:

Contract the torso, arms in Element Air position.

[4 COUNTS]:

Extend the legs into half pike or pike, while hands come slightly behind the pelvis on the floor for support. Extend the spine on the diagonal.

[4 COUNTS]:

Transition legs into 4th position, while in the air, arms in Four Directions.

[4 COUNTS]:

Twist the body, facing front—lower the legs into fourth position onto the floor (left leg forward, right leg behind), vertical spine.

[4 COUNTS]:

Release head and chest forward, over front leg, palms touching the floor.

[4 COUNTS]:

Return to vertical spine, arms in Four Directions.

[8 COUNTS]:

Extend back leg (right leg) completely, place fingertips of the hands on the floor for support.

[4 COUNTS]:
Return to 4th position.

[8 COUNTS]:
Roll to the right, legs pass through parallel position with both knees bent, continue towards the back wall, cross the left leg over the right to stand.

END SEQUENCE

[4 COUNTS]:
Plié [bent knees].

[4 COUNTS]:
Extend legs.

Messages | Past, Present and Future

Begin:
Feet in first base position (feet touching). Spine is vertical, arms behind back at sacrum, awareness of the *Triangle of Balance.*

[2 COUNTS]:
Plié [bent knees], extend arms towards the Earth, lengthen arms pass Four Directions into High V position.

[2 COUNTS]:
Extend legs, arms to Element Fire.

[2 COUNTS]:
Extend elbows, flex wrists—palm flat towards the Universe.

[2 COUNTS]:
Reach arms down to Four Directions position, wrist remains flexed, fingertips reaching towards the Earth, with palms flat (facing out).

[4 COUNTS]:
Extend wrist, palm facing flat to the front.

[4 COUNTS]:
Bend elbows until arms reach Element Water.

[4 COUNTS]:
Element Air.

[4 COUNTS]:
From Element Air, rotate wrist so fingertips move down and forward, fingertips point towards the front, and palms face out.

[4 COUNTS]:
Extend elbows, fingertips reach forward.

[4 COUNTS]:
Flex wrists, bend elbows, crossing at the center, fingertips touch shoulder on left side and right side.

[4 COUNTS]:
Open arms to the side, wrists remain flexed.

[4 COUNTS]:
Cross arms at the center again to touch shoulders (change arms so that the bottom arm is on top).

[4 COUNTS]:
Extend arms to Four Directions.

[4 COUNTS]:
Relax wrists, fingertips relax towards the Earth.

[4 COUNTS]:
Lift arms towards the Universe (High V with wrist relaxed).

[4 COUNTS]:
Plié [bent knees]. Bend elbows to lower arms.

[4 COUNTS]:
Arms return to lower back—*Triangle of Balance*.
Repeat sequence in:
1st position (feet) | Open triangle feet
2nd position (feet) in parallel
2nd position (feet) in outward rotation

END SEQUENCE

[4 COUNTS]:
Plié [bent knees] in second position, arms in the Four Directions.

[4 COUNTS]:
Rotate and walk feet in to parallel 2nd, to 1st position, and first base position.

[4 COUNTS]:
Bend elbows and extend legs.

Pliés with Flatback

Begin:
2nd position parallel, vertical spine. Arms along the side of the body.

[4 COUNTS]:

Roll down, extending the body forwards, towards the Earth from the waist, arms reaching in front in the *Triangle of Balance,* elbows extended.

[4 COUNTS]:

Separate hands and extend fingertips along the floor until spine reaches diagonal flatback.

[4 COUNTS]:

Plié [bent knees], reach the arms and palms of the hands up towards the Universe (as if splashing water up), spine extended on a high diagonal.

[4 COUNTS]:

Release arms and torso back down towards the Earth (signaling the energy of the Earth) deeper plié.

[4 COUNTS]:

Extend fingertips along the floor (hands separated, in two parallel lines) with flatback on the low diagonal, extend legs.

[4 COUNTS]:

Lift flatback to horizontal position (parallel to floor). Arms in line with ears, reaching forward.

[4 COUNTS]:

Initiating with a contraction in the lower abdominals, roll up the spine to vertical position with arms in front of heart chakra, parallel to the floor.

[4 COUNTS]:

Plié [bent knees], vertical spine.

[4 COUNTS]:

Flatback, torso horizontal towards the Earth—maintain plié [bent knees]. Arms in line with the ears.

[4 COUNTS]:

Extend legs.

[4 COUNTS]:

Initiating with a contraction in the lower abdominals, roll up the spine to vertical position with arms in front of heart chakra, parallel to the floor.

[4 COUNTS]:

Plié [bent knees], vertical spine.

[4 COUNTS]:

Flatback, torso horizontal towards the Earth—maintain plié [bent knees]. Arms in line with the ears.

[4 COUNTS]:

Extend legs.

[4 COUNTS]:
Initiating with a contraction in the lower abdominals, roll up the spine to vertical position with arms in front of heart chakra, parallel to the floor.

[4 COUNTS]:
Projection. High release arms remain in front of heart chakra, parallel to floor.

[4 COUNTS]:
Plié [bent knees], maintaining Projection (high release).

[4 COUNTS]:
Flatback, torso horizontal towards the Earth—maintain plié [bent knees], arms in line with ears.

[2 COUNTS]:
Arms salute Element Air—eyes focus forward.

[4 COUNTS]:
Open arms to Four Directions (horizontal to the Earth).

[4 COUNTS]:
Drop head and arms towards the Earth—hands grab hold to elbows.

[4 COUNTS]:
Knees remain in plié [bent], roll up to vertical spine—arms remain over the head (hands holding onto elbows).

[4 COUNTS]:
Open arms to Four Directions extend knees.

[4 COUNTS]:
Lower arms.

Pliés with Flatback (Extended Version)

Begin:
2nd position parallel, vertical spine. Arms along the side of the body.

[4 COUNTS]:
Roll down, extending the body forwards, towards the Earth from the waist, arms reaching in front in the *Triangle of Balance,* elbows extended.

[4 COUNTS]:
Separate hands and extend fingertips along the floor until spine reaches diagonal flatback.

[4 COUNTS]:
Plié [bent knees], reach the arms and palms of the hands up towards the Universe (as if splashing water up), spine extended on a high diagonal.

[4 COUNTS]:
Release arms and torso back down towards the Earth (signaling the energy of the Earth) deeper plié.

[4 COUNTS]:
Extend fingertips along the floor (hands separated, in two parallel lines) with flatback on the low diagonal, extend legs.

[4 COUNTS]:
Lift flatback to horizontal position. Arms in line with ears, reaching forward.

[4 COUNTS]:
Initiating with a contraction in the lower abdominals, roll up the spine to vertical position with arms in front of heart chakra, parallel to the floor.

[4 COUNTS]:
Plié [bent knees], vertical spine.

[4 COUNTS]:
Flatback, torso horizontal towards the Earth—maintain plié [bent knees]. Arms in line with the ears.

[4 COUNTS]:
Extend legs.

[4 COUNTS]:
Initiating with a contraction in the lower abdominals, roll up the spine to vertical position with arms in front of heart chakra, parallel to the floor.

[4 COUNTS]:
Plié [bent knees], vertical spine.

[4 COUNTS]:
Flatback, torso horizontal towards the Earth—maintain plié [bent knees]. Arms in line with the ears.

[4 COUNTS]:
Extend legs.

[4 COUNTS]:
Initiating with a contraction in the lower abdominals, roll up the spine to vertical position with arms in front of heart chakra, parallel to the floor.

[4 COUNTS]:
Projection high release arms remain in front of heart chakra, parallel to floor.

[4 COUNTS]:
Plié [bent knees], maintaining Projection (high release).

[4 COUNTS]:
Flatback, torso horizontal towards the Earth—maintain plié [bent knees], arms in line with ears

[2 COUNTS]:
Arms salute Element Air—eyes focus forward.

[4 COUNTS]:
Open arms to Four Directions (horizontal to the Earth).

[4 COUNTS]:
Drop head and arms towards the Earth—hands grab hold to elbows.

[4 COUNTS]:
Knees remain in plié [bent knees], roll up to vertical spine—arms remain over the head (hands holding onto elbows).

[4 COUNTS]:
Extend legs.

[2 COUNTS]:
Force arch right foot, right hand in Lotus position, extending elbow reaching towards the Universe.

[2 COUNTS]:
Return hand and foot.

[2 COUNTS]:
Forced arch left foot, left hand in Lotus position, extending elbow reaching towards the Universe.

[2 COUNTS]:
Return hand and foot.

[4 COUNTS]:
Plié [bent knees], roll through feet into relevé [lift heels]—Element Fire hands above head, lower heels.

[4 COUNTS]:
Plié [bent knees], and lift feet into forced arch position, lower heels, extend knees, maintain Element Fire arms.

[4 COUNTS]:
Relevé [lift heels].

[4 COUNTS]:
Lower heels, and plié.

[4 COUNTS]:
Flatback, torso horizontal towards the Earth—maintain plié [bent knees]—arms remain in Element Fire, elbows in line with ears.

[4 COUNTS]:
Arms salute Element Air—head focuses forward.

[4 COUNTS]:
Open arms to Four Directions (horizontal to the Earth).

[4 COUNTS]:
Drop head and arms towards the Earth—hands grab hold to elbows.

[4 COUNTS]:
Plié [bent knees], roll up to vertical spine and extend legs simultaneously—arms remain over the head (hands holding onto elbows).

[4 COUNTS]:
Relevé [lift heels], arms in Element Fire, body in Projection (high release).

[4 COUNTS]:
Plié [bent knees], drop head and arms towards the Earth—(maintaining Element Fire) passing in front of the torso. Extend legs—open arms to Four Elements roll up to vertical spine.

[4 COUNTS]:
Relevé [lift heels] arms in Four Elements.

[4 COUNTS]:
Extend torso to high release Projection and open arms to Four Directions.

[4 COUNTS]:
Plié [bent knees], drop head and arms toward the Earth, hands grab onto elbows. Roll up to vertical spine, extend legs and relevé simultaneously.

[4 COUNTS]:
Maintain relevé [lift heels], to arms to Element Fire, body in Projection (high release).

[4 COUNTS]:
Plié [bent knees], drop head and arms towards the Earth—(arms in Element Fire) passing in front of the torso. Extend legs—open arms to Four Elements roll up to vertical spine—relevé [lift heels].

[4 COUNTS]:
Maintain relevé [lift heels] arms in Four Elements.

[4 COUNTS]:
Extend body to Projection (high release), arms to Four Directions.

[2 COUNTS]:
Plié, flatback, arms side in Four Directions with palms facing down.

[2 COUNTS]:
Flex wrist, vertical spine in plié—fingertips reach back, palms facing out with arms extending from the shoulders.

[4 COUNTS]:
Plié [bent knees], cross arms in front of the body.

[4 COUNTS]:
Open arms side and extend legs.

[4 COUNTS]:
Plié [bent knees], cross arms in front of the body, wrists flexed.

[4 COUNTS]:
Open arms side and extend legs.

[4 COUNTS]:
Plié [bent knees], cross arms in front of the body, extend legs—cross arms above your head (removing a t-shirt action).

[4 COUNTS]:
Salute the *Triangle of Inspiration* above the head—open arms to Four Directions.

END SEQUENCE

[4 COUNTS]:
Plié [bent knees], arms in Four Directions.

[4 COUNTS]:
Bend elbows and extend legs.

Body Circles with Contraction

Begin:
Feet in 1st base position, vertical spine. Arms along the side of the body.

[4 COUNTS]:
Plié [bent knees], contraction, 1st position arms (encircling solar plexus).

[2 COUNTS]:
With arms in remaining in 1st position, extend the knees and circle the torso, to the right side of the body.

[2 COUNTS]:
Continue circling the torso back, into Projection (heart reaching towards sky).

[2 COUNTS]:
Circle torso to the left.

[1 COUNT]:
Plié [bent knees], contract center and forward, smoothly and sharply.

[2 COUNTS]:
Reverse the circle—arms remain in 1st position, extend the knees and circle the torso to the left side.

[2 COUNTS]:
Continue circling the torso back, into Projection (heart reaching towards sky).

[2 COUNTS]:
Circle torso to the right.

[1 COUNT]:
Plié [bent knees], contract center and forward, smoothly and sharply.

[4 COUNTS]:
Repeat movement of the torso—circling in the direction of the right side with arms opening to Four Directions, palms facing upwards towards the Universe:
When circling right, the left arm reaches towards the right side of the body, over the head, before opening into Four Directions (palms facing up) as the heart reaches up towards the sky. The right arm reaches, over the head, towards the left side of the body, as the torso continues to circle to the left. The arms return to 1st position, with plié [bent knees], contraction at the center.

[4 COUNTS]:
Extend legs into relevé [lift heels]. Arms move in front of the body, above the head into 5th position (encircling the crown chakra), verticality.

[4 COUNTS]:
Arms open, passing through the Four Directions to return to 1st base position. Plié [bent knees], contraction, arms encircling solar plexus.

[4 COUNTS]:
Relevé [lift heels], arms move in front of the body, above the head into 5th position (encircling the crown chakra), verticality.

[4 COUNTS]:
Arms open, passing through the Four Directions to return to 1st base position. Plié [bent knees], contraction, arms encircling solar plexus.
Repeat the ENTIRE sequence, starting with the left side.

Body Circles with Contraction and Passé

Begin:

Feet in 1st base position, vertical spine. Arms along the side of the body.

[4 COUNTS]:

Plié [bent knees], contraction, 1st position arms (encircling solar plexus).

[2 COUNTS]:

With arms remaining in 1st position, extend the knees and circle the torso, to the right side of the body.

[2 COUNTS]:

Continue circling the torso back, into Projection (heart reaching towards sky).

[2 COUNTS]:

Circle torso to the left.

[1 COUNT]:

Plié [bent knees], contract center and forward, smoothly and sharply.

[2 COUNTS]:

Reverse the circle—arms remain in 1st position, extend the knees and circle the torso to the left side.

[2 COUNTS]:

Continue circling the torso back, into Projection (heart reaching towards sky).

[2 COUNTS]:

Circle torso to the right.

[1 COUNT]:

Plié [bent knees], contract center and forward, smoothly and sharply.

[4 COUNTS]:

Repeat movement of the torso—circling in the direction of the right side with arms opening to Four Directions, palms facing upwards towards the Universe:

When circling right, the left arm reaches towards the right side of the body, over the head, before opening into Four Directions (palms facing up) as the heart reaches up towards the sky. The right arm reaches over the head, towards the left side of the body, as the torso continues to circle to the left. The arms return to 1st position, with plié [bent knees], contraction at the center.

[4 COUNTS]:

Extend legs into relevé [lift heels]. Arms move in front of the body, above the head into 5th position (encircling the crown chakra), verticality.

[4 COUNTS]:

Arms open, passing through the Four Directions to return to 1st base position. Plié [bent knees], contraction, arms encircling solar plexus.

[4 COUNTS]:

Passé right leg, arms move in front of the body, above the head into 5th position (encircling the crown chakra), verticality.

[4 COUNTS]:

Arms open, passing through the Four Directions to return to 1st base position. Plié [bent knees], contraction, arms encircling solar plexus.

Repeat the ENTIRE sequence, starting with the left side. Passé the left leg when starting with the left.

Four Directions and Four Elements

Begin:

Feet in first base position, vertical spine, arms hanging at the side of the body.

[2 COUNTS]:

Element Earth position.

[2 COUNTS]:

Element Water position.

[2 COUNTS]:

Element Air position.

[2 COUNTS]:

Element Water position.

[2 COUNTS]:

With palms facing the sternum, cross right hand on top of left hand.

[2 COUNTS]:

Element Fire position in front of sternum, elbows reaching side.

[2 COUNTS]:

Lift Element Fire hands over the head.

[2 COUNTS]:

Open arms into Four Directions.

[4 COUNTS]:

Bend elbows into Four Elements.

[4 COUNTS]:

Extend elbows into Four Directions.

[4 COUNTS]:

Bend elbows into Four Elements.

[4 COUNTS]:
Extend elbows into Four Directions.

[4 COUNTS]:
Bend elbows into Four Elements.

[4 COUNTS]:
Elbows reach up towards the Universe (inward rotation of the shoulder).

[4 COUNTS]:
Elbows lower towards the Earth (outward rotation of the shoulder).

[4 COUNTS]:
Elbows reach up towards the Universe.

[4 COUNTS]:
Elbows lower towards the Earth.

[4 COUNTS]:
Elbows reach up towards the Universe.

[4 COUNTS]:
Continue extending arms towards the universe (arms parallel reaching towards the sky).

[4 COUNTS]:
Open arms to Four Directions.

[4 COUNTS]:
Plié.

[4 COUNTS]:
Extend the legs and lower the arms to the sides of the body.

Arm Circles

[4 COUNTS]:
Contraction, plié [bent knees], arms lower in front of the body, palms facing upwards (in scooping position).

[4 COUNTS]:
Extend arms forward, on the low diagonal, palms facing down.

[4 COUNTS]:
Extend knees, arms circle forward and up, towards the Universe. Torso extends into Projection (heart reaches towards the Universe). Continue the arm circle behind the body.

[4 COUNTS]:
Contraction, plié [bent knees], continue arms circling down, and forward, scooping under.

[4 COUNTS]:
Extend knees, arms circle up towards the Universe. Torso extends into Projection (heart reaches towards the universe). Continue the arm circle behind the body.

[4 COUNTS]:
Contraction, plié [bent knees], continue arms circling down, and forward, scooping under.

[4 COUNTS]:
Reverse the arm circle, extend legs, arms extend down and behind the body. Arms continue to circle back. Torso extends into Projection (heart reaches towards the universe), arms into High V back.

[4 COUNTS]:
Continue fingertips towards the Universe (both arms parallel reaching upwards).

[4 COUNTS]:
Contraction, plié [bent knees], continue arms circling forward and down, scooping under.

[4 COUNTS]:
Extend legs, arms extend down and behind the body. Arms continue to circle back. Torso extends into Projection high arch (heart reaches towards the universe), arms into High V back.

[4 COUNTS]:
Continue fingertips towards the Universe (both arms parallel reaching upwards).

[4 COUNTS]:
Contraction, plié [bent knees], continue arms circling forward and down, scooping under.

[4 COUNTS]:
Rotate arms, arms are extended on the low diagonal and palms are facing down.

[4 COUNTS]:
Extend the knees and rest the arms along the sides of the body.

Articulations of the Lower Body

Begin:
Feet in first base position, vertical spine, arms are along the side of the body with palms facing in towards thighs.

[5 COUNTS]:
Plié [bent knees], arms in Element Earth.

[5 COUNTS]:
Extend legs, arms in Element Water.

[5 COUNTS]:
Arms in Element Air.

[5 COUNTS]:
From Element Air, rotate wrist so fingertips move down and forward, fingertips point towards the front, and palms face out.

[5 COUNTS]:
Open arms to Four Elements.

[5 COUNTS]:
Plié [bent knees], simultaneously stretch right foot to forced arch position.

[5 COUNTS]:
Extend legs, return to first base feet.

[5 COUNTS]:
Plié [bent knees], simultaneously stretch left foot to forced arch position.

[5 COUNTS]:
Extend legs, return to first base feet.

[5 COUNTS]:
Plié [bent knees], simultaneously stretch right foot to forced arch position.

[5 COUNTS]:
Extend standing leg and passé right foot (parallel).

[5 COUNTS]:
Flex right foot and slide down left leg in plié [bent knees].

[5 COUNTS]:
Extend both legs.
Repeat passé on left side.

[5 COUNTS]:
Plié [bent knees], simultaneously stretch right foot to forced arch position.

[5 COUNTS]:
Extend standing leg and passé right foot (parallel).

[5 COUNTS]:
Maintaining the triangle of the arms, elbows reach down towards the Earth, plié standing leg [bend left knee], hands grab hold onto right leg (just below the knee).

[5 COUNTS]:
Lift right leg higher with support of arms in the triangles, elbows reach side, extend standing left leg, point foot towards the Earth.

[5 COUNTS]:
Release right leg into passé, arms in Four Elements.

[5 COUNTS]:
Flex right foot and slide down left leg in plié [bent knees].

[5 COUNTS]:
Extend both legs.
Repeat left.

Passé and Extensions

Begin:
Feet in first base position, vertical spine, arms are along the side of the body with palms facing in towards thighs.

[5 COUNTS]:
Plié [bent knees], arms in Element Earth.

[5 COUNTS]:
Extend legs, arms in Element Water.

[5 COUNTS]:
Arms in Element Air.

[5 COUNTS]:
Moving through Element Air, rotate hand and forearm so that fingertips point towards the front, and palms face out.

[5 COUNTS]:
Open arms to Four Elements.

[5 COUNTS]:
Plié [bent knees], simultaneously stretch right foot to forced arch position.

[5 COUNTS]:
Extend standing leg and passé right foot (parallel).

[5 COUNTS]:
Plié standing leg, flex right foot and developpé right leg in parallel (extend forward from the knee).

[5 COUNTS]:
Return right leg to passé, extend standing leg.

[5 COUNTS]:
Flex right foot and slide down left leg in plié [bent knees].

[5 COUNTS]:
Extend both legs.
Repeat left.

[5 COUNTS]:
Plié [bent knees], simultaneously stretch right foot to forced arch position.

[5 COUNTS]:
Extend standing leg and passé right foot (parallel).

[5 COUNTS]:
Developpé right leg in parallel (extend forward from the knee).

[5 COUNTS]:
Return right leg to passé.

[5 COUNTS]:
Flex right foot and slide down left leg in plié [bent knees].

[5 COUNTS]:
Extend both legs.
Repeat left.
End Sequence

[4 COUNTS]:
Right leg in passé, foot flexed, arms in Appreciation to the front.

[4 COUNTS]:
Lower right foot to the Earth with plié [bent knees], lower arms.

[4 COUNTS]:
Bend elbows and extend legs.

Développé Combination with Walks

Begin:
Feet in 1st base position, vertical spine. Arms along the side of the body.

[5 COUNTS]:
Plié [bent knees], arms in Element Earth.

[5 COUNTS]:
Extend legs, arms in Element Water.

[5 COUNTS]:
Arms in Element Air.

[5 COUNTS]:
From Element Air, rotate wrist so fingertips move down and forward, fingertips point towards the front, and palms face out.

[5 COUNTS]:
Open arms to Four Elements.

[5 COUNTS]:
Plié [bent knees], simultaneously stretch right foot to forced arch position.

[5 COUNTS]:
Extend standing leg and passé right foot (parallel).

[5 COUNTS]:
Plié the standing leg [bend knee], flex right foot and développé (extend leg) parallel forward.

[5 COUNTS]:
Left knee remains in plié [bent knees], lower right heel down.

[5 COUNTS]:
Extend left knee (straight), transferring weight up-and-over onto right leg, bend right knee, foot flat on the Earth.

[5 COUNTS]:
Transferring weight back onto left leg with plié (left), extend right knee (straight), while sliding right foot along the Earth into first base position, both legs extended.

[5 COUNTS]:
Plié [bent knees], simultaneously stretch right foot to forced arch position.

[5 COUNTS]:
Extend standing leg and passé right foot (parallel).

[5 COUNTS]:
Développé right leg (foot pointed), standing leg is extended (straight).

[5 COUNTS]:
Return right leg to passé.

[5 COUNTS]:
Plié [bend knee] standing leg, flex right foot in passé.

[5 COUNTS]:
Développé right leg forward in parallel (foot flexed), standing leg remains in plié [bent knees].

[5 COUNTS]:
Remain in plié [bent knees], lower right heel down.

[5 COUNTS]:
Extend left knee (straight), transferring weight up-and-over onto right leg, plié [bent knees] right leg, foot flat on the Earth.

[5 COUNTS]:
Lift left heel (into high arch), extend right knee, arms reach side through Four Directions, reaching up towards the Universe.

[5 COUNTS]:
Plié [bent knees] (weight over front/right leg), left foot in high arch, arms lower in front of body in scooping position (palms facing up).

[5 COUNTS]:
Rotate left leg open into 2nd position (lower left heel), torso follows in space—body facing left wall, arms in Four Elements.

[5 COUNTS]:
Remain in plié [bent knees], lift left heel into forced arch.

[5 COUNTS]:
Rotate body to face front, right leg forward—weight forward on right leg, right foot flat on the floor, left foot in high arch, arms in Four Elements.

[5 COUNTS]:
Extend left knee, left heel reaches towards the Earth, extend right knee.

[5 COUNTS]:
Open arms into Four Directions, chest into Projection (heart reaches towards the Universe), arms continue to extend into High V (lengthening from the arch).

[5 COUNTS]:
Small lunge forward, right leg in plié, arms in Four Directions. Verticality.

[5 COUNTS]:
Passé left leg (without moving placement of right leg in parallel).

[5 COUNTS]:
Flex left foot (standing right leg remains in plié [bent]), lower left foot, sliding along right leg.

[5 COUNTS]:
Plié [bent knees].

[5 COUNTS]:
Straighten legs.

[5 COUNTS]:
Walk backwards, leading with the right leg.

[5 COUNTS]:
Walk forwards, leading with the right leg.

[5 COUNTS]:
Walk around in a circle toward the right, leading with the right leg.

[5 COUNTS]:
Walk around in a circle toward the left, leading with the left leg.
Repeat entire sequence to the left.

END SEQUENCE

[4 COUNTS]:
Right leg in passé, foot flexed, arms in Appreciation to the front.

[4 COUNTS]:
Lower right foot to the Earth with plié [bent knees], lower arms.

[4 COUNTS]:
Bend elbows and extend legs.

Across the Floor

Progressions across the floor are completed in *Familias* (Families) of four dancers in each line. Normally, the *Familias* move straight across the space, towards the musicians, unless otherwise noted. Once the progression reaches the opposite side of the room, the dancers divide in the center, two to the right and two to the left, to return back to the starting location.

Runs with Element Symbols

Begin:
1st base position, vertical spine, arms are along the side of the body with palms facing in towards thighs.
*Note: Runs across, maintain plié [bent knees] throughout.

[16 COUNTS]:
Runs across with arms in Element Earth.

[16 COUNTS]:
Runs across with arms in Element Water.

[16 COUNTS]:
Runs across with arms in Element Air.

[16 COUNTS]:
Runs across with arms in Element Fire.

[16 COUNTS]:
Runs across with arms in Four Directions.

Runs Backwards with Element Symbols

Begin:

Facing backwards, first base position, vertical spine, arms are along the side of the body with palms facing in towards thighs.

*Note: Runs backwards across, maintain plié [bent knees] throughout.

[16 COUNTS]:
Runs backward with arms in Element Earth.

[16 COUNTS]:
Runs backward with arms in Element Water.

[16 COUNTS]:
Runs backward with arms in Element Air.

[16 COUNTS]:
Runs backward with arms in Element Fire.

[16 COUNTS]:
Runs backward with arms in Four Directions.

Passé and Four Element Arms

Begin:

2nd position parallel, vertical spine, arms open to Four Elements.

[2 COUNTS]:
Step left foot forward (extended), passé right knee parallel, arms remain in Four Elements. Foot pointed.

[2 COUNTS]:
Step right in plié, step left in plié, arms remain in Four Elements.

[2 COUNTS]:
Step right foot forward (extended), passé left leg parallel, arms remain in Four Elements.

[2 COUNTS]:
Step left in plié, step right in plié, arms remain in Four Elements.
Repeat right and left.

Passé and Four Element Arms with Piqué

Begin:

2nd position parallel, vertical spine, arms open to Four Elements.

[2 COUNTS]:
Piqué onto left foot (extended), passé right knee parallel, arms remain in Four Elements. Foot pointed.

[2 COUNTS]:
Step right in plié, step left in plié, arms remain in Four Elements.

[2 COUNTS]:
Piqué onto right foot (extended), passé left leg parallel, arms remain in Four Elements.

[2 COUNTS]:
Step left in plié, step right in plié, arms remain in Four Elements.
Repeat right and left

Battements in Attitude (Parallel)

Begin:
Small lunge, left leg forward, right leg extended in back, vertical spine, arms in Four Directions with wrists flexed (fingertips are pointing towards the Universe).

[2 COUNTS]:
Battement right leg to the front in parallel position, right knee in attitude, foot flexed, standing leg in plié [bent].

[2 COUNTS]:
Step right in plié, step left in plié.

[2 COUNTS]:
Step right, battement left leg to the front in parallel position, left knee in attitude, foot flexed, standing leg in plié [bent].

[2 COUNTS]:
Step left in plié, step right in plié.
Repeat right and left.

Battements with Legs Extended (Parallel)

Begin:
Small lunge, left leg forward, right leg extended in back, vertical spine, arms in Four Directions.

[2 COUNTS]:
Battement right leg to the front in parallel position, right knee extended, foot pointed, standing leg extended.

[2 COUNTS]:
Step right in plié, step left in plié.

[2 COUNTS]:
Step right, battement left leg to the front in parallel position, left knee extended, foot pointed, standing leg extended.

[2 COUNTS]:
Step left in plié, step right in plié.
Repeat right and left.

Choreography Sequence

Create a choreography sequence/movement combination incorporating the skills obtained from the training technique. The choreography sequence serves as an opportunity for deeper exploration of discovery, self-expression and self-determination through movement. The *Body Universe* is fully engaged and responsive.

Ending

- With feet in 1st base position, rub the hands together in front of the heart chakra to draw energy from the body
- Open to Appreciation
- Use a short section of any the conversations to center the body
- Bring arms into the *Triangle of Balance* position behind the sacrum
- Salute:
    ◊ Body/Self
    ◊ Dancers in the space
    ◊ Musicians
    ◊ Observes
    ◊ Main entrance/exit
    ◊ Teacher(s)

Intermediate/Level II

Opening Sequence

Begin:
Center floor, feet in first base position (feet touching). Spine is vertical, arms are along the side of the body with palms facing in towards thighs. Eyes are closed.

- Centering thoughts
- Connect the body to the triangles

Tempo: Described counts are suggested for foundational development of movement phrases.

Internalization

CONNECT THE ELEMENTS

Scanning the body starting from the soles of the feet connecting to the earth below. Feeling stabilization, security, and balance. In this position dancers should be aware of their weight distributed evenly through the feet. The energy of the earth in the feet is drawn up through the legs along the backs of the knees, elongated through the hip flexors, and arrives into the pelvis where elements water is recognized. The water is present in the core of the body where contractions are initiated. Visualize water flowing throughout the body in various forms, including through the blood vessels and veins. The essence of water releases any tensions that may be present throughout the body. Energy from the core of the body continue up through the spine and diaphragm into the chest cavity where the heart and lungs are housed. Attention is given to the elements air, which enters and leaves our lungs as we breathe, allowing our heart to beat continuously. The person should feel the air on their skin as they stand in space. The energy from the chest continues up through the back of the neck, releasing any tension in the jaw. The energy shoots out through the top of the head connecting to the sky, sun and universe above. Imagine the heat from the sun on the crown of the head connecting the body to element fire. Acknowledging the connection of the four elements throughout the body starts the illumination of the *Body Universe*.

Inhale through the nose, and exhale with plié [bent knees] in first base position. After the breath has fully exited the body, straighten both legs into verticality.

BODY UNIVERSE | THREE TRIANGLES

From the top of your head to your shoulders imagine the *Triangle of Inspiration,* offering perception and visualizations for movement. Set the intention for the dance.

From the shoulders down to the navel, imagine the *Triangle of Expression* allowing freedom of movement and the dancer's creative voice to speak.

From the hips to the base of the feet imagine the *Triangle of Balance,* providing stability, harmony, and security.

Inhale through the nose, and exhale with plié [bent knees] in first base position. After the breath has fully exited the body, straighten both legs into verticality.

Open eyes (slowly).

Saluting the *Body Universe*

Begin:

Feet in first base position (feet touching). Spine is vertical, arms are along the side of the body with palms facing in towards thighs.

SALUTING THE TRIANGLE OF INSPIRATION

[4 COUNTS]:

Slowly bend elbows towards the side, allowing the hands to glide up the side of the thigh, until the wrist reaches the hip. Elbows continue pointing side

[4 COUNTS]:

Reverse the action by gliding the palms back down the side of the thigh until elbows are no longer bent.

SALUTING THE TRIANGLE OF EXPRESSION

[4 COUNTS]:

Repeat arms with plié [bent knees].

[4 COUNTS]:

Straighten the legs and arms.

SALUTING THE TRIANGLE OF BALANCE

[4 COUNTS]:

Repeat arms without plié [bent knees].

[4 COUNTS]:

Straighten the arms.

SALUTING THE BODY

[4 COUNTS]:

With elbows straight, the palms of the hands draw towards each other, wrapping around just under the gluteus. Fingertips pointing towards the Earth below.

[4 COUNTS]:

The elbows bend allowing the palms to glide over the gluteus until elbows are bent and are facing completely side. Palms are resting on hips and fingertips are pointing inwards, towards the spine. The thumb reaches forward in line with the hip socket, leaving the fingertips back (embracing the gluteus).

[4 COUNTS]:
Elbows remain in place, bent towards the side. The hand rotates downwards until fingertips point towards the Earth.

[4 COUNTS]:
Elbows straighten as the palms glide alongside the thigh.

Center Sequences

Four Elements

Begin:
Feet in first base position (feet touching). Spine is vertical, arms are along the side of the body with palms facing in towards thighs.

[3 COUNTS]:
Plié [bent knees], arms in Element Earth.

[3 COUNTS]:
Extend legs, arms in Element Water.

[3 COUNTS]:
Arms in Element Air.

[3 COUNTS]:
Return arms to Element Water.

[3 COUNTS]:
Right hand crosses over left, flex wrist, fingertips are pointing forward with palms facing out, elbows side.

[3 COUNTS]:
Maintain shape, move arms overhead to Element Fire.

[3 COUNTS]:
Extend elbows, rotate wrists so that both palms are flat, facing forward, (right palm touches backside of left hand) extend fingertips up towards the Universe, relevé.

[3 COUNTS]:
Plié [bent knees], feet flat and lower the shape of the arms in front of heart.

[3 COUNTS]:
Open arms to Four Elements.

[3 COUNTS]:

Drop elbows towards the Earth, palms acknowledge space (palms facing forward towards space in Appreciation).

[3 COUNTS]:
Extend knees, extend and lengthen arms down, by the side of the body.

Opening the Channels (Chakras) Part I

Begin:
Feet in first base position (feet touching). Spine is vertical, arms are along the side of the body with palms facing in towards thighs.

[4 COUNTS]:
Slowly bend elbows, palms facing the front of the thighs. Element Earth. Elbows continue to reach side as fingertips touch each other in front of the heart. Element Water. Shoulders are pressing down.

[4 COUNTS]:
Palms face the body as the elbows continue reaching up—elbows same level as the ears. Palms scan in front of the face and pass over the forehead, stopping over the crown of the head.

[4 COUNTS]:
Flex wrists until the palms face each other and fingertips reach up towards the Universe. Element Fire. There is space between the two palms.

[4 COUNTS]:
Extend the elbows completely, fingertips reach towards the Universe.

[4 COUNTS]:
Flex the wrists, arms open to the side of the body—stopping at shoulder level—fingertips reaching towards the Earth. Projection, heart reaching towards the Universe.

[4 COUNTS]:
Arms retrace movement until palms face the Universe above the head. Vertical spine.

[4 COUNTS]:
Flip palms over, elbows remain in place as fingertips move down towards the forehead.

[4 COUNTS]:
Hands reach the sternum with backs of hands are touching, elbows are reaching up. Element Water.

[4 COUNTS]:
Rotate wrists so that palms face each other (not touching), elbows move down below shoulder level.

[4 COUNTS]:
Extend elbows, fingertips reach towards the Earth.

[4 COUNTS]:
Plié [bent knees] bringing arms to Element Earth.

[4 COUNTS]:
Contraction, knees remain in plié [bent], arms parallel to the floor, extended front from shoulders.

[4 COUNTS]:
Retract position, Element Earth, vertical spine.

[4 COUNTS]:
Extend legs, hands to Element Water.

[4 COUNTS]:
High contraction, legs remain extended, arms parallel to the floor, extended front from shoulders.

[4 COUNTS]:
Retract position, vertical spine, Element Water.

[4 COUNTS]:
Flex wrist, fingers point towards the Earth, elbows side.

[4 COUNTS]:
Reach fingers towards the Earth, extend elbows.

[4 COUNTS]:
Three shoulder rolls (shoulders rolling front, upwards and back).

[4 COUNTS]:
Plié [bent knees], reach arms out in front of the heart extending from the shoulders, palms facing up, Projection.

[4 COUNTS]:
Heart pouring forward towards the Earth until chest is over thighs and fingertips touch the floor on each side of the body.

[4 COUNTS]:
Circle fingertips from the sides of the body to the front of the toes, gathering the seeds from the Earth.

[4 COUNTS]:
Roll up, extending the knees simultaneously into vertical spine.
Repeat sequence in:
1st position (feet) | Open triangle feet
2nd position (feet) in parallel
2nd position (feet) in outward rotation

END SEQUENCE
[4 COUNTS]:

Plié [bent knees] in second position, arms in the Four Directions, rotate and walk feet in to parallel 2nd, to 1st position, and first base position.

[4 COUNTS]:
Bend elbows and extend legs.

Opening the Channels (Chakras) Part II

Begin:
Feet in first base position (feet touching). Spine is vertical, arms are along the side of the body with palms facing in towards thighs.

[4 COUNTS]:
Slowly bend elbows, palms facing the front of the thighs. Element Earth. Elbows continue to reach side as fingertips touch each other in front of the heart. Element Water. Shoulders are pressing down.

[4 COUNTS]:
Palms face the body as the elbows continue reaching up—elbows same level as the ears. Palms scan in front of the face and pass over the forehead, stopping over the crown of the head.

[4 COUNTS]:
Flex wrists until the palms face each other and fingertips reach up towards the universe. Element Fire. Maintain the space between the two palms.

[4 COUNTS]:
Extend the elbows completely, fingertips reach towards the Universe.

[4 COUNTS]:
Rotate outward from the shoulders, press palms down toward the Earth—arms are extended to the Four Directions.

[12 COUNTS]:
Arms in Four Directions, plié [bent knees] 3 times.

[4 COUNTS]:
Bend the elbows on the fourth plié [bent knees].

[4 COUNTS]:
Straighten the knees, lower arms to the sides of the body. Roll down the front of the body until the hand touch the floor, palms flat on the floor and fingertips pointing towards each other.

[12 COUNTS]:
Plié [bent knees] 3 times.

[2 COUNTS]:
Remain in plié [bent knees], sharply open hands side—from the

elbow—until the fingertips are touching the floor and palms are facing outwards.

[4 COUNTS]:
Remain in plié [bent knees], contract from the 2nd chakra, roll up to vertical spine.

[4 COUNTS]:
Extend knees while simultaneously rotating the arms from the shoulder socket so that arms are in a High V position.

[8 COUNTS]:
Plié [bent knees] 2 times.

[8 COUNTS]:
Relevé [lift heels] 2 times.

[4 COUNTS]:
Plié [bent knees], arms point to the Four Directions. Rotate legs to 1st position (open triangle feet).

[4 COUNTS]:
Deepen plié [bent knees].

[4 COUNTS]:
Extend arms and legs simultaneously.
Repeat sequence in:
1st position (feet) | Open triangle feet
2nd position (feet) in parallel
2nd position (feet) in outward rotation

END SEQUENCE

[4 COUNTS]:
Plié [bent knees] in second position, arms in the Four Directions, rotate and walk feet in to parallel 2nd, to 1st position, and first base position.

[4 COUNTS]:
Bend elbows and extend legs.

Messages | Past, Present and Future—Part I

Begin:
Arms behind back at sacrum, awareness of the *Triangle of Balance*.

[2 COUNTS]:
Plié [bent knees], extend right arm towards the Earth, lengthen right arm into the High V position.

[2 COUNTS]:
Extend legs, right arm to Element Fire.

[2 COUNTS]:
Extend elbow, flex wrist—palm flat towards the Universe.

[2 COUNTS]:
Reach right arm down to Four Directions position, wrist remains flexed, fingertips reaching towards the Earth, with palm flat (facing out).

[2 COUNTS]:
Extend wrist, palm facing flat to the front.

[2 COUNTS]:
Bend right elbow, right hand in Element Water.

[2 COUNTS]:
Element Air.

[2 COUNTS]:
From Element Air, rotate wrist so fingertips move down and forward, fingertips point towards the front, and palm face out.

[2 COUNTS]:
Extend elbow, fingertips reach forward.

[2 COUNTS]:
Flex wrist, bend elbow, fingertips touch shoulder on left side.

[2 COUNTS]:
Extend right arm to Four Directions position.

[2 COUNTS]:
Relax wrist, fingertips relax towards the Earth.

[2 COUNTS]:
Lift arm towards the Universe (High V with wrist relaxed).

[2 COUNTS]:
Bend elbow to lower arm.

[2 COUNTS]:
Right arm returns to lower back—*Triangle of Balance*.
Repeat left.
Repeat with right and left arms together.
Repeat sequence in:
1st position (feet) | Open triangle feet
2nd position (feet) in parallel
2nd position (feet) in outward rotation

END SEQUENCE

[4 COUNTS]:
Plié [bent knees] in second position, arms in the Four Directions.

[4 COUNTS]:

Rotate and walk feet in to parallel, to 1st position, and first base position.

[4 COUNTS]:
Bend elbows and extend legs.

Messages | Past, Present and Future—Part II

Begin:
Arms behind back at sacrum, awareness of the *Triangle of Balance*.

[2 COUNTS]:
Plié [bent knees], extend right arm towards the Earth, lengthen right arm into the High V position.

[2 COUNTS]:
Extend legs, right arm to Element Fire.

[2 COUNTS]:
Extend elbow, flex wrist—palm flat towards the Universe.

[2 COUNTS]:
Reach right arm down to Four Directions position, wrist remains flexed, fingertips reaching towards the Earth, with palm flat (facing out).

[2 COUNTS]:
Extend wrist, palm facing flat to the front.

[2 COUNTS]:
Bend right elbow, right hand in Element Water.

[2 COUNTS]:
Element Air.

[2 COUNTS]:
From Element Air, rotate wrist so fingertips move down and forward, fingertips point towards the front, and palm face out.

[2 COUNTS]:
Extend elbow, fingertips reach forward.

[2 COUNTS]:
Flex wrist, bend elbow, fingertips touch shoulder on left side.

[2 COUNTS]:
Extend right arms to reach in Four Directions position.

[2 COUNTS]:
Relax wrist, fingertips relax towards the Earth.

[2 COUNTS]:
Lift arm towards the Universe (High V with wrist relaxed).

[2 COUNTS]:
Bend elbow to lower arm.

[2 COUNTS]:
Right arm returns to lower back—*Triangle of Balance.*
Repeat left.
Repeat with right and left arms together.

[2 COUNTS]:
Plié [bent knees], arms reach towards the Earth.

[2 COUNTS]:
Extend legs, arms move through Four Directions towards the Universe.

[2 COUNTS]:
Plié [bent knees], arms in 5th position (Encircling Crown Chakra).

[2 COUNTS]:
Flatback forward in plié. Arms overhead (wrist extended), Projection (heart reaching forward).

[2 COUNTS]:
Bend completely over at the waist, place palms on the floor, fingertips pointing inwards towards each other, extend legs simultaneously.

[2 COUNTS]:
Legs remain extended, contract from the 2nd chakra—roll up to vertical spine. Hands remain in place over head, palms facing the Universe.
Repeat the following 3 times:

[2 COUNTS]:
Flatback forward in plié. Arms overhead (wrist extended), arch chest (heart reaching forward).

[2 COUNTS]:
Bend completely over at the waist, place palms on the floor, fingertips pointing inwards towards each other, extend legs simultaneously.

[2 COUNTS]:
Legs remain extended, contract from the 2nd chakra—roll up to vertical spine. Hands remain in place over head, palms facing the Universe.

[2 COUNTS]:
Plié [bent knees], arms overheard, palms facing the Universe.

[4 COUNTS]:
Plié [bent knees], spiral torso to the right, palms facing Universe, pelvis and lower body remains square, facing front.

[4 COUNTS]:
Return center.

[4 COUNTS]:
Plié [bent knees], spiral torso to the left side, palms facing Universe, pelvis and lower body remains square, facing front.

[4 COUNTS]:
Return center.

[2 COUNTS]:
Extend legs, reaching palms towards the Universe.

[1 COUNT]:
Rotate wrist to 5th position (palms down).

[4 COUNTS]:
Spiral torso to the right side, right arm remains in 5th position, left arm opens side, palm facing Universe, pelvis and lower body remains facing front.

[4 COUNTS]:
Return body front, arms in 5th position.

[4 COUNTS]:
Spiral torso to the left side, left arm remains in 5th position, right arm opens side, palm facing Universe, pelvis and lower body remain facing front.

[4 COUNTS]:
Return body front, arms in 5th position.

[2 COUNTS]:
Salute the *Triangle of Inspiration* above the head.

[4 COUNTS]:
Open arms to Four Directions.

TRANSITION
[4 COUNTS]:
Plié [bent knees], arms in Four Directions, rotate feet and legs to 1st position.

[4 COUNTS]:
Bend elbows and extend legs.
Repeat sequence in:
1st position (feet) | Open triangle feet
2nd position (feet) in parallel
2nd position (feet) in outward rotation

END SEQUENCE
[4 COUNTS]:

Plié [bent knees] in second position, arms in the Four Directions, rotate and walk feet in to parallel 2nd, to 1st position, and first base position.

[4 COUNTS]:
Bend elbows and extend legs.

Pliés with Flatback

Begin:
2nd position parallel, vertical spine. Arms in *Triangle of Balance* in front of the body.

[4 COUNTS]:
Roll down, extending the body forwards, towards the Earth from the waist, arms reaching in front in the *Triangle of Balance,* elbows extended.

[4 COUNTS]:
Separate hands and extend fingertips along the floor until spine reaches diagonal flatback.

[4 COUNTS]:
Plié [bent knees], reach the arms and palms of the hands up towards the Universe (as if splashing water up), spine extended on a high diagonal.

[4 COUNTS]:
Release arms and torso back down towards the Earth (signaling the energy of the Earth) deeper plié.

[4 COUNTS]:
Extend fingertips along the floor (hands separated, in two parallel lines) with flatback on the low diagonal, extend legs.

[4 COUNTS]:
Lift flatback to horizontal position (parallel to the Earth). Arms in line with ears, reaching forward.

[4 COUNTS]:
Initiating with a contraction in the lower abdominals, roll up the spine to vertical position with arms in front of heart chakra, parallel to the floor.

[4 COUNTS]:
Plié [bent knees], vertical spine.

[4 COUNTS]:
Flatback, torso horizontal towards the Earth—maintain plié [bent knees], arms in line with ears.

[4 COUNTS]:
Extend legs.

[4 COUNTS]:

Initiating with a contraction in the lower abdominals, roll up the spine to vertical position with arms in front of heart chakra, parallel to the floor.

[4 COUNTS]:
Plié [bent knees], vertical spine.

[4 COUNTS]:
Flatback, torso horizontal towards the Earth—maintain plié [bent knees], arms in line with ears.

[4 COUNTS]:
Extend legs.

[4 COUNTS]:
Initiating with a contraction in the lower abdominals, roll up the spine to vertical position with arms in front of heart chakra, parallel to the floor.

[4 COUNTS]:
Projection (high release) arms remain in front of heart chakra, parallel to floor.

[4 COUNTS]:
Plié [bent knees], maintaining Projection.

[4 COUNTS]:
Flatback, torso horizontal towards the Earth—maintain plié [bent knees], arms in line with ears.

[2 COUNTS]:
Arms in Element Air—head focus forward.

[4 COUNTS]:
Open arms to Four Directions (horizontal to the Earth).

[4 COUNTS]:
Drop head and arms towards the Earth—hands grab hold to elbows.

[4 COUNTS]:
Knees remain in plié [bent], roll up to vertical spine—arms remain over the head (hands holding onto elbows).

[4 COUNTS]:
Extend knees, hands continue to hold onto elbows.

[4 COUNTS]:
Relevé, arms in Element Fire above the head, elbows in line with ears.

[4 COUNTS]:
Lower heels.

[4 COUNTS]:
Relevé.

[4 COUNTS]:
Lower heels.

[4 COUNTS]:
Relevé.

[8 COUNTS]:
Remain in relevé, open arms to Four Elements.

[4 COUNTS]:
Open arms to Four Directions.

[4 COUNTS]:
Lower heels.

[4 COUNTS]:
Lower arms.

Pliés with Flatback (Extended Version)

Begin:
2nd position parallel, vertical spine. Arms in *Triangle of Balance* in front of the body.

[4 COUNTS]:
Roll down, extending the body forwards, towards the Earth from the waist, arms reaching in front in the *Triangle of Balance,* elbows extended.

[4 COUNTS]:
Separate hands and extend fingertips along the floor until spine reaches diagonal flatback.

[4 COUNTS]:
Plié [bent knees], reach the arms and palms of the hands up towards the Universe (as if splashing water up), spine extended on a high diagonal.

[4 COUNTS]:
Release arms and torso back down towards the Earth (signaling the energy to the Earth) deeper plié.

[4 COUNTS]:
Extend fingertips along the floor (hands separated, in two parallel lines) with flatback on the low diagonal, extend legs.

[4 COUNTS]:
Lift flatback to horizontal position (parallel to the Earth). Arms in line with ears, reaching forward.

[4 COUNTS]:
Initiating with a contraction in the lower abdominals, roll up the spine to vertical position with arms in front of heart chakra, parallel to the floor.

[4 COUNTS]:
Plié [bent knees], vertical spine.

[4 COUNTS]:
Flatback, torso horizontal towards the Earth—maintain plié [bent knees], arms in line with ears.

[4 COUNTS]:
Extend legs.

[4 COUNTS]:
Initiating with a contraction in the lower abdominals, roll up the spine to vertical position with arms in front of heart chakra, parallel to the floor.

[4 COUNTS]:
Plié [bent knees], vertical spine.

[4 COUNTS]:
Flatback, torso horizontal towards the Earth—maintain plié [bent knees], arms in line with ears.

[4 COUNTS]:
Extend legs.

[4 COUNTS]:
Initiating with a contraction in the lower abdominals, roll up the spine to vertical position with arms in front of heart chakra, parallel to the floor.

[4 COUNTS]:
Projection, arms remain in front of heart chakra, parallel to floor.

[4 COUNTS]:
Plié [bent knees], maintain Projection.

[4 COUNTS]:
Flatback, torso horizontal towards the Earth—maintain plié [bent knees], arms in line with ears.

[2 COUNTS]:
Arms salute Element Air—head focus forward.

[4 COUNTS]:
Open arms to Four Directions (horizontal to the Earth).

[4 COUNTS]:
Drop head and arms towards the Earth—hands grab hold to elbows.

[4 COUNTS]:
Knees remain in plié [bent], roll up to vertical spine—arms remain over the head (hands holding onto elbows).

[4 COUNTS]:
Extend legs.

[2 COUNTS]:
Force arch right foot, right hand in Lotus position, extending elbow reaching towards the Universe.

[2 COUNTS]:
Return hand and foot.

[2 COUNTS]:
Forced arch left foot—left hand in Lotus position, extending elbow reaching towards the Universe.

[2 COUNTS]:
Return hand and foot.

[4 COUNTS]:
Plié [bent knees], roll through feet into relevé [lift heels], with legs extended—Element Fire hands above head.

[4 COUNTS]:
Grande plié [bend knees deeply] with heels off of the floor (forced arch feet).

[4 COUNTS]:
Extend legs, continue into relevé [lift heels higher].

[4 COUNTS]:
Lower heels, and plié.

[4 COUNTS]:
Flatback, torso horizontal towards the Earth—maintain plié [bent knees], hands remain in Element Fire.

[4 COUNTS]:
Arms salute Element Air—head focuses forward.

[4 COUNTS]:
Open arms to Four Directions (horizontal to the Earth).

[4 COUNTS]:
Drop head and arms towards the Earth—hands grab hold to elbows.

[4 COUNTS]:
Plié [bent knees], roll up to vertical spine and extend legs simultaneously—arms remain over the head (hands holding onto elbows).

[4 COUNTS]:
Relevé [lift heels], salute Element Fire in Projection (high release).

[4 COUNTS]:
Plié [bent knees], heart drops towards the Earth. Arms in Element Fire, passing in front of the torso. Head over the Earth. Extend legs—open arms to Four Elements roll up to vertical spine.

[4 COUNTS]:
Relevé [lift heels] arms in Four Elements.

[4 COUNTS]:
Open to Four Directions and Projection (high release).

[4 COUNTS]:
Plié [bent knees], drop heart toward the Earth, head follows. Hands grab onto elbows. Roll up to vertical spine, extend legs and relevé simultaneously.

[4 COUNTS]:
In relevé [lift heels], salute Element Fire in Projection (high release).

[4 COUNTS]:
Plié [bent knees], heart drops towards the Earth. Arms in Element Fire, passing in front of the torso. Head over the Earth. Extend legs—open arms to Four Elements roll up to vertical spine, relevé [lift heels].

[4 COUNTS]:
Relevé [lift heels] arms in Four Elements.

[4 COUNTS]:
Open to Four Directions in Projection (high release).

[2 COUNTS]:
Plié, flatback, arms side in Four Directions with palms facing down.

[2 COUNTS]:
Flex wrists, vertical spine in plié—fingertips reach back, palms facing out with arms side.

[4 COUNTS]:
Plié [bent knees], cross arms in front of the body.

[4 COUNTS]:
Open arms to Four Directions and extend legs.

[4 COUNTS]:
Plié [bent knees], cross arms in front of the body, opposite arm on top.

[4 COUNTS]:
Open arms to Four Directions and extend legs.

[4 COUNTS]:
Plié [bent knees], cross arms in front of the body, extend legs—cross arms above your head (removing a t-shirt action).

[4 COUNTS]:
Salute the *Triangle of Inspiration* above the head—open arms to Four Directions.

END SEQUENCE

[4 COUNTS]:
Plié [bent knees], arms in Four Directions.

[4 COUNTS]:
Bend elbows and extend legs.

Flat Back—Abbreviated 2nd Position (Outward Rotation)

Begin:
Second position turnout, vertical spine, arms in *Triangle of Balance* in front of the body.

[4 COUNTS]:
Roll down, extending the body forwards, towards the Earth from the waist, arms reaching in front in the *Triangle of Balance,* elbows extended.

[4 COUNTS]:
Separate hands and extend fingertips along the floor until spine reaches diagonal flatback.

[4 COUNTS]:
Plié in 2nd position [bent knees] in outward rotation, extend flatback to horizontal, arms in line with ears.

[4 COUNTS]:
Remain in 2nd position plié [bent knees], vertical spine, backs of hands press on the inside of knees, elbows extended. (Signal of open of rotation of the hips and legs).

[4 COUNTS]:
Knees remain in plié [bent], flatback forward, extend arms forward, parallel to the Earth, in line with ears..

[4 COUNTS]:
Extend legs, remain in flatback

[4 COUNTS]:
Initiating with a contraction in the lower abdominals, roll up the spine to vertical position with arms in front of heart chakra, parallel to the floor.

[4 COUNTS]:
Plié [bent knees] in 2nd position, vertical spine.

[4 COUNTS]:
Knees remain in plié [bent], flatback forward, extend arms forward, parallel to the Earth, in line with ears.

[4 COUNTS]:
Extend legs.

[4 COUNTS]:
Initiating with a contraction in the lower abdominals, roll up the spine to vertical position with arms in front of heart chakra, parallel to the floor.

[4 COUNTS]:
Projection (high release) arms remain in front of heart chakra, parallel to floor.

[4 COUNTS]:
2nd position plié [bent knees], maintain Projection.

[4 COUNTS]:
Flatback, torso horizontal towards the Earth—over with plié [bent knees], arms in line with ears.

[2 COUNTS]:
Arms salute Element Air— head focus forward.

[4 COUNTS]:
Open arms to Four Directions (horizontal to the Earth).

[4 COUNTS]:
Drop head and arms towards the Earth—hands grab hold to elbows.

[4 COUNTS]:
Knees remain in plié [bent], roll up to vertical spine—hand are over the head (holding onto elbows).

[4 COUNTS]:
Extend knees, hands continue to hold onto elbows.

[4 COUNTS]:
Relevé, arms into Element Fire above head.

[4 COUNTS]:
Lower heels.

[4 COUNTS]:
Relevé.

[4 COUNTS]:
Lower heels.

[4 COUNTS]:
Relevé.

[8 COUNTS]:
Remain in relevé, open arms to Four Elements.

[4 COUNTS]:
Open arms to Four Directions.

[4 COUNTS]:
Lower heels.
[4 COUNTS]:
Lower arms.

Flat Back—Extended 2nd Position
(Outward Rotation)

Begin:
Second position turnout, vertical spine, arms in *Triangle of Balance* in front of the body.

[4 COUNTS]:
Roll down, extending the body forwards, towards the Earth from the waist, arms reaching in front in the *Triangle of Balance,* elbows extended.

[4 COUNTS]:
Separate hands and extend fingertips along the floor until spine reaches diagonal flatback.

[4 COUNTS]:
Plié in 2nd position [bend knees in outward rotation], extend flatback to horizontal, arms in line with ears.

[4 COUNTS]:
Remain in 2nd position plié [bent knees], vertical spine, backs of hands press on the inside of knees, elbows extended. (Signal of open of rotation of the hips and legs).

[4 COUNTS]:
Knees remain in plié [bent], flatback forward, extend arms forward, parallel to the Earth, in line with ears.

[4 COUNTS]:
Extend legs, remain in flatback.

[4 COUNTS]:
Initiating with a contraction in the lower abdominals, roll up the spine to vertical position with arms in front of heart chakra, parallel to the floor.

[4 COUNTS]:
Plié [bent knees] in 2nd position, vertical spine.

[4 COUNTS]:
Knees remain in plié [bent], flatback forward, extend arms forward, parallel to the Earth, in line with ears.

[4 COUNTS]:
Extend legs.

[4 COUNTS]:
Initiating with a contraction in the lower abdominals, roll up the spine to vertical position with arms in front of heart chakra, parallel to the floor.

[4 COUNTS]:
Projection (high release) arms remain in front of heart chakra, parallel to floor.

[4 COUNTS]:
2nd position plié [bent knees], maintain Projection.

[4 COUNTS]:
Flatback, torso horizontal towards the Earth—over with plié [bent knees], arms in line with ears.

[2 COUNTS]:
Arms salute Element Air—head focus forward.

[4 COUNTS]:
Open arms to Four Directions (horizontal to the Earth).

[4 COUNTS]:
Drop head and arms towards the Earth—hands grab hold to elbows.

[4 COUNTS]:
Knees remain in plié [bent], roll up to vertical spine—hand are over the head (holding onto elbows).

[4 COUNTS]:
Extend knees, hands continue to hold onto elbows.

[2 COUNTS]:
Force arch right foot (outward rotation), right hand in Lotus position, extending elbow reaching towards the Universe.

[2 COUNTS]:
Return hand and foot.

[2 COUNTS]:
Forced arch left leg (outward rotation), left hand in Lotus position, extending elbow reaching towards the Universe.

[2 COUNTS]:
Return hand and foot.

[4 COUNTS]:
Plié [bent knees], roll through feet into relevé [lift heels] and extend legs—Element Fire hands above head.

[4 COUNTS]:
Grande plié [bend knees deeply] in 2nd position, with heels off of the floor.

[4 COUNTS]:
Extend legs, continue into relevé [lift heels].

[4 COUNTS]:
Lower heels, and plié.

[4 COUNTS]:
Flatback, torso horizontal towards the Earth—over with plié [bent knees]—hands remain in Element Fire.

[4 COUNTS]:
Arms salute Element Air—head focus forward.

[4 COUNTS]:
Open arms to Four Directions (horizontal to the Earth).

[4 COUNTS]:
Drop head and arms towards the Earth—hands grab hold to elbows.

[4 COUNTS]:
Plié [bent knees], roll up to vertical spine and extend legs simultaneously—hands are over the head (holding onto elbows).

[4 COUNTS]:
Relevé [lift heels], salute Element Fire, Projection.

[4 COUNTS]:
Plié [bent knees], heart drops towards the Earth. Arms in Element Fire passing in front of the torso. Head over the Earth. Extend legs—open arms to Four Elements roll up to vertical spine, relevé [lift heels].

[4 COUNTS]:
Relevé [lift heels] arms in Four Elements.

[4 COUNTS]:
Open to Four Directions and Projection .

[4 COUNTS]:
Plié [bent knees], drop heart toward the Earth, head follows. Hands grab onto elbows. Roll up to vertical spine, extend legs and relevé simultaneously.

[4 COUNTS]:
In relevé [lift heels], salute Element Fire in Projection.

[4 COUNTS]:
Plié [bent knees], heart drops towards the Earth. Arms in Element Fire passing in front of the torso. Head over the Earth. Extend legs—open arms to Four Elements roll up to vertical spine, relevé [lift heels].

[4 COUNTS]:
Relevé [lift heels] arms in Four Elements.

[4 COUNTS]:
Open to Four Directions in Projection.

[4 COUNTS]:
Plié, flatback, arms side in Four Directions with palms facing down.

[2 COUNTS]:
Flex wrists, vertical spine in plié—fingertips reach back, palms facing out with arms side.

[4 COUNTS]:
Plié [bent knees], cross arms in front of the body.

[4 COUNTS]:
Open arms to Four Directions and extend legs.

[4 COUNTS]:
Plié [bent knees], cross arms in front of the body opposite arm on top.

[4 COUNTS]:
Open arms to Four Directions and extend legs.

[4 COUNTS]:
Plié [bent knees], cross arms in front of the body, extend legs—cross arms above your head (removing a t-shirt action).

[4 COUNTS]:
Salute the *Triangle of Inspiration* above the head—open arms to Four Directions.

END SEQUENCE

[4 COUNTS]:
Plié [bent knees], arms in Four Directions.

[4 COUNTS]:
Bend elbows and extend legs.

Body Circles with Contraction and Passé

Begin:
Feet in 1st base position, vertical spine. Arms along the side of the body.

[4 COUNTS]:
Plié [bent knees], contraction, 1st position arms (encircling solar plexus).

[2 COUNTS]:
With arms in 1st position, extend the knees and circle the torso, to the right side of the body.

[2 COUNTS]:
Continue circling the torso back, into Projection (heart reaching towards sky).

[2 COUNTS]:
Circle torso to the left.

[1 COUNT]:
Plié [bent knees], contract center and forward, smoothly and sharply.

[2 COUNTS]:
Reverse the circle—arms remain in 1st position, extend the knees and circle the torso to the left side.

[2 COUNTS]:
Continue circling the torso back, into Projection (heart reaching towards sky).

[2 COUNTS]:
Circle torso to the right

[1 COUNT]:
Plié [bent knees], contract center and forward, smoothly and sharply.

[4 COUNTS]:
Repeat movement of the torso—circling in the direction of the right side with arms opening to Four Directions, palms facing upwards towards the Universe.

When circling right, the left arm reaches towards the right side of the body, over the head, before opening into Four Directions (palms facing up) as the heart reaches up towards the sky. The right arm reaches, over the head, towards the left side of the body, as the torso continues to circle to the left. The arms return to 1st position, with plié [bent knees], contraction at the center.

[4 COUNTS]:
Extend legs into relevé [lift heels]. Arms move in front of the body, above the head into 5th position (encircling the crown chakra), verticality.

[4 COUNTS]:
Arms open, passing through the Four Directions to return to 1st base position. Plié [bent knees], contraction, arms encircling the solar plexus.

[4 COUNTS]:
Passé right leg, arms move in front of the body, above the head into 5th position (encircling the crown chakra), verticality.

[4 COUNTS]:
Arms open, passing through the Four Directions to return to 1st base position. Plié [bent knees], contraction, arms encircling the solar plexus.

Repeat the ENTIRE sequence, starting with the left side. Passé the left leg when starting with the left.

END SEQUENCE

[4 COUNTS]:
Plié [bent knees], lift arms in Four Directions, vertical spine.

[4 COUNTS]:
Right leg in passé, foot flexed, arms in Appreciation to the front.

[4 COUNTS]:
Lower right foot to the Earth with plié [bent knees], lower arms.

[4 COUNTS]:
Bend elbows and extend legs.

Body Circles with Contraction, Passé and Pirouettes

Begin:
Feet in 1st base position, vertical spine. Arms along the side of the body.

[4 COUNTS]:
Plié [bent knees], contraction, 1st position arms (encircling solar plexus).

[2 COUNTS]:
With arms in 1st position, extend the knees and circle the torso, to the right side of the body.

[2 COUNTS]:
Continue circling the torso back, into Projection (heart reaching towards sky).

[2 COUNTS]:
Circle torso to the left.

[1 COUNT]:
Plié [bent knees], contract center and forward, smoothly and sharply.

[2 COUNTS]:
Reverse the circle—arms remain in 1st position, extend the knees and circle the torso to the left side.

[2 COUNTS]:
Continue circling the torso back, into Projection (heart reaching towards sky).

[2 COUNTS]:
Circle torso to the right.

[1 COUNT]:
Plié [bent knees], contract center and forward, smoothly and sharply.

[4 COUNTS]:
Repeat movement of the torso—circling in the direction of the right side with arms opening to Four Directions, palms facing upwards towards the Universe:

When circling right, the left arm reaches towards the right side of the body, over the head, before opening into Four Directions (palms facing up) as the heart reaches up towards the sky. The right arm reaches, over the head, towards the left side of the body, as the torso continues to circle to the left. The arms return to 1st position, with plié [bent knees], contraction at the center.

[4 COUNTS]:
Extend left leg in relevé, passé right leg, arms move in front of the body, above the head into 5th position (encircling the crown chakra), verticality.

[4 COUNTS]:
Arms open, passing through the Four Directions to return to 1st base position. Plié [bent knees], contraction, encircling the solar plexus.

[4 COUNTS]:
Pirouette (right leg in passé, turning to the right) arms move in front of the body, above the head into 5th position (encircling the crown chakra), verticality.

[4 COUNTS]:
Arms open, passing through the Four Directions to return to 1st base position. Plié [bent knees], contraction, encircling the solar plexus.

Repeat ENTIRE sequence, starting with the left side (pirouette to the left).

END SEQUENCE
[4 COUNTS]:
Plié [bent knees], lift arms in the Four Directions, vertical spine.

[4 COUNTS]:
Right leg in passé, foot flexed, arms in Appreciation to the front .

[4 COUNTS]:
Lower right foot to the Earth with plié [bent knees], lower arms.

[4 COUNTS]:
Bend elbows and extend legs.

Four Directions and Four Elements

Begin:
Feet in first base position, vertical spine, arms hanging at the side of the body.

[2 COUNTS]:
Element Earth position.

[2 COUNTS]:
Element Water position.

[2 COUNTS]:
Element Air position.

[2 COUNTS]:
Element Water position.

[2 COUNTS]:
With palms facing the sternum, cross right hand on top of left hand.

[2 COUNTS]:
Element Fire position in front of sternum, fingertips pointing forward.

[2 COUNTS]:
Lift Element Fire hands over the head.

[2 COUNTS]:
Slightly extend elbows, rotate wrists so that both palms are flat, facing forward, (right palm touches backside of left hand) extend fingertips up towards the Universe, Duality.

[2 COUNTS]:
Open arms into Four Directions.

[4 COUNTS]:
Bend elbows into Four Elements.

[4 COUNTS]:
Extend elbows into Four Directions..

[4 COUNTS]:
Bend elbows into Four Elements

[4 COUNTS]:
Extend elbows into Four Directions.

[4 COUNTS]:
Bend elbows into Four Elements.

[4 COUNTS]:
Elbows reach up towards the Universe (inward rotation of the shoulder).

[4 COUNTS]:
Elbows lower towards the Earth (outward rotation of the shoulder).

[4 COUNTS]:
Elbows reach up towards the Universe.

[4 COUNTS]:
Elbows lower towards the Earth.

[4 COUNTS]:
Elbows reach up towards the Universe.

[4 COUNTS]:
Continue extending arms towards the Universe (arms parallel reaching towards the sky).

[4 COUNTS]:
Contraction, plié [bent knees], arms lower in front of the body, palms facing upwards (in scooping position).

[4 COUNTS]:
Extend arms forward, on the low diagonal, palms facing down.

[4 COUNTS]:
Extend knees, arms circle forward and up, towards the Universe. Torso extends into Projection (heart reaches towards the universe). Continue the arm circle behind the body.

[4 COUNTS]:
Contraction, plié [bent knees], continue arms circling back, down, and forward, scooping under.

[4 COUNTS]:
Extend knees, arms circle up towards the Universe. Torso extends into Projection (heart reaches towards the universe). Continue the arm circle behind the body.

[4 COUNTS]:
Contraction, plié [bent knees], continue arms circling back, down, and forward, scooping under.

[4 COUNTS]:
Reverse the arm circle, extend legs, arms extend down and behind the body. Arms continue to circle back. Torso extends into Projection (heart reaches towards the universe), arms into High V back.

[4 COUNTS]:
Continue fingertips towards the Universe (both arms parallel reaching upwards).

[4 COUNTS]:

Contraction, plié [bent knees], continue arms circling forward and down, scooping under.

[4 COUNTS]:
Extend legs, arms extend down and behind the body. Arms continue to circle back. Torso extends into Projection (heart reaches towards the universe), arms into High V back.

[4 COUNTS]:
Continue fingertips towards the Universe (both arms parallel reaching upwards).

[4 COUNTS]:
Contraction, plié [bent knees], continue arms circling forward and down, scooping under.

[4 COUNTS]:
Rotate arms, arms extended are on the low diagonal and palms are facing down.

[4 COUNTS]:
Extend the knees and rest the arms along the sides of the body.

Articulations of the Lower Body

Begin:
Feet in first base position, vertical spine, arms are along the side of the body with palms facing in towards thighs.

[5 COUNTS]:
Plié [bent knees], arms to Element Earth.

[5 COUNTS]:
Extend legs, arms Element Water.

[5 COUNTS]:
Arms in Element Air.

[5 COUNTS]:
From Element Air, rotate wrist so fingertips move down and forward, fingertips point towards the front, and palms face out.

[5 COUNTS]:
Open arms to Four Elements.

[5 COUNTS]:
Plié [bent knees], simultaneously stretch right foot to forced arch position.

[5 COUNTS]:
Extend legs, return to first base feet.
Repeat left.

[5 COUNTS]:
Plié [bent knees], simultaneously stretch right foot to forced arch position.

[5 COUNTS]:
Extend standing leg and passé right foot (parallel).

[5 COUNTS]:
Flex right foot and slide down left leg in plié [bent knees].

[5 COUNTS]:
Extend both legs.
Repeat left.

[5 COUNTS]:
Plié [bent knees], simultaneously stretch right foot to forced arch position.

[5 COUNTS]:
Extend standing leg and passé right foot (parallel).

[5 COUNTS]:
Maintaining the triangle of the arms, elbows reach down towards the Earth, plié standing leg [bend left knee], hands grab hold onto right leg (just below the knee).

[5 COUNTS]:
Lift right leg higher with support of arms in the triangles, elbows reach side, extend standing left leg, point foot towards the Earth.

[5 COUNTS]:
Release right leg into passé, arms in Four Elements.

[5 COUNTS]:
Flex right foot and slide down left leg in plié [bent knees].

[5 COUNTS]:
Extend both legs.
Repeat left.

[5 COUNTS]:
Plié [bent knees], simultaneously stretch right foot to forced arch position.

[5 COUNTS]:
Extend standing leg and passé right foot (parallel).

[5 COUNTS]:
Plié standing leg, flex right foot and developpé right leg in parallel (extend forward from the knee).

[5 COUNTS]:
Return right leg to passé, extend standing leg.

[5 COUNTS]:
Flex right foot and slide down left leg in plié [bent knees].

[5 COUNTS]:
Extend both legs.
Repeat left.

[5 COUNTS]:
Plié [bent knees], simultaneously stretch right foot to forced arch position.

[5 COUNTS]:
Extend standing leg and passé right foot (parallel).

[5 COUNTS]:
Developpé right leg in parallel (extend forward from the knee).

[5 COUNTS]:
Return right leg to passé.

[5 COUNTS]:
Flex right foot and slide down left leg in plié [bent knees].

[5 COUNTS]:
Extend both legs.
Repeat left.
Repeat ENTIRE sequence in 1st position (open triangle feet), turnout position of the legs.

Développé with Walks

Begin:
Feet in 1st base position, vertical spine. Arms along the side of the body.

[5 COUNTS]:
Plié [bent knees], arms to Element Earth.

[5 COUNTS]:
Extend legs, arms in Element Water.

[5 COUNTS]:
Arms in Element Air.

[5 COUNTS]:
From Element Air, rotate wrist so fingertips move down and forward, fingertips point towards the front, and palms face out.

[5 COUNTS]:
Open arms to Four Elements.

[5 COUNTS]:
Plié [bent knees], simultaneously stretch right foot to forced arch position.

[5 COUNTS]:
Extend standing leg and passé right foot (parallel).

[5 COUNTS]:
Plié the standing leg [bend knee], flex right foot, développé (extend leg) parallel forward.

[5 COUNTS]:
Left knee remains in plié [bent], lower right heel down.

[5 COUNTS]:
Extend left knee (straight), transferring weight up-and-over onto right leg, bend right knee, foot flat on the Earth.

[5 COUNTS]:
Transferring weight back onto left leg with plié (left), extend right knee (straight), while sliding right foot along the Earth into first base position, both legs extended.

[5 COUNTS]:
Plié [bent knees], simultaneously stretch right foot to forced arch position.

[5 COUNTS]:
Extend standing leg and passé right foot (parallel).

[5 COUNTS]:
Développé right leg (foot pointed) standing leg is extended (straight).

[5 COUNTS]:
Return right leg to passé.

[5 COUNTS]:
Plié [bend knee] standing leg, flex right foot in passé.

[5 COUNTS]:
Développé right leg forward in parallel (foot flexed), standing leg remains in plié [bent].

[5 COUNTS]:
Remain in plié [bent], lower right heel down.

[5 COUNTS]:
Extend left knee (straight), transferring weight up-and-over onto right leg, plié [bend] right leg, foot flat on the Earth.

[5 COUNTS]:

Lift left heel (into high arch), extend right knee, arms reach side through Four Directions, reaching up towards the Universe.

[5 COUNTS]:
Plié [bent knees] (weight over front/right leg), left foot in high arch, arms lower in front of body in scooping position (palms facing up).

[5 COUNTS]:
Rotate left leg open into 2nd position (lower left heel), torso follows in space—*body facing left wall*, arms in Four Elements.

[5 COUNTS]:
Knees remain in plié [bent], lift left heel into forced arch.

[5 COUNTS]:
Rotate body *to face front*, right leg forward—weight forward on right leg, right foot flat on the floor, left foot in high arch, arms in Four Elements.

[5 COUNTS]:
Extend left knee, left heel reaches towards the Earth.

[5 COUNTS]:
Extend right knee.

[5 COUNTS]:
Open arms into Four Directions, chest into Projection (heart reaches towards the Universe), arms continue to extend into High V (lengthening from the arch).

[5 COUNTS]:
Small lunge forward, right leg in plié, arms in Four Directions.

[5 COUNTS]:
Passé left leg (without moving placement of right leg in parallel).

[5 COUNTS]:
Flex left foot (standing right leg remains in plié [bent]), lower left foot, sliding along right leg.

[5 COUNTS]:
Plié [bent knees].

[5 COUNTS]:
Straighten legs. Lower arms along the side of the body.

[5 COUNTS]:
Walk backwards, leading with the right leg.

[5 COUNTS]:
Walk forwards, leading with the right leg.

[5 COUNTS]:
Walk around in a circle toward the right, leading with the right leg.

[5 COUNTS]:
Walk around in a circle toward the left, leading with the left leg.
Repeat entire sequence to the left.

END SEQUENCE
[4 COUNTS]: Right leg in passé, foot flexed, arms in Appreciation to
the front.

[4 COUNTS]: Lower right foot to the Earth with plié [bent knees],
lower arms.

[4 COUNTS]: Bend elbows and extend legs.

Flatback Combination with Développé

Begin:
Feet in 1st base position, vertical spine. Arms along the side of the
body.

DIRECTION: FACING FRONT
[4 COUNTS]:
Plié [bent knees], arms in Element Earth, rotate legs into 1st position
(Open triangle feet). Now facing *Diagonal Right.*

[4 COUNTS]:
Extend legs, arms in Element Water.

[4 COUNTS]:
Arms in Element Air.

[4 COUNTS]:
Moving through Element Air, rotate hand and forearm so that fingertips point towards the front, and palms face out.

DIRECTION: FACING DIAGONAL RIGHT
[4 COUNTS]:
Open arms to Four Directions feet in 1st position (Open triangle feet)
to the right diagonal.

DIRECTION: FACING DIAGONAL RIGHT
[2 COUNTS]:
Plié [bent knees], lower right arm down pointing towards the Earth,
flex wrist, right arm moves up in front of body to heart level.

[2 COUNTS]:
Grande plié [bend knees deeply], simultaneously, right arm lifts overhead—palm towards the Universe

DIRECTION: FACING FRONT

[4 COUNTS]:
Rotate right leg inwards (both legs into 4th position parallel, left leg slightly forward) simultaneously, arm circle through Four Directions and down reaching towards the Earth. Both palms face inwards towards each other—at heart level, extend knees, vertical spine.

[4 COUNTS]:
Arms continue to lengthen up towards the Universe overhead, palms facing inwards.

[4 COUNTS]:
Flatback forward, arms in line with ears.

[4 COUNTS]:
Body maintains flatback, arms half-circle (lowering down, towards the Earth, brushing sides of legs, until fingertips reach towards the back wall, arms in line with flatback).

[4 COUNTS]:
Contraction (initiating at the 2nd chakra), flex wrist (fingertips reach towards the center of the body).

[4 COUNTS]:
Roll up into vertical spine, arms move forward and up until palms face upwards towards the Universe, knees remain extended.

DIRECTION: FACING DIAGONAL RIGHT

[4 COUNTS]:
Rotate right leg into 1st position (Open triangle feet), plié, arms open into Four Directions.

[2 COUNTS]:
Plié [bent knees], lower right arm down pointing towards the Earth, flex wrist, right arm moves up in front of body to heart level.

[2 COUNTS]:
Grande plié [bend knees deeply], simultaneously right arm lifts overhead—palm towards the Universe.

DIRECTION: FACING FRONT

[4 COUNTS]:
Rotate right leg inwards (both legs into 4th position parallel, left leg slightly forward), simultaneously, arm circle through Four Directions and down reaching towards the Earth. Both palms face inwards towards each other—at heart level, extend knees, vertical spine.

[4 COUNTS]:
Arms continue to lengthen up towards the Universe overhead, palms facing inwards.

[4 COUNTS]:
Relevé [lift heels].

[4 COUNTS]:
Lower relevé.

[4 COUNTS]:
Flatback forward, arms in line with ears.

[4 COUNTS]:
Body maintains flatback, arms half-circle (lowering towards the Earth, brushing sides of legs, until fingertips reach towards the back wall, arms in line with flatback).

[2 COUNTS]:
Contraction (initiating at the 2nd chakra), remaining in parallel, plié [bent knees], right foot into high arch (lift heel), flex wrists (fingertips reach towards the center of the body).

[4 COUNTS]:
Maintaining contraction and high arch in back foot, lift torso towards verticality, move arms from the sides of the body around into 1st position (in front of the heart), wrist flexed with palms facing outward.

Direction: Facing Diagonal Right

[4 COUNTS]:
Rotate right leg into 1st position (Open triangle feet), release into vertical spine, plié, open arms into Four Directions.

[2 COUNTS]:
Plié [bent knees], lower right arm down pointing towards the Earth, flex wrist, right arm moves up in front of body to heart level.

[2 COUNTS]:
Grande plié [bend knees deeply], simultaneously right arm lifts overhead—palm towards the Universe.

Direction: Facing Front

[4 COUNTS]:
Rotate right leg inwards (both legs into 4th position parallel, left leg slightly forward) simultaneously, arm circle through Four Directions and down reaching towards the Earth. Both palms face inwards towards each other—at heart level, extend knees, vertical spine.

[4 COUNTS]:
Arms continue to lengthen up towards the Universe overhead, palms facing inwards.

[4 COUNTS]:
Plié.

[4 COUNTS]:
Extend knees.

[4 COUNTS]:
Relevé [lift heels].

[4 COUNTS]:
Flatback forward, lower heels, arms in line with ears.

[4 COUNTS]:
Body maintains flatback, arms half-circle (lowering towards the Earth, brushing sides of legs, until fingertips reach towards the back wall, arms in line with flatback).

[2 COUNTS]:
Sharply—plié [bent knees], right foot into high arch behind, spine in contraction, head in alignment with spine, extend parallel arms on the low diagonal forward, palms facing inwards.

[2 COUNTS]:
Maintain plié [bent knees] with right foot in high arch, vertical spine, arms parallel at heart level, palms facing inward.

[2 COUNTS]:
Initiating from the 2nd chakra, undulate torso forward allowing the head to follow.

[2 COUNTS]:
Contract the upper spine forward and over, maintain arms in parallel position.

[2 COUNTS]:
Vertical spine.

[2 COUNTS]:
Initiating from the 2nd chakra, undulate torso forward allowing the head to follow.

[2 COUNTS]:
Contract the upper spine forward and over, maintain arms in parallel position.

[2 COUNTS]:
Vertical spine.

[2 COUNTS]:
Initiating from the 2nd chakra, undulate torso forward allowing the head to follow.

[2 COUNTS]:
Contract the upper spine forward and over, lower arms in parallel position towards the Earth.

[4 COUNTS]:
Extend knees, roll up through the spine, torso into Projection, arms reach into High V position.

[2 COUNTS]:
Plié [bent knees], arms remain in high V, flip palms over, elbows remain in line with ears as fingertips move down towards the sternum.

[2 COUNTS]:
Continue hands reaching down towards the Earth, backs of hands are touching, elbows are reaching up.

[4 COUNTS]:
Flatback on low diagonal, arms open to parallel position on the low diagonal (extending the line of the torso), palms facing inwards, extend the knees.

[4 COUNTS]:
Relax the spine and palms touch the Earth, fingertips point inward towards each other.

[4 COUNTS]:
Roll up to vertical spine, arms relaxed on sides of body.

DIRECTION: FACING FRONT

Arms remain along the sides of the body, palms facing inwards.

[2 COUNTS]:
Passé right leg parallel, base leg extended.

[2 COUNTS]:
Right foot steps backward, passé left leg parallel.

[4 COUNTS]:
Plié [bend knee] right leg, développé left leg parallel forward, foot pointed.

[2 COUNTS]:
Step forward onto left leg (extended), passé right leg parallel.

[2 COUNTS]:
Right foot steps backward, passé left leg parallel.

[4 COUNTS]:
Right knee extended, développé left leg parallel forward, foot pointed.

[2 COUNTS]:
Relevé [lift heel] right foot.

[2 COUNTS]:
Piqué forward onto left leg, passé right leg parallel.

[2 COUNTS]:
Right foot steps backward, passé left leg parallel.

[4 COUNTS]:
Right knee extended, développé left leg parallel forward, foot pointed.

[2 COUNTS]:
Relevé [lift heel] right foot.

[2 COUNTS]:
Piqué forward onto left leg, passé right leg parallel.

[2 COUNTS]:
Plié [bent knees], flex right foot.

[2 COUNTS]:
Slide right foot, down left leg in plié.

[2 COUNTS]:
1st base position, legs extended.

TRANSITION

[2 COUNTS]:
Plié [bent knees].

DIRECTION: FACING DIAGONAL LEFT

[4 COUNTS]:
Rotate legs to 1st position, arms in Four Directions.

[4 COUNTS]:
Bend elbows, extend legs and arms (arms by sides of body).
Repeat left side.

Push Ups and Pirouettes

Begin:
Feet in 2nd position parallel, vertical spine. Arms along the side of the body.

DIRECTION: SIDE WALL (RIGHT)

[2 COUNTS]:

Plié [bent knees], Projection, arms extended parallel forward at heart level with Lotus hands.

[2 COUNTS]:
Continue plié and reach forward until heels lift and shoot body out and forward onto the floor into plank position, arms in line with shoulders.

[16 COUNTS]:
Eight push-ups (1 count down, 1 count up).

[4 COUNTS]:
Lower the body to the floor as one unit.

[4 COUNTS]:
Initiating from the tailbone, push back into the child's pose (pelvis resting over heels, forehead resting on the floor, arms stretched forward).

[4 COUNTS]:
Relax into child's pose.

[2 COUNTS]:
Tuck toes under, move hands to the sides of the shoulders on the floor (preparation).

[2 COUNTS]:
Push back onto both feet flat on the floor, legs full extended, torso in flatback reaching on the low diagonal, arms in line with ears—reaching towards the Earth—on the low diagonal.

[4 COUNTS]:
Remaining in flatback, arms circle forward, up towards the Universe, back and down, grabbing the upper thighs (below the gluteus).

[4 COUNTS]:
Slide hands down legs (towards the ankles) to stretch.

[4 COUNTS]:
Roll up to vertical spine.

[2 COUNTS]:
Plié [bent knees].

[2 COUNTS]:
Relevé [lift heel] left foot, passé right leg.

[2 COUNTS]:
Return right leg to maintain relevé [lift heels], both legs.

[2 COUNTS]:
Lower heels.

[2 COUNTS]:
Plié [bent knees].

[2 COUNTS]:
Pirouette turn (one and a half turn to the right), right leg passé.

DIRECTION: SIDE WALL (LEFT)

[2 COUNTS]:
Relevé [lift heel].

[2 COUNTS]:
Lower heels.
Repeat plié, relevé, passé section on the left side (end pirouette turn facing front).
Repeat entire sequence. Start facing the left wall.

Across the Floor

Progressions across the floor are completed in *Familias* (Families) of four dancers in each line. Normally, the *Famlilias* move straight across the space, towards the musicians, unless otherwise noted. Once the progression reaches the opposite side of the room, the dancers divide in the center, two to the right and two to the left, to return back to the starting location.

Runs with Element Symbols

Begin:
1st base position, vertical spine, arms are along the side of the body with palms facing in towards thighs.
Note: Runs across, maintain plié [bent] knees throughout.

[2 COUNTS]:
Run right, left—arms in Element Earth.

[2 COUNTS]:
Run right, left—arms in Element Water.

[2 COUNTS]:
Run right, left—arms in Element Air.

[2 COUNTS]:
Run right, left—arms in Element Fire.

[4 COUNTS]:
Run right, left, right, left—Lower Fire arms in front of heart and slowly open to the Four Elements.

Runs Backwards with Element Symbols

Begin:
Facing backwards, first base position, vertical spine, arms are along the side of the body with palms facing in towards thighs.
*Note: Runs backwards across, maintain plié [bent knees] throughout.
[2 COUNTS]:
Run backwards right, left—arms in Element Earth.
[2 COUNTS]:
Run backwards right, left—arms in Element Water.
[2 COUNTS]:
Run backwards right, left—arms in Element Air.
[2 COUNTS]:
Run backwards right, left—arms in Element Fire.
[4 COUNTS]:
Run backwards right, left, right, left—Lower Fire arms in front of heart and slowly open to the Four Elements.

Passé and Four Element Arms with Piqué

Begin:
2nd position parallel, vertical spine, arms open to Four Elements.
[2 COUNTS]:
Piqué onto left foot, passé right knee parallel, arms remain in Four Elements.
[2 COUNTS]:
Step right in plié, step left in plié, arms remain in Four Elements.
[2 COUNTS]:
Piqué onto right foot, passé left leg parallel, arms remain in Four Elements.
[2 COUNTS]:
Step left in plié, step right in plié, arms remain in Four Elements.
Repeat right and left across the floor

Passé and Four Element Arms with Pirouettes

Begin:
2nd position parallel, vertical spine, arms open to Four Elements.
Preparation:
[and ... COUNT]:

Arms close slightly, with elbows reaching side (fingertips meet in front of heart).

[2 COUNTS]

Piqué turn (onto left foot, pirouette turn right), passé right leg parallel, arms in Four Elements.

[2 COUNTS]:

Step right in plié, step left in plié, arms close slightly with elbows reaching side (fingertips meet in front of heart).

[2 COUNTS]:

Piqué turn (onto right foot, pirouette turn left), passé left leg parallel, arms in Four Elements.

[2 COUNTS]:

Step left in plié, step right in plié, arms close slightly with elbows reaching side (fingertips meet in front of heart).

Repeat right and left across the floor.

Battements in Attitude (Parallel)

Begin:

Small lunge, left leg forward, right leg extended in back, vertical spine, arms in Four Directions with wrists flexed (fingertips are pointing towards the Universe).

[2 COUNTS]:

Battement right leg to the front in parallel position, right knee in attitude, foot flexed, standing leg in plié [bent].

[2 COUNTS]:

Step right in plié, step left in plié.

[2 COUNTS]:

Step right, battement left leg to the front in parallel position, left knee in attitude, foot flexed, standing leg in plié [bent].

[2 COUNTS]:

Step left in plié, step right in plié.

Repeat right and left.

Battements with Legs Extended (Parallel)

Begin:

Small lunge, left leg forward, right leg extended in back, vertical spine, arms in Four Directions.

[2 COUNTS]:

Battement right leg to the front in parallel position, right knee extended, foot pointed, standing leg extended.

[2 COUNTS]:
Step right in plié, step left in plié.

[2 COUNTS]:
Step right, battement left leg to the front in parallel position, left knee extended, foot pointed, standing leg extended.

[2 COUNTS]:
Step left in plié, step right in plié.
Repeat right and left.

Battements with Legs Extended in Outward Rotation

Begin:
Small lunge, left leg forward, right leg extended in back with the heel connected to the Earth, vertical spine reaching towards the Universe, arms in Four Directions.

Note: Movement is performed in turn out/outward rotation.

[2 COUNTS]:
Battement right leg to the front (passing through 1st position) in outward rotation, right knee extended, foot pointed, standing leg extended.

[2 COUNTS]:
Step right in plié, step left in plié in outward rotation.

[2 COUNTS]:
Step right, battement left leg to the front (passing through 1st position) in turned out position, left knee extended, foot pointed, standing leg extended.

[2 COUNTS]:
Step left in plié, step right in plié in outward rotation.
Repeat right and left.

Choreography Sequence

Create a choreography sequence/movement combination incorporating the skills obtained from the training technique. The choreography sequence serves as an opportunity for deeper exploration of discovery, self-expression and self-determination through movement. The *Body Universe* is fully engaged and responsive.

Ending

- Rub the hands together in front of the heart chakra to draw energy from the body
- Open to Appreciation
- Use a short section of any the conversations to center the body
- Bring arms into the *Triangle of Balance* position behind the sacrum
- Salute:
  ◊ Body/Self
  ◊ Dancers in the space
  ◊ Musicians
  ◊ Observes
  ◊ Main entrance/exit
  ◊ Teacher(s)

Advanced/Level III (Professionals and Silvestre Technique Instructors)

Opening Sequence

Begin:
Center floor, feet in first base position (feet touching). Spine is vertical, arms are along the side of the body with palms facing in towards thighs. Eyes are closed.

- Centering thoughts
- Connect the body to the triangles

Tempo: Described counts are suggested for foundational development of movement phrases.

Internalization

CONNECT THE ELEMENTS

Scanning the body starting from the soles of the feet connecting to the earth below. Feeling stabilization, security, and balance. In this position dancers should be aware of their weight distributed evenly through the feet. The energy of the earth in the feet is drawn up through the legs along the backs of the knees, elongated through the hip flexors, and arrives into the pelvis where elements water is recognized. The water is present in the core of the body where contractions are initiated. Visualize water flowing throughout the body in various forms, including through the blood vessels and veins. The essence of water releases any tensions that may be present throughout the body. Energy from the core of the body continue up through the spine and diaphragm into the chest cavity where the heart and lungs are housed. Attention is given to the elements air, which enters and leaves our lungs as we breathe, allowing our heart to beat continuously. The person should feel the air on their skin as they stand in space. The energy from the chest continues up through the back of the neck, releasing any tension in the jaw. The energy shoots out through the top of the head connecting to the sky, sun and universe above. Imagine the heat from the sun on the crown of the head connecting the body to element fire. Acknowledging the connection of the four elements throughout the body starts the illumination of the *Body Universe*.

Inhale through the nose, and exhale with plié [bent knees] in first base position. After the breath has fully exited the body, straighten both legs into verticality.

BODY UNIVERSE OF THREE TRIANGLES

From the top of your head to your shoulders imagine the *Triangle of Inspiration*, offering perception and visualizations for movement. Set the intention for the dance.

From the shoulders down to the navel, imagine the *Triangle of Expression* allowing freedom of movement and the dancer's creative voice to speak.

From the hips to the base of the feet imagine the *Triangle of Balance*, providing stability, harmony, and security.

Inhale through the nose, and exhale with plié [bent knees] in first base position. After the breath has fully exited the body, straighten both legs into verticality.

Open eyes (slowly).

Saluting the *Body Universe*

Begin:

Feet in first base position (feet touching). Spine is vertical, arms are along the side of the body with palms facing in towards thighs.

SALUTING THE TRIANGLE OF INSPIRATION
[4 COUNTS]:

Slowly bend elbows towards the side, allowing the hands to glide up the side of the thigh, until the wrist reaches the hip. Elbows continue pointing side.

[4 COUNTS]:
Reverse the action by gliding the palms back down the side of the thigh until elbows are no longer bent.

SALUTING THE TRIANGLE OF EXPRESSION

[4 COUNTS]:
Repeat arms with plié [bent knees].

[4 COUNTS]:
Straighten the legs and arms.

SALUTING THE TRIANGLE OF BALANCE

[4 COUNTS]:
Repeat arms without plié [bent knees].

[4 COUNTS]:
Straighten the arms.

SALUTING THE BODY

[4 COUNTS]:
With elbows straight, the palms of the hands draw towards each other, wrapping around just under the gluteus. Fingertips pointing towards the Earth below.

[4 COUNTS]:
The elbows bend allowing the palms to glide over the gluteus until elbows are bent and are facing completely side. Palms are resting on hips and fingertips are pointing inwards, towards the spine. The thumb reaches forward in line with the hip socket, leaving the fingertips back (embracing the gluteus).

[4 COUNTS]:
Elbows remain in place, bent towards the side. The hand rotates downwards until fingertips point towards the Earth.

[4 COUNTS]:
Elbows straighten as the palms glide alongside the thigh.

Center Sequences

Opening the Channels (Chakras) Part I

Begin:

Feet in first base position (feet touching). Spine is vertical, arms are along the side of the body with palms facing in towards thighs.

[4 COUNTS]:
Slowly bend elbows, palms facing the front of the thighs. Element Earth. Elbows continue to reach side as fingertips touch each other in front of the heart. Element Water. Shoulders are pressing down.

[4 COUNTS]:
Palms face the body as the elbows continue reaching up—elbows same level as the ears. Palms scan in front of the face and pass over the forehead, stopping over the crown of the head.

[4 COUNTS]:
Flex wrists until the palms face each other and fingertips reach up towards the Universe. Element Fire. There is space between the two palms.

[4 COUNTS]:
Extend the elbows completely, fingertips reach towards the Universe.

[4 COUNTS]:
Flex the wrists, arms open to the side of the body—stopping at shoulder level—fingertips reaching towards the Earth. Projection heart reaching towards the Universe.

[4 COUNTS]:
Arms retrace movement until palms face the Universe above the head. Vertical spine.

[4 COUNTS]:
Flip palms over, elbows remain in place as fingertips move down towards the forehead.

[4 COUNTS]:
Hands reach the sternum with backs of hands are touching, elbows are reaching up. Element Water.

[4 COUNTS]:
Rotate wrists so that palms face each other (not touching), elbows extend slightly down below shoulder level.

[4 COUNTS]:
Extend elbows, fingertips reach towards the Earth.

[4 COUNTS]:
Plié [bent knees] bringing arms to Element Earth.

[4 COUNTS]:
Contraction knees remain in plié [bent], arms parallel to the floor, extended front from shoulders.

[4 COUNTS]:
Retract position, Element Earth, vertical spine.

[4 COUNTS]:
Extend legs, hands to Element Water.

[[4 COUNTS]:
High Contraction, legs remain extended, arms parallel to the floor, extended front from shoulders.

[4 COUNTS]:
Retract position, vertical spine, Element Water.

[4 COUNTS]:
Flex wrist, fingers point towards the Earth, elbows side.

[4 COUNTS]:
Reach fingers towards the Earth, extend elbows.

[4 COUNTS]:
Three shoulder rolls (shoulders rolling front, upwards and back).

[4 COUNTS]:
Plié [bent knees], reach arms out in front of the heart extending from the shoulders, palms facing up, Projection.

[4 COUNTS]:
Heart pouring forward towards the Earth until chest is over thighs and fingertips touch the floor on each side of the body.

[4 COUNTS]:
Circle fingertips from the sides of the body to the front of the toes, gathering the seeds from the Earth.

[4 COUNTS]:
Roll up, extending the knees simultaneously to reach vertical spine.
Repeat sequence in:
1st position
2nd position parallel
2nd position

END SEQUENCE

[4 COUNTS]:
Plié [bent knees] in second position, arms in the Four Directions, rotate and walk feet in to 2nd position parallel, to 1st position, and 1st base position.

[4 COUNTS]:
Bend elbows and extend legs and arms.

Opening the Channels (Chakras) Part II

Begin:

Feet in first base position (feet touching). Spine is vertical, arms are along the side of the body with palms facing in towards thighs.

[4 COUNTS]:

Slowly bend elbows, palms facing the front of the thighs. Element Earth. Elbows continue to reach side as fingertips touch each other in front of the heart. Element Water. Shoulders are pressing down.

[4 COUNTS]:

Palms face the body as the elbows continue reaching up—elbows same level as the ears. Palms scan in front of the face and pass over the forehead, stopping over the crown of the head.

[4 COUNTS]:

Flex wrists until the palms face each other and fingertips reach up towards the Universe. Element Fire. There is space between the two palms.

[4 COUNTS]:

Extend the elbows completely, fingertips reach towards the Universe.

[4 COUNTS]:

Rotate outward from the shoulders, press palms down toward the Earth—arms are extended to the Four Directions.

[12 COUNTS]:

Arms in Four Directions, plié [bent knees] 3 times

[4 COUNTS]:

On the fourth plié [bent knees], bend the elbows.

[4 COUNTS]:

Straighten the knees, lower arms to the sides of the body. Roll down the front of the body until the hands touch the floor. Palms flat on the floor and fingertips pointing towards each other.

[12 COUNTS]:

Plié [bent knees] 3 times.

[2 COUNTS]:

Remain in plié [bent knees], sharply open hands side—from the elbow—until the fingertips are touching the floor and palms are facing outwards.

[4 COUNTS]:

Remain in plié [bent knees], contract from the 2nd chakra, roll up to vertical spine.

[4 COUNTS]:

Extend knees while simultaneously rotating the arms from the shoulder socket so that arms are in a High V position.

[8 COUNTS]:
Plié [bent knees] 2 times.

[8 COUNTS]:
Relevé [lift heels] 2 times.

[4 COUNTS]:
Plié [bent knees], arms point to the Four Directions. Rotate legs to 1st position (Open triangle feet).

[4 COUNTS]:
Bend elbows and extend legs.
Repeat sequence in:
1st position (feet) | Open triangle feet
2nd position (feet) in parallel
2nd position (feet) in outward rotation

END SEQUENCE

[4 COUNTS]:
Plié [bent knees] in second position, arms in the Four Directions, rotate and walk feet in to 2nd position parallel, to 1st position, and first base position.

[4 COUNTS]:
Bend elbows and extend legs.

Messages | Past, Present and Future—Part I and II

Begin:
Arms behind back at sacrum, awareness of the *Triangle of Balance*.

[2 COUNTS]:
Plié [bent knees], extend right arm towards the Earth, lengthen right arm into the High V position.

[2 COUNTS]:
Extend legs, right arm to Element Fire.

[2 COUNTS]:
Extend elbow, flex wrist—palm flat towards the Universe.

[2 COUNTS]:
Reach right arm down to Four Directions position, wrist remains flexed, fingertips reaching towards the Earth, with palm flat (facing out).

[2 COUNTS]:
Extend wrist, palm facing flat to the front.

[2 COUNTS]:
Bend right elbow, right hand in Element Water.

[2 COUNTS]:
Element Air.

[2 COUNTS]:
From Element Air, rotate wrist so fingertips move down and forward, fingertips point towards the front, and palm faces out.

[2 COUNTS]:
Extend elbow, fingertip reach forward.

[2 COUNTS]:
Flex wrist, bend elbow, fingertips touch shoulder on left side.

[2 COUNTS]:
Extend right arm to Four Directions position.

[2 COUNTS]:
Relax wrist, fingertips relax towards the Earth.

[2 COUNTS]:
Lift arm towards the Universe (High V with wrist relaxed).

[2 COUNTS]:
Bend elbow to lower arm.

[2 COUNTS]:
Right arm returns to lower back—*Triangle of Balance.*

[2 COUNTS]:
Plié [bent knees], right arm reaches towards the Earth.

[2 COUNTS]:
Extend legs, right arm moves through Four Directions towards the Universe

[2 COUNTS]:
Plié [bent knees], right arm in 5th position, encircling the crown chakra.

[4 COUNTS]:
Flatback forward in plié, right arm in line with right ear (wrist extended), Projection (heart reaching forward).

[2 COUNTS]:
Bend completely over at the waist with right palm on the floor, fingertip pointing inward towards the center, legs extend simultaneously.

[2 COUNTS]:
Contract from the 2nd chakra—roll up to vertical spine. Right hand remain in place over head, palm facing the Universe.

Repeat the following:

[2 COUNTS]:

Flatback forward in plié, right arm in line with right ear (wrist extended), Projection (heart reaching forward).

[2 COUNTS]:

Bend completely over at the waist with right palm on the floor, fingertip pointing inward towards the center, legs extend simultaneously.

[2 COUNTS]:

Contract from the 2nd chakra—roll up to vertical spine. Right hand remain in place over head, palm facing the Universe.

[2 COUNTS]:

Plié [bent knees], left hand passes through Four Directions to meet right hand over head, palms facing the Universe.

[1 COUNT]:

Plié [bent knees], spiral torso to the right, palms facing Universe, pelvis and lower body remains square, facing front.

[1 COUNT]:

Return center.

[1 COUNTS]:

Plié [bent knees], spiral torso to the left side, palms facing Universe, pelvis and lower body remains square, facing front.

[1 COUNT]:

Return center.

[2 COUNTS]:

Extend legs, reaching palms towards the Universe.

[1 COUNT]:

Rotate wrist to 5th position (palm down).

[4 COUNTS]:

Relevé, legs extended, spiral torso to the right side, arms remains in 5th position, pelvis square.

[4 COUNTS]:

Remain in relevé, return body front, arms in 5th position.

[4 COUNTS]:

Remain in relevé, spiral torso to the left side, arms remains in 5th position, pelvis square.

[4 COUNTS]:

Remain in relevé, return body front, arms in 5th position.

[4 COUNTS]:

Lower relevé, spiral torso to the right side, right arm remains in 5th position, left arm opens side, palm facing Universe, pelvis and lower body remains square, facing front.

[4 COUNTS]:
Return body front, both arms in 5th position.

[4 COUNTS]:
Spiral torso to the left side, left arm remains in 5th position, right arm opens side, palm facing Universe, pelvis and lower body remains square, facing front.

[4 COUNTS]:
Return body front, arms in 5th position.

[2 COUNTS]:
Salute the *Triangle of Inspiration* above the head, relevé.

[4 COUNTS]:
Open arms to Four Directions.

TRANSITION

[4 COUNTS]:
Plié [bent knees], arms in Four Directions, rotate feet and legs to 1st position.

[4 COUNTS]:
Bend elbows and extend legs.
Repeat sequence in:
1st position (feet) | Open triangle feet
2nd position (feet) in parallel
2nd position (feet) in outward rotation

END SEQUENCE

[4 COUNTS]:
Plié [bent knees] in second position, arms in the Four Directions, rotate and walk feet in to 2nd position parallel, to 1st position, and first base position.

[4 COUNTS]:
Bend elbows and extend legs.

Pliés with Flatback (Extended Version)

Begin:
2nd position parallel, vertical spine. Arms along the side of the body.

[4 COUNTS]:
Roll down, extending the body forwards, towards the Earth from the waist, arms reaching in front in the *Triangle of Balance,* elbows extended.

[4 COUNTS]:
Separate hands and extend fingertips along the floor until spine reaches diagonal flatback.

[4 COUNTS]:
Plié [bent knees], reach the arms and palms of the hands up towards the Universe (as if splashing water up), spine extended on a high diagonal.

[4 COUNTS]:
Release arms and torso back down towards the Earth (signaling the energy to the Earth) deeper plié.

[4 COUNTS]:
Extend fingertips along the floor (hands separated, in two parallel lines) with flatback on the low diagonal, extend legs.

[4 COUNTS]:
Lift flatback to horizontal position. Arms in line with ears, reaching forward.

[4 COUNTS]:
Initiating with a contraction in the lower abdominals, roll up the spine to vertical position with arms in front of heart chakra, parallel to the floor.

[4 COUNTS]:
Plié [bent knees], vertical spine.

[4 COUNTS]:
Flatback, torso horizontal towards the Earth—maintain plié [bent knees].

[4 COUNTS]:
Extend legs.

[4 COUNTS]:
Initiating with a contraction in the lower abdominals, roll up the spine to vertical position with arms in front of heart chakra, parallel to the floor.

[4 COUNTS]:
Plié [bent knees], vertical spine.

[4 COUNTS]:
Flatback, torso horizontal towards the Earth—maintain plié [bent knees].

[4 COUNTS]:
Extend legs.

[4 COUNTS]:
Initiating with a contraction in the lower abdominals, roll up the spine to vertical position with arms in front of heart chakra, parallel to the floor.

[4 COUNTS]:
Projection (high release) arms remain in front of heart chakra, parallel to floor.

[4 COUNTS]:
Plié [bent knees], maintaining Projection.

[4 COUNTS]:
Flatback, torso horizontal towards the Earth—maintain plié [bent knees], arms in line with ears.

[2 COUNTS]:
Arms salute Element Air—head focuses forward.

[4 COUNTS]:
Forced arch (lift heels off the floor), maintain plié.

[4 COUNTS]:
Deepen forced arch and plié.

[4 COUNTS]:
Lower heels to the floor.

[4 COUNTS]:
Forced arch (lift heels off the floor), maintain plié.

[4 COUNTS]:
Deepen forced arch and plié.

[4 COUNTS]:
Lower heels to the floor.

[4 COUNTS]:
Open arms to Four Directions (horizontal to the Earth).

[4 COUNTS]:
Drop head and arms towards the Earth—hands grab hold to elbows.

[4 COUNTS]:
Knees remain in plié [bent], roll up to vertical spine—hands are over the head (holding onto elbows).

[4 COUNTS]:
Extend legs.

[2 COUNTS]:
Force arch right foot, right hand in Lotus position, extending elbow, reaching fingers towards the Universe.

[2 COUNTS]:
Return hand and foot.

[2 COUNTS]:

Forced arch left foot—left hand in Lotus position, extending elbow, reaching fingers towards the Universe.

[2 COUNTS]:
Return hand and foot.

[4 COUNTS]:
Relevé.

[4 COUNTS]:
Lower heels.

[4 COUNTS]:
Relevé.

[4 COUNTS]:
Lower heels.

[8 COUNTS]:
Plié [bent knees], roll through feet into relevé [lift heels]. Extend legs.—Element Fire above the head

[4 COUNTS]:
Grande plié [bend knees deeply] with heels off of the floor (forced arch).

[4 COUNTS]:
Extend legs, continue into relevé [lift heels].

[4 COUNTS]:
Lower heels, and plié, arms remain in Element Fire.

[4 COUNTS]:
Flatback, torso horizontal towards the Earth—remain in plié [bent knees]—hands remain in Element Fire.

[4 COUNTS]:
Arms salute Element Air—head focuses forward.

[4 COUNTS]:
Open arms to Four Directions (horizontal to the Earth).

[4 COUNTS]:
Drop head and arms towards the Earth—hands grab hold to elbows.

[4 COUNTS]:
Plié [bent knees], roll up to vertical spine and extend legs simultaneously—arms remain over the head (hands holding onto elbows).

[4 COUNTS]:
Relevé [lift heels], salute Element Fire in Projection (high release).

[4 COUNTS]:
Plié [bent knees], heart drops towards the Earth. Arms in Element Fire

passing in front of the torso. Head over the Earth. Extend legs—open arms to Four Elements roll up to vertical spine, relevé [lift heels].

[4 COUNTS]:
Relevé [lift heels] arms in Four Elements.

[4 COUNTS]:
Open to Four Directions and Projection (high release).

[4 COUNTS]:
Plié [bent knees], drop heart toward the Earth, head follows. Hands grab onto elbows. Roll up to vertical spine, extend legs and relevé simultaneously.

[4 COUNTS]:
In relevé [lift heels], salute Element Fire in Projection.

[4 COUNTS]:
Plié [bent knees], heart drops towards the Earth. Arms in Element Fire passing in front of the torso. Head over the Earth. Extend legs—open arms to Four Elements pull up to vertical spine, relevé [lift heels].

[4 COUNTS]:
Relevé [lift heels] arms in Four Elements.

[4 COUNTS]:
Open to Four Directions in Projection.

[2 COUNTS]:
Plié, flatback, arms side in Four Directions with palms facing down.

[2 COUNTS]:
Flex wrist, vertical spine in plié—fingertips reach back, palms facing out with arms side.

[4 COUNTS]:
Deepen plié [bent knees], cross arms in front of the body.

[4 COUNTS]:
Open arms to Four Directions and extend legs.

[4 COUNTS]:
Plié [bent knees], cross arms in front of the body, opposite arm on top.

[4 COUNTS]:
Open arms to Four Directions and extend legs.

[4 COUNTS]:
Plié [bent knees], cross arms in front of the body, extend legs—cross arms above your head (removing a t-shirt action).

[4 COUNTS]:
Salute the *Triangle of Inspiration* above the head—Open arms to Four Directions.

End Sequence

[4 COUNTS]: Plié [bent knees], arms in Four Directions.

[4 COUNTS]: Bend elbows and extend legs.

Flat Back—Extended 2nd Position (Outward Rotation)

Begin:
Second position turned out, vertical spine, arms in *Triangle of Balance* in front of the body.

[4 COUNTS]:
Roll down, extending the body forwards, towards the Earth from the waist, arms reaching in front in the *Triangle of Balance,* elbows extended.

[4 COUNTS]:
Separate hands and extend fingertips along the floor until spine reaches diagonal flatback.

[4 COUNTS]:
Plié [bent knees] in 2nd position turned out, vertical spine, backs of hands press on the inside of knees. (Signal of open of rotation of the hips and legs).

[4 COUNTS]:
Knees remain in plié [bent], flatback forward, extend arms forward, in line with ears.

[4 COUNTS]:
Extend legs, remain in flatback.

[4 COUNTS]:
Initiating with a contraction in the lower abdominals, roll up the spine to vertical position with arms in front of heart chakra, parallel to the floor.

[4 COUNTS]:
Plié [bent knees] in 2nd position, vertical spine.

[4 COUNTS]:
Knees remain in plié [bent], flatback forward, arms remain forward, in line with ears.

[4 COUNTS]:
Extend legs.

[4 COUNTS]:
Initiating with a contraction in the lower abdominals, roll up the spine to vertical position with arms in front of heart chakra, parallel to the floor.

[4 COUNTS]:
Projection (high release) arms remain in front of heart chakra, parallel to floor.

[4 COUNTS]:
2nd position plié [bent knees], maintain Projection.

[4 COUNTS]:
Flatback, torso horizontal towards the Earth—deepen plié [bent knees], arms in line with ears.

[2 COUNTS]:
Arms salute Element Air—head focuses forward.

[4 COUNTS]:
Open arms to Four Directions (horizontal to the Earth).

[4 COUNTS]:
Drop head and arms towards the Earth—hands grab hold to elbows.

[4 COUNTS]:
Knees remain in plié [bent], roll up to vertical spine—hands are over the head (holding onto elbows).

[4 COUNTS]:
Extend knees, hands continue to hold onto elbows.

[2 COUNTS]:
Force arch right foot (outward rotation), right hand in Lotus position.

[2 COUNTS]:
Return hand and foot.

[2 COUNTS]:
Force arch left foot (outward rotation), left hand in Lotus position.

[2 COUNTS]:
Return hand and foot.

[4 COUNTS]:
Plié [bent knees], roll through feet into relevé [lift heels]—Element Fire hands above head. Extend legs.

[4 COUNTS]:
Grande plié [bend knees deeply] in 2nd position, with heels off of the floor—forced arch.

[4 COUNTS]:
Extend legs, continue into relevé [lift heels].

[4 COUNTS]:
Lower heels, and plié.

[4 COUNTS]:
Flatback, torso horizontal towards the Earth—over with plié [bent knees]—arms maintain Element Fire.

[4 COUNTS]:
Arms salute Element Air—head focuses forward.

[4 COUNTS]:
Open arms to Four Directions (horizontal to the Earth).

[4 COUNTS]:
Drop head and arms towards the Earth—hands grab hold to elbows.

[4 COUNTS]:
Plié [bent knees], roll up to vertical spine and extend legs simultaneously—hands are over the head (holding onto elbows).

[4 COUNTS]:
Relevé [lift heels], salute Element Fire in Projection.

[4 COUNTS]:
Plié [bent knees], heart drops towards the Earth. Arms in Element Fire passing in front of the torso. Head over the Earth. Extend legs—open arms to Four Elements roll up to vertical spine, relevé [lift heels].

[4 COUNTS]:
Relevé [lift heels] arms in Four Elements.

[4 COUNTS]:
Open to Four Directions and Projection.

[4 COUNTS]:
Plié [bent knees], drop heart toward the Earth, head follows. Hands grab onto elbows. Roll up to vertical spine, extend legs and relevé simultaneously.

[4 COUNTS]:
In relevé [lift heels], salute Element Fire in Projection.

[4 COUNTS]:
Plié [bent knees], heart drops towards the Earth. Arms in Element Fire passing in front of the torso. Head over the Earth. Extend legs—open arms to Four Elements roll up to vertical spine, relevé [lift heels].

[4 COUNTS]:
Relevé [lift heels] arms in Four Elements.

[4 COUNTS]:
Open to Four Directions in Projection.

[4 COUNTS]:
Plié, flatback, arms side in Four Directions with palms facing down.

[2 COUNTS]:
Flex wrist, vertical spine in plié—fingertips reach back, palms facing out with arms side.

[4 COUNTS]:
Plié [bent knees], cross arms in front of the body.

[4 COUNTS]:
Open arms to Four Directions and extend legs.

[4 COUNTS]:
Plié [bent knees], cross arms in front of the body, opposite arm on top.

[4 COUNTS]:
Open arms to Four Directions and extend legs.

[4 COUNTS]:
Plié [bent knees], cross arms in front of the body, extend legs—cross arms above your head (removing a t-shirt action).

[4 COUNTS]:
Salute the *Triangle of Inspiration* above the head—Open arms to Four Directions.

END SEQUENCE

[4 COUNTS]: Plié [bent knees], arms in Four Directions.

[4 COUNTS]: Bend elbows and extend legs.

Body Circles with Contraction, Passé and Pirouettes

Begin:
Feet in 1st base position, vertical spine. Arms along the side of the body.

[4 COUNTS]:
Plié [bent knees], contraction, 1st position arms (encircling solar plexus).

[2 COUNTS]:
With arms in 1st position, extend the knees and circle the torso, to the right side of the body.

[2 COUNTS]:
Continue circling the torso back, into Projection (heart reaching towards sky).

[2 COUNTS]:
Circle torso to the left.

[1 COUNT]:
Plié [bent knees], contract center and forward, smoothly and sharply.

[2 COUNTS]:
Reverse the circle—arms remain in 1st position, extend the knees and circle the torso to the left side.

[2 COUNTS]:
Continue circling the torso back, into Projection (heart reaching towards sky).

[2 COUNTS]:
Circle torso to the right.

[1 COUNT]:
Plié [bent knees], contract center and forward, smoothly and sharply.

[4 COUNTS]:
Repeat movement of the torso—circling in the direction of the right side with arms opening to Four Directions, palms facing upwards towards the Universe:
When circling right, the left arm reaches towards the right side of the body, over the head, before opening into Four Directions (palms facing up) as the heart reaches up towards the sky. The right arm reaches, over the head, towards the left side of the body, as the torso continues to circle to the left. The arms return to 1st position, with plié [bent knees], contraction at the center.

[4 COUNTS]:
Extend left leg and relevé, passé right leg, arms move in front of the body, above the head into 5th position (encircling the crown chakra), verticality.

[4 COUNTS]:
Arms open, passing through the Four Directions to return to 1st base position. Plié [bent knees], contraction, arms encircling the solar plexus.

[4 COUNTS]:
Pirouette (right leg in passé, turning to the right) arms move in front of the body, above the head into 5th position (encircling the crown chakra), verticality.

[4 COUNTS]:
Arms open, passing through the Four Directions to return to 1st base position. Plié [bent knees], contraction, arms encircling the solar plexus.
Repeat ENTIRE sequence, starting with the left side (pirouette to the left).

END SEQUENCE

[4 COUNTS]:
Plié [bent knees], lift arms to Four Directions, vertical spine.

[4 COUNTS]:
Right leg in passé, foot flexed, arms in Appreciation to the front.

[4 COUNTS]:
Lower right foot to the Earth with plié [bent knees], lower arms.

[4 COUNTS]:
Left leg in passé, foot flexed, arms in Appreciation to the front.

[4 COUNTS]:
Lower left foot to the Earth with plié [bent knees], lower arms.

[4 COUNTS]:
Bend elbows and extend legs.

Body Circles with Contraction, Passé and Pirouettes

Begin:
Feet in 1st base position, vertical spine. Arms along the side of the body.

[4 COUNTS]:
Plié [bent knees], contraction, 1st position arms (encircling solar plexus).

[2 COUNTS]:
With arms in 1st position, extend the knees and circle the torso, to the right side of the body.

[2 COUNTS]:
Continue circling the torso back, into Projection (heart reaching towards sky).

[2 COUNTS]:
Circle torso to the left.

[1 COUNT]:
Plié [bent knees], contract center and forward, smoothly and sharply.

[2 COUNTS]:
Reverse the circle—arms remain in 1st position, extend the knees and circle the torso to the left side.

[2 COUNTS]:
Continue circling the torso back, into Projection (heart reaching towards sky).

[2 COUNTS]:
Circle torso to the right.

[1 COUNT]:
Plié [bent knees], contract center and forward, smoothly and sharply.

[4 COUNTS]:
Repeat movement of the torso—circling in the direction of the right side with arms opening to Four Directions, palms facing upwards towards the Universe:

When circling right, the left arm reaches towards the right side of the body, over the head, before opening into Four Directions (palms facing up) as the heart reaches up towards the sky. The right arm reaches, over the head, towards the left side of the body, as the torso continues to circle to the left. The arms return to 1st position, with plié [bent knees], contraction at the center.

[4 COUNTS]:
Pirouette (right leg in passé, turning to the right) arms move in front of the body, above the head into 5th position (encircling the crown chakra), verticality.

[4 COUNTS]:
Arms open, passing through the Four Directions to return to 1st base position. Plié [bent knees], contraction, arms encircling the solar plexus.

[4 COUNTS]:
Pirouette (right leg in passé, turning to the right) arms move in front of the body, above the head into 5th position (encircling the crown chakra), verticality.

[4 COUNTS]:
Arms open, passing through the Four Directions to return to 1st base position. Plié [bent knees], contraction, arms encircling the solar plexus.

Repeat ENTIRE sequence, starting with the left side (pirouette to the left).

END SEQUENCE

[4 COUNTS]:
Plié [bent knees], lift arms to Four Directions, vertical spine.

[4 COUNTS]:
Right leg in passé, foot flexed, arms in Appreciation to the front.

[4 COUNTS]:
Lower right foot to the Earth with plié [bent knees], lower arms.

[4 COUNTS]:
Left leg in passé, foot flexed, arms in Appreciation to the front.

[4 COUNTS]:
Lower left foot to the Earth with plié [bent knees], lower arms.

[4 COUNTS]:
Bend elbows and extend legs.

Four Directions and Four Elements

Begin:
Feet in 1st base position, vertical spine, arms hanging at the side of the body.

[2 COUNTS]:
Element Earth position.

[2 COUNTS]:
Element Water position.

[2 COUNTS]:
Element Air position.

[2 COUNTS]:
Element Water position.

[2 COUNTS]:
With palms facing the sternum, cross right hand on top of left hand.

[2 COUNTS]:
Element Fire position in front of sternum.

[2 COUNTS]:
Lift Element Fire hands over the head.

[2 COUNTS]:
Open arms into Four Directions.

[4 COUNTS]:
Bend elbows into Four Elements.

[4 COUNTS]:
Extend elbows into Four Directions.

[4 COUNTS]:
Bend elbows into Four Elements.

[4 COUNTS]:
Extend elbows into Four Directions.

[4 COUNTS]:
Bend elbows into Four Elements.

[4 COUNTS]:
Elbows reach up towards the Universe (inward rotation of the shoulder).

[4 COUNTS]:
Elbows lower towards the Earth (outward rotation of the shoulder).

[4 COUNTS]:
Elbows reach up towards the Universe.

[4 COUNTS]:
Elbows lower towards the Earth.

[4 COUNTS]:
Elbows reach up towards the Universe.

[4 COUNTS]:
Continue extending arms towards the Universe (arms parallel reaching towards the sky).

[4 COUNTS]:
Contraction, plié [bent knees], arms lower in front of the body, palms facing upwards (in scooping position).

[4 COUNTS]:
Extend arms forward, on the low diagonal, palms facing down.

[4 COUNTS]:
Extend knees, arms circle forward and up, towards the Universe. Torso extends into Projections (heart reaches towards the Universe). Continue the arm circle behind the body.

[4 COUNTS]:
Contraction, plié [bent knees], continue arms circling down, and forward, scooping under.

[4 COUNTS]:
Extend knees, arms circle up towards the Universe. Torso extends into Projection (heart reaches towards the universe). Continue the arm circle behind the body.

[4 COUNTS]:
Contraction, plié [bent knees], continue arms circling down, and forward, scooping under.

[4 COUNTS]:
Reverse the arm circle, extend legs, arms extend down and behind the body. Arms continue to circle back. Torso extends into Projection (heart reaches towards the universe), arms into High V back.

[4 COUNTS]:
Continue fingertips towards the Universe (both arms parallel reaching upwards).

[4 COUNTS]:

Contraction, plié [bent knees], continue arms circling forward and down, scooping under.

[4 COUNTS]:
Extend legs, arms extend down and behind the body. Arms continue to circle back. Torso extends into Projection (heart reaches towards the Universe), arms into High V back.

[4 COUNTS]:
Continue fingertips towards the Universe (both arms parallel reaching upwards).

[4 COUNTS]:
Contraction, plié [bent knees], continue arms circling forward and down, scooping under.

[4 COUNTS]:
Rotate arms, arms reach towards the low diagonal with palms are facing down.

[4 COUNTS]:
Extend the knees and rest the arms along the sides of the body.

Flatback Combination with Développé

Begin:
Feet in 1st base position, vertical spine. Arms along the side of the body.

DIRECTION: FACING FRONT

[4 COUNTS]:
Plié [bent knees], arms in Element Earth, rotate legs into 1st position (Open triangle feet).

[4 COUNTS]:
Extend legs, arms in Element Water.

[4 COUNTS]:
Arms in Element Air.

[4 COUNTS]:
From Element Air, rotate wrist so fingertips move down and forward, fingertips point towards the front, and palms face out.

DIRECTION: FACING DIAGONAL RIGHT

[4 COUNTS]:
Open arms to Four Directions, feet in 1st position (Open triangle feet) to the right diagonal.

DIRECTION: FACING DIAGONAL RIGHT

[2 COUNTS]:
Plié [bent knees], arms in Four Directions.

[2 COUNTS]:
Plié [bent knees], lower right arm down pointing towards the Earth, flex right wrist, right arm moves up in front of body to heart level.

[2 COUNTS]:
Grande plié [bend knees deeply], simultaneously, right arm lifts overhead—palm towards the Universe.

DIRECTION: FACING FRONT

[2 COUNTS]:
Rotate right leg inwards (both legs into 4th position parallel, left leg forward in 4th position parallel) simultaneously, right arm circle through Four Directions and both arms reach down towards the Earth. Both palms face inwards towards each other—at heart level, extend knees, vertical spine.

[4 COUNTS]:
Arms continue to lengthen up towards the Universe overhead, palms facing inwards.

[4 COUNTS]:
Flatback forward, arms in line with ears.

[4 COUNTS]:
Body maintains flatback, arms half-circle (lowering down forward, towards the Earth, brushing sides of legs, until fingertips reach towards the back wall, arms in line with flatback).

[4 COUNTS]:
Contraction (initiating at the 2nd chakra), flex wrist (fingertips reach towards the center of the body).

[4 COUNTS]:
Roll up into vertical spine, arms move forward and up until palms face upwards towards the Universe, knees remain extended.

DIRECTION: FACING DIAGONAL RIGHT

[4 COUNTS]:
Rotate right leg into 1st position (Open triangle feet), plié, arms open into Four Directions.

[2 COUNTS]:
Plié [bent knees], lower right arm down pointing towards the Earth, flex right wrist, right arm moves up in front of body to heart level.

[2 COUNTS]:
Grande plié [bend knees deeply], simultaneously, right arm lifts overhead—palm towards the Universe.

DIRECTION: FACING FRONT

[4 COUNTS]:
Rotate right leg inwards (both legs into 4th position parallel, left leg forward in 4th position parallel), simultaneously, right arm circle through Four Directions and both arms reach down towards the Earth. Both palms face inwards towards each other—at heart level, extend knees, vertical spine.

[4 COUNTS]:
Arms continue to lengthen up towards the Universe overhead, palms facing inwards.

[4 COUNTS]:
Plié.

[4 COUNTS]:
Extend legs.

[4 COUNTS]:
Relevé [lift heels].

[4 COUNTS]:
Flatback forward, lower relevé slowly, arms in line with ears.

[4 COUNTS]:
Body maintains flatback, arms half-circle (lowering down forward, towards the Earth, brushing sides of legs, until fingertips reach towards the back wall, arms in line with flatback).

[2 COUNTS]:
Contraction (initiating at the 2nd chakra), remaining in parallel, plié [bent knees], right foot into high arch [lift heel], flex wrists (fingertips reach towards the center of the body).

[4 COUNTS]:
Maintaining contraction and right foot in high arch, lift torso towards verticality, arms extend to the sides of the body, palms facing back.

[2 COUNTS]:
Vertical spine, arms reach around into 1st position (in front of the heart), wrist flexed with palms facing outward .

DIRECTION: FACING DIAGONAL RIGHT

[4 COUNTS]:
Rotate right leg into 1st position (Open triangle feet), plié, open arms into Four Directions.

[2 COUNTS]:

Plié [bent knees], lower right arm down pointing towards the Earth, flex right wrist, right arm moves up in front of body to heart level.

[2 COUNTS]:

Grande plié [bend knees deeply], simultaneously, right arm lifts overhead—palm towards the Universe.

DIRECTION: FACING FRONT

[4 COUNTS]:

Rotate right leg inwards (both legs into 4th position parallel, left leg forward in 4th position parallel) simultaneously, right arm circle through Four Directions and down reaching towards the Earth. Both palms face inwards towards each other—at heart level, extend knees, vertical spine.

[4 COUNTS]:

Arms continue to lengthen up towards the Universe overhead, palms facing inwards.

[3 COUNTS]:

Relevé.

[3 COUNTS]:

Passé right leg and flex wrists, palms facing towards the Universe.

[3 COUNTS]:

Return leg and hand position.

[3 COUNTS]:

Passé left leg and flex wrists, palms facing towards the Universe.

[3 COUNTS]:

Return leg and hand position.

[4 COUNTS]:

Flatback forward, lower heels, arms in line with ears.

[4 COUNTS]:

Body maintains flatback, arms half-circle (lowering down forward, towards the Earth, brushing sides of legs, until fingertips reach towards the back wall, arms in line with flatback).

[2 COUNTS]:

Sharply—plié [bent knees], right foot into high arch behind, spine in contraction, head in alignment with spine, extend parallel arms on the low diagonal forward, palms facing inwards.

[2 COUNTS]:

Maintain plié [bent knees] with right foot in high arch, vertical spine, arms parallel at heart level, palms facing inward.

[2 COUNTS]:
Initiating from the 2nd chakra, undulate torso forward allowing the head to follow.

[2 COUNTS]:
Contract the upper spine forward and over, maintain arms in parallel position.

[2 COUNTS]:
Vertical spine.

[2 COUNTS]:
Initiating from the 2nd chakra, undulate torso forward allowing the head to follow.

[2 COUNTS]:
Contract the upper spine forward and over, maintain arms in parallel position.

[2 COUNTS]:
Vertical spine.

[2 COUNTS]:
Initiating from the 2nd chakra, undulate torso forward allowing the head to follow.

[2 COUNTS]:
Contract the upper spine forward and over, lower arms in parallel position towards the Earth.

[4 COUNTS]:
Extend knees, place both heels flat on the Earth, roll up through the spine, torso into Projection, arms reach into High V position.

[2 COUNTS]:
Plié [bent knees], remain in high arch, flip palms over, elbows remain in place as fingertips move down towards the sternum.

[2 COUNTS]:
Continue hands reaching down towards the Earth, backs of hands are touching, elbows are reaching up.

[2 COUNTS]:
Flatback on low diagonal, arms open to parallel position on the low diagonal (extending the line of the torso), palms facing inwards, extend the knees.

[4 COUNTS]:
Relax the spine and arms towards the Earth (hanging).

[4 COUNTS]:
Roll up to vertical spine, arms hanging on sides of body.

DIRECTION: FACING FRONT

*Arms remain along the sides of the body, palms facing inwards.

[2 COUNTS]:
Passé right leg parallel, base leg extended.

[2 COUNTS]:
Right foot steps backward, passé left leg parallel.

[4 COUNTS]:
Plié [bend knee] right leg, développé left leg parallel forward, foot pointed.

[2 COUNTS]:
Step forward onto left leg (extended), passé right leg parallel.

[2 COUNTS]:
Right foot steps backward, passé left leg parallel.

[4 COUNTS]:
Right knee extended, développé left leg parallel forward, foot pointed.

[2 COUNTS]:
Relevé [lift heel] right foot.

[2 COUNTS]:
Piqué forward onto left leg, passé right leg parallel.

[2 COUNTS]:
Right foot steps backward, passé left leg parallel.

[4 COUNTS]:
Right knee extended, développé left leg parallel forward, foot pointed.

[2 COUNTS]:
Relevé [lift heel] right foot.
Repeat: piqué and développé—4 times in 1 COUNT.

PREPARATION FOR LEFT SIDE

[2 COUNTS]:
Piqué forward onto left leg, passé right leg parallel..

[2 COUNTS]:
Plié [bent knees], flex right foot

[2 COUNTS]:
Slide right foot, down left leg in plié.

[2 COUNTS]:
1st base position, legs extended.
Repeat entire sequence on the left side.
After piqué and développé sequence left, passé right leg, rotate body to the right-side wall. 2nd position parallel.

DIRECTION CHANGE: SIDE WALL (RIGHT)

[2 COUNTS]:
Plié [bent knees], torso in Projection, arms extended parallel forward at heart level with Lotus hands.

[2 COUNTS]:
Continue plié and reach forward until heels lift, shoot body out and forward onto the floor into plank position.

[16 COUNTS]:
Eight push-ups (1 count down, 1 count up).

[4 COUNTS]:
Lower the body, placed flat on the floor.

[4 COUNTS]:
Initiating from the tailbone, push back into the child's pose.

[4 COUNTS]:
Relax into child's pose.

[2 COUNTS]:
Tuck toes under, move hands to the sides of the shoulders on the floor (preparation).

[2 COUNTS]:
Push back onto both feet flat on the floor, legs full extended, torso in flatback reaching on the low diagonal, arms in line with ears—reaching towards the Earth—on the low diagonal.

[4 COUNTS]:
Remaining in flatback, arms circle up towards the Universe, back and down, grabbing the upper thighs (below the gluteus).

[4 COUNTS]:
Slide hands down legs (towards the ankles) to stretch.

[4 COUNTS]:
Roll up to vertical spine.

[2 COUNTS]:
Plié [bent knees].

[2 COUNTS]:
Relevé [lift heel] left foot, passé right leg.

[2 COUNTS]:
Return right leg to maintain relevé [lift heels], both legs.

[2 COUNTS]:
Lower heels.

[2 COUNTS]:
Plié [bent knees].

[2 COUNTS]:
Pirouette turn (one and a half turn to the right), right leg passé.

DIRECTION: SIDE WALL (LEFT)

[2 COUNTS]:
Relevé [lift heel].

[2 COUNTS]:
Lower heels.
Repeat entire sequence. Start facing the left wall.

Turns in Center

Begin:
Feet in 1st position (Open triangle feet), vertical spine. Arms along the side of the body.

[2 COUNTS]:
Plié [bent knees], open to 2nd position plié, arms Four Directions.

[2 COUNTS]:
Extend knees and simultaneously turn right *facing right wall* into 4th position feet (right leg forward) turnout, arms Four Directions.

[2 COUNTS]:
Plié [bent knees].

[2 COUNTS]:
Passé right leg, arms in Element Air.

[2 COUNTS]:
Lower right leg into 4th position relevé, arms Four Directions.

[2 COUNTS]:
Plié [bent knees].

[2 COUNTS]:
Pirouette (turn) right with right leg in passé, arms in Element Air.

DIRECTION: END FACING FRONT

[2 COUNTS]:
1st position relevé [bent knees], arms Four Directions, 2nd position plié.

[2 COUNTS]:
Extend knees and simultaneously turn left facing left wall into 4th position feet (left leg forward) turnout, arms Four Directions.

[2 COUNTS]:
Plié [bent knees].

[2 COUNTS]:
Passé left leg, arms in Element Air.

[2 COUNTS]:
Lower left leg into 4th position relevé, arms Four Directions.

[2 COUNTS]:
Plié [bent knees].

[2 COUNTS]:
Pirouette (turn) left with left leg in passé, arms in Element Air.

DIRECTION: END FACING FRONT

[2 COUNTS]:
1st position relevé [bent knees], arms Four Directions.

END SEQUENCE

[2 COUNTS]: Plié. Draw legs into 1st base position, arms in Element Air.

[2 COUNTS]: Open arms into Appreciation forward.

Across the Floor

Progressions across the floor are completed in *Familias* (Families) of four dancers in each line. Normally, the *Famlilias* move straight across the space, towards the musicians, unless otherwise noted. Once the progression reaches the opposite side of the room, the dancers divide in the center, two to the right and two to the left, to return back to the starting location.

Passé and Four Element Arms with Pirouettes

Begin:
2nd position parallel, vertical spine, arms open to Four Elements.
Preparation:

[and.... COUNT]:
Arms close slightly, with elbows reaching side (fingertips meet in front of heart).

[2 COUNTS]
Piqué turn (onto left foot, 2 pirouette turns right), passé right leg parallel, arms in Four Elements.

[2 COUNTS]:

Step right in plié, step left in plié, arms close slightly with elbows reaching side (fingertips meet in front of heart).

[2 COUNTS]:
Piqué turn (onto right foot, 2 pirouette turns left), passé right leg parallel, arms in Four Elements.

[2 COUNTS]:
Step left in plié, step right in plié, arms close slightly with elbows reaching side (fingertips meet in front of heart).

Repeat right and left across the floor

Battements in Attitude (Parallel)

Begin:
Small lunge, left leg forward, right leg extended in back, vertical spine, arms in Four Directions with wrists flexed (fingertips are pointing towards the Universe).

[2 COUNTS]:
Battement right leg to the front in parallel position, right knee in attitude, foot flexed, standing leg in plié [bent].

[2 COUNTS]:
Step right in plié, step left in plié.

[2 COUNTS]:
Step right, battement left leg to the front in parallel position, left knee in attitude, foot flexed, standing leg in plié [bent].

[2 COUNTS]:
Step left in plié, step right in plié.
Repeat right and left.

Battements with Legs Extended (Parallel)

Begin:
Small lunge, left leg forward, right leg extended in back, vertical spine, arms in Four Directions.

[2 COUNTS]:
Battement right leg to the front in parallel position, right knee extended, foot pointed, standing leg extended.

[2 COUNTS]:
Step right in plié, step left in plié.

[2 COUNTS]:
Step right, battement left leg to the front in parallel position, left knee extended, foot pointed, standing leg extended.

[2 COUNTS]:
Step left in plié, step right in plié.
Repeat right and left.

Battements with Legs Extended in Parallel, Piqué

Begin:
Small lunge, left leg forward, right leg extended in back, vertical spine, arms in Four Directions.

[2 COUNTS]:
Battement right leg to the front in parallel position, right knee extended, foot pointed, standing leg extended, left foot relevé.

[2 COUNTS]:
Step right in plié, step left in plié.

[2 COUNTS]:
Piqué right [lift heel], battement left leg to the front in parallel position, left knee extended, pointed, standing leg extended.

[2 COUNTS]:
Step left in plié, step right in plié.
Repeat right and left.

Battements with Legs Extended in Outward Rotation

Begin:
Small lunge, left leg forward, right leg extended in back with the heel connected to the Earth, vertical spine reaching towards the Universe, arms in Four Directions.
Note: Movement is performed in turn out/outward rotation.

[2 COUNTS]:
Battement right leg to the front (passing through 1st position) in outward rotation, right knee extended, foot pointed, standing leg extended.

[2 COUNTS]:
Step right in plié, step left in plié in outward rotation.

[2 COUNTS]:
Step right, battement left leg to the front (passing through 1st position) in turned out position, left knee extended, foot pointed, standing leg extended.

[2 COUNTS]:
Step left in plié, step right in plié in outward rotation.
Repeat right and left

Battements with Legs Extended
in Outward Rotation, Piqué

Begin:
Small lunge, left leg forward, right leg extended in back with the heel connected to the Earth, vertical spine reaching towards the Universe, arms in Four Directions.

Note: Movement is performed in turn out/outward rotation.

[2 COUNTS]:
Battement right leg to the front (passing through 1st position) in turned out position, right knee extended, foot pointed, standing leg extended and relevé.

[2 COUNTS]:
Step right in plié, step left in plié in outward rotation.

[2 COUNTS]:
Piqué right [lift heel], battement left leg to the front (passing through 1st position) in turned out position, left knee extended, foot pointed, standing leg extended.

[2 COUNTS]:
Step right, step left, step left in plié in outward rotation.
Repeat right and left.

Battements Side in Attitude

Begin:
Small lunge, left leg forward, right leg extended in back, vertical spine, arms in Four Directions with wrists flexed (fingertips are pointing towards the Universe).

Note: Movement is performed in turn out/outward rotation.

[2 COUNTS]:
Battement right leg to the side of the body (passing through 1st position), right knee in attitude [bent], foot flexed, standing leg in plié [bend knee].

[2 COUNTS]:
Step right in plié, step left in plié.

[2 COUNTS]:
Step right (passing through 1st position), battement left leg to the side of the body (passing through 1st position) left knee in attitude [bent], foot flexed, standing leg in plié [bend knee].

[2 COUNTS]:

Step left in plié, step right in plié.
Repeat right and left

Battements Side with Legs Extended in Outward Rotation

Begin:
Small lunge, left leg forward, right leg extended in back, vertical spine, arms in Four Directions.

Note: Movement is performed in turn out/outward rotation.

[2 COUNTS]:
Battement right leg to the side of the body (passing through 1st position), right knee extended, foot pointed, standing leg extended.

[2 COUNTS]:
Step right in plié, step left in plié in outward rotation.

[2 COUNTS]:
Step right (passing through 1st position), battement left leg to the side of the body (passing through 1st position), left knee extended, foot pointed, standing leg extended.

[2 COUNTS]:
Step left in plié, step right in plié in outward rotation.
Repeat right and left.

Battements Side with Legs Extended in Outward Rotation, Piqué

Begin:
Small lunge, left leg forward, right leg extended in back, vertical spine, arms in Four Directions.

Note: Movement is performed in turn out/outward rotation.

[2 COUNTS]:
Battement right leg to the side (passing through 1st position) into second position, right knee extended, foot pointed, standing leg extended in relevé.

[2 COUNTS]:
Step right in plié, step left in plié in outward rotation.

[2 COUNTS]:
Piqué right [lift heel], (passing through 1st position), battement left leg to the side (passing through 1st position) into second position, left knee extended, foot pointed, standing leg extended.

[2 COUNTS]:
Step left in plié, step right in plié in outward rotation.
Repeat right and left.

Choreography Sequence

Create a choreography sequence/movement combination incorporating the skills obtained from the training technique. The choreography sequence serves as an opportunity for deeper exploration of discovery, self-expression and self-determination through movement. The *Body Universe* is fully engaged and responsive.

Ending

- Rub the hands together in front of the heart chakra to draw energy from the body
- Open to Appreciation
- Use a short section of any the conversations to center the body
- Bring arms into the *Triangle of Balance* position behind the sacrum
- Salute:
    ◊ Body/Self
    ◊ Dancers in the space
    ◊ Musicians
    ◊ Observers
    ◊ Main entrance/exit or doorway
    ◊ Teacher(s)

Activating the Chakras Through Movement

Movement conversations from Silvestre Dance Technique may support the body and mind to attain higher consciousness. The movement conversations activate all the chakras of the body simultaneously; however, this section provides detailed descriptions and examples of how specific movements can stimulate and open some of the major energy centers of the body.

Root Chakra

The first chakra is the body's root support. It draws energy from the earth, which supports the opening of the chakra. Physical contact with the earth sends energy through the legs stimulating the root chakra. The root chakra connects the individual with their reality on Earth.

SEQUENCE

Exercise: Opening Chakra sequence
Advantages: Connection to the Earth for balance and stabilization
Standing with toes pointing forward and feet hip width apart in parallel position. The spine is vertical; arms are along the side of the body with palms facing in towards thighs. Bend knees, arch the chest, and extend the heart forward towards the Earth, until the chest is over the thighs and fingertips touch the floor on each side of the body. Roll up, Extending the knees simultaneously to reach vertical spine. Repeat. Lengthen the arms side into Four Directions, bend and straighten the knees four times slowly. Bend at the elbows and straighten the arms towards the Earth. Initiating with the crown of the head, roll the body down toward the Earth, articulating through the spine. Place the palms flat on the floor with the fingertips pointing towards each other (if palms don't touch the Earth, reach fingertips towards it). Bend and straighten the knees three times slowly. Maintaining bent knees, sharply open hands side—from the elbow—until the fingertips are touching the floor and palms are facing outwards. Roll up to vertical spine. Repeat the sequence three times.

Standing with toes pointing forward and feet hip width apart in parallel position. The spine is vertical; arms parallel over the head. With legs bent, arch the chest and reach the torso forward, bending completely over from the waist. The arms swoop down to touch the Earth. With the crown of the head extended down towards the Earth, straighten the legs, and roll up the spine quickly. Releasing energy down towards the Earth. Repeat 4 times.

Sacral Chakra

The second chakra awakens one's sensibilities and empathy towards others. The sacral chakra is associated with compassion. A heightened sacral chakra may allow a person to experience vivid dreams connecting to one's past, present and future. For some, the womb is a sacred space for astral travel. Creative seeds are planted and manifest from the sacral chakra. Higher conscious is elevated through the sacral chakra.

SEQUENCE

Exercise: Flatbacks, Contractions and Undulations

Advantages: Brings energy in the pelvis, stretches the lower back

Standing with toes pointing forward and feet touching in first base position. The spine is vertical; arms are along the sides of the body with palms facing in towards thighs. Bend forward at the waist, so that the torso reaches forward into a tabletop (flatback) position. Arms simultaneously drop forward towards the Earth and brush backwards, in line with the spine. From the tabletop/flatback position, contract the lower abdominals, and with straight legs, roll up into vertical spine. Arms lift above the head, afterwards they press down into Four Directions. Bend knees and the elbows, and straighten the legs and the arms along the sides of the body. Repeat.

Bend forward at the waist, so that the torso reaches forward into a tabletop (flatback) position. Arms simultaneously drop forward towards the Earth and brush backwards, in line with the spine. Bend both legs, extend the spine diagonally forward (high diagonal) with the head in alignment with the spine. Extend parallel arms on the low diagonal forward, palms facing inwards. Maintaining bent legs, lift up to vertical spine with arms parallel at heart level, palms facing inwards. Initiating from the pelvis, undulate through the body, up the spine, allowing the head to follow. Afterwards, curve the upper spine and head over to the front with arms in parallel position. Repeat—undulate forward through the spine. Repeat—curve forward and undulation, three times. Lift up to vertical spine. Open the arms side to Four Directions. Bend knees and the elbows, straighten the legs and the arms along the sides of the body.

Solar Plexus Chakra

The third chakra, known as the solar plexus chakra, cultivates the power within. It is the chakra of self-empowerment and assertion. The solar plexus chakra stimulates one's personal understanding and realization. It is the key to self-acceptance and one's conscious power to transform. The solar plexus opens the power of choice of the divine self. When one's solar plexus chakra is balanced, the individual is able to make clear decisions. Through the cultivation of this chakra, the unconscious becomes conscious, thoughts become words, and words become action. Self-empowerment can be created through connection to nature. The third chakra can be activated for higher consciousness through self-knowledge and wisdom.

Sequence

Exercise: Pike backwards and Stretches on the Floor
Hands can be placed on the floor if support is needed
Advantages: Strengthens core, releases blocked energy around the organs

Sitting with legs straight along the floor in front of the body in parallel position, toes pointed. Vertical spine, arms along the side of the body. With arms reaching to the sides, lift both legs off of the floor, engaging the abdominals; the torso leans slightly back on the diagonal (pike). Hold the pike position for four counts. Roll backwards on the spine, allow the legs to follow the direction of the body back, reaching up towards the sky. Place the back of the shoulders on the floor, with legs together in parallel, over the heart; reach the toes towards the floor behind the head. With the pelvis lifted (use the arms/hands to assist the back if necessary) and spine elongated, rotate the legs outwards and bend the knees into a diamond shape. Lift the legs upward slowly, until the pointed toes reach towards the universe, maintaining the outward rotation/diamond shape legs. Gently roll down through the spine (from the cervical spine to the lumbar spine and sacrum) until sitting tall on the sits bones (ischial tuberosity). The legs remain in the diamond shape and the torso is in vertical spine. Bending forward at the waist with an elongated spine, the head reaches down towards feet and stretches for eight counts. Lift the torso to vertical spine and extend the legs forward in parallel simultaneously. Repeat the entire sequence four times.

Heart Chakra

The heart chakra is linked to freedom and unity. When this chakra is well balanced, quality relationships and acceptance of others is achievable. Inner peace is attainable through a balanced heart chakra. The heart connects to all parts of the body, delivering the flow of oxygen (air) and water (blood). The heart chakra provides the potential to make outward connections with nature and communities of people.

SEQUENCES

Exercise: Arm circles

Four Elements and Four Directions

Advantages: Releases muscle tension of the chest. Extends energy of the heart out through the arms and fingers. Opens the vertebrae, decompressing the spine.

Standing with toes pointing forward and feet touching in first base position. The spine is vertical; arms are along the sides of the body with palms facing in towards thighs. Bending the knees, initiate a contraction from the middle abdominals, moving arms slightly forward. Straighten the knees and circle the torso to the right, arching the spine towards the right side of the body. Continue the arching circle, with a high arch backwards with the heart open towards the universe and continue to circle to the left side. Bend knees and contract forward and center. Reverse the full body circle, repeating towards the left side. Repeat the movement, arching the torso towards the right side, with the arms in Four Directions—with palms facing up (when going to the right, the left arm reaches towards the right side of the body, over the head, before opening wide to Four Directions). The right arm reaches towards the left side of the body, over the head, as the torso arches left and returns to the contraction position with bent knees, center. Arms remain along the sides of the body in contraction.

Repeat the entire sequence, starting the arch to the left side. To finish, lift the torso to vertical spine with legs straight and arms along the side of the body.

Standing with toes pointing forward and feet touching in first base position. The spine is vertical; arms in Four Directions. Bend the elbows into Four Elements, extend the elbows into Four Directions. Bend the elbows again into Four Elements, extend into Four Directions, focusing on opening the heart and scapula. Bend the elbows into Four Elements and reach elbows up towards the universe. Lower the elbows down towards the Earth, reach elbows up towards the universe, lower elbows down towards the Earth. Contract forward from the middle abdominals, with bent knees. Lower arms in front of the body with palms facing upward (in a scooping position). Extend the knees, circle the arms up towards the universe. Continue the arm circle behind the body, arching the torso backwards while opening the heart towards the universe, continue the arm circle down, behind the body, contract the spine and bend knees. Repeat the arm circles: 7 times.

Reverse the arm circles—starting with bent knees, in contraction. Extend the legs and extend the arms when passing the legs. Continue to circle the arms behind the body, into a high arch with arms reaching back into a High V position with the heart reaching towards the universe. Reach the fingertips towards the universe (both arms parallel reaching upwards). Arms continue forward, sweeping down in front of the body bending the knees and contracting the torso. Repeat the reverse arm circles 7 times. To finish, lift up to vertical spine with legs straight and arms along the side of the body.

Throat Chakra

The throat chakra extends from oneself outwards into the world. It is the center for oral communication. The body communicates through cells and sensors; messages travel to nerves and provide information. Our nervous system is the communication center of our body, powered by electrical energy, which is fire. The throat chakra is also a fire chakra. The throat is the pathway providing information from the self into the world. The fifth chakra is a center of self-expression. Transcendence begins to occur from within the body to the outer world through communication, supported by the throat chakra. The fifth chakra is the gateway from the self to the world. The subconscious and conscious thought manifest into spoken word at the throat chakra. These words are vibrations of the body. Sound occurs through vibrations that travel through the air. In *Wheels of Life,* Anodea Judith explains that "all vibrations are characterized by rhythm, a repeated, regular pattern of movement through time and space. These rhythmical patterns are deeply ingrained functions of our consciousness" (Judith, 2012, p. 246).

SEQUENCE

Exercise: Opening Chakras and Pike backwards

Advantages: Releases tension held in the neck. Opens the flow of energy from the *Triangle of Inspiration* to the *Triangle of Expression* and *Balance.*

Standing with toes pointing forward and feet touching in first base position. The spine is vertical; arms above the head in open Element Fire position. There is space between the two palms. Extend the elbows completely reaching towards the universe. Flex the wrists and open the arms to the side of the body, stopping at shoulder level. Simultaneously, arch the upper torso so that the heart reaches towards the universe the throat is exposed to the sky. The fingertips should point towards the Earth. Retract the arm movement until palms point towards the universe above the head. Flip the palms over, allow the elbows remain in place as fingertips move down towards the forehead. Continue reaching the hands down until they reach the sternum with the backs of the hands touching. Flip the palms so that they face each other (not touching) and the elbows move down to shoulder level. Extend the elbows, while the fingertips reach towards the Earth.

Roll the shoulders backwards three times. Bend both knees and arch the chest forward. The heart reaches forward towards the Earth until chest is over the thighs and fingertips touch the floor on each side of the body. Circle the fingertips from the sides of the body to the front of the toes. With knees remaining bent, roll up the spine, articulating through one vertebra at a time. Straighten the knees simultaneously to reach vertical spine. Repeat the entire sequence.

Lift up to vertical spine with legs straight and arms along the side of the body, to finish.

Sitting with legs straight along the floor in front of the body in parallel position, toes pointed. Vertical spine, arms along the side of the body.

With arms reaching to the sides in Four Directions, lift both legs off of the floor, engaging the abdominals; the torso leans slightly back on the diagonal (pike). Hold the pike position for four counts. Roll backwards on the spine, allow the legs to follow the direction of the body back, reaching up towards the sky. Place the back of the shoulders on the floor, with legs together in parallel, over the heart. Reach the toes towards the floor behind the head. With the pelvis lifted (use the arms/hands to support the back, if necessary) and spine elongated, rotate the legs outwards and bend the knees into a diamond shape. Lift the legs upward slowly, until the pointed toes reach towards the universe, maintaining the outward rotation/diamond shape legs. Gently roll down through the spine (from the cervical spine to the lumbar spine and sacrum) until sitting tall on the sits bones (ischial tuberosity). The legs remain in the diamond shape and the torso is in vertical spine. Bending forward at the waist with an elongated spine, the head reaches down towards feet and stretches for eight counts. Lift the torso to vertical spine and extend the legs forward in parallel simultaneously. Repeat the entire sequence four times.

Third Eye Chakra

The third eye chakra, sometimes referred to as the first eye chakra, is the center for intuition and perception. When this chakra is balanced, psychic abilities may be heightened. One's awareness of self and others is made clear. With a well aligned sixth chakra, one's imagination may be amplified through visualizations and foresight.

SEQUENCE

Exercise: Child's Pose and Inverted Stretch

Advantages: Increases blood flow to the pineal gland. Upper body strengthening, stretches the lumber spine and hamstrings.

Standing with toes pointing forward and feet touching in first base position. The spine is vertical; arms reaching forward, in front of the sternum with palms facing up. Bend the knees and bend forward at the waist; the back elongates as it moves forward, and the arms reach down towards the Earth. When the fingertips touch the Earth, slide out into plank position. Gently lower the body down towards the Earth. Initiating from the tailbone, push back into child's pose (knees bent, pelvis over the ankles, forehead/third eye resting on the Earth) with the arms stretching forward. Relax in child's pose. Tuck the toes under, place the hands to the sides of the shoulders on the floor and push back onto both feet. The feet are flat on the floor and both legs are extended. The crown of the head is reaching towards the Earth. Maintain this position and stretch the body; try to reach the third eye closer towards the legs. Bend the knees and slowly roll up the spine, one vertebra at a time. Repeat.

Crown Chakra

A balanced crown chakra may bring forth transcendence. A person is able to acknowledge their true self. A strong seventh chakra is often demonstrated through wisdom. Varying levels of consciousness may be experienced.

SEQUENCE

Exercise: Element Fire and Inversion

Advantages: Stretches the pectoral (chest), latissimus dorsi, abdominal, psoas muscles (spine and thigh), and hamstring muscles. Decompresses the spine. Helps to stabilize breathing and function of the nervous system. Increases awareness.

Standing with toes pointing forward and feet touching in first base position. The spine is vertical; elbows bent, palms facing chest, in front of sternum. Cross the right hand on top of the left and flex the wrist; point the fingertips front with the palms facing out—Element Fire. Lift the shape overhead, elbows reach towards the side, and the fingertips reach towards the sky. Inhale and extend the elbows, rotate the wrist so that the palms are flat, facing forward (the right palm touches the backside of the left hand). Exhale and bend the knees, lowering the shape of the arms in front of the heart. Lower the arms down to the sides of the body. Roll down through the spine. Place the hands on the Earth or reach the fingertips towards the Earth (the hands can hold onto the back of the leg at the calf muscle if needed). Inhale. Exhale, bending the knees slowly. Inhale and extend the knees. Exhale, bending the knees slowly. Inhale and extend the knees. Repeat once more. Bend the knees and gently roll up the spine.

VII

Methodology and Pedagogy

"We talk about nature, but are often times afraid to, or don't experience nature."—Rosangela Silvestre (Williams, 2011–2014)

Methodology and Pedagogy

Silvestre Technique connects gestures that symbolize African-Brazilian culture. Orixá movement is not folkloric dance; it is a sacred dance. Dance can be seen from different angles as spirituality can be seen from different angles. Seeing a flower from various viewpoints would be a unique understanding for everyone; maintaining a flexible perspective is an important concept to grasp while teaching Silvestre Technique. In Silvestre training, participants are not completing exercises but instead, talking to their bodies. Rosangela declares that "The only way to discover dance is through movement" and these movement conversations with the body are influenced by the *Triangle of Inspiration* (Williams, 2011–2014). Participants training in Silvestre Technique can deepen their artistic development as they recognize the body's potential while visualizing the manifestation of movement. "We are human. Bring that to everywhere you go"—when we enter the space to teach, whether it is ourselves or others, we must remember that we are human, and as humans we are capable (Williams, 2011–2014). This is one of the greatest lessons that Silvestre Technique has taught me.

Rosangela instructs the teachers of the technique to explain the training in a variety of ways: scientifically, intuitively, visually, and physically. People learn from various pedagogy methods. Having multiple layers of learning deepens the absorption of knowledge. There is a standard of teaching, which utilizes diverse tools for learning styles in the methodological process of Silvestre Technique. When the teacher is present to train others, the instructor has a technique class. Rosangela asks Silvestre teachers to question themselves. "Are you training others? Or sharing movement? You

232

can study methodology academically, but you must learn how to apply it to each group that you will teach" (Williams, 2011–2014). She has taught me that methodology should be used as a means to improve. Effective teachers must have a method or structure to teach others and must have a foundation for the class to have structure.

Rosangela continues to guide her students about the responsibilities of teaching. Through my studies with her I have learned that teachers should know the body muscles and joints in order to push their students to work. Teachers must know the physicality of the dancers' bodies and gain tools to express to students how to use the body and develop it. Rosangela explains, "When teaching you must break everything down" (Williams, 2011–2014). Instructors should investigate what parts of the body initiate movement. The movement should be repeated several times and basic steps should be used when working with beginners. When teaching, it is vital to do what comes naturally first. Instructors of Silvestre Technique use words that correspond to nature to explain the symbology of what occurs within the body. The body conversations in Silvestre Technique movement can be slow, very fast, or medium pace. It is important to connect to the four elements to enrich and guide movement. When the dynamics change the connections to the elements remains.

Language is imperative in teaching Silvestre Technique in order not to discredit or misinform the dancer. Oftentimes, when students hear dance vocabulary their bodies become tense. For this reason, it is imperative for movement to be demonstrated first in Silvestre training. Teachers explain what the body is doing. Instructors are encouraged not to tell students that what they are doing is wrong, instead we say, "it can be better" or "that's for a different dance." Vocabulary is particularly important: "give," "share," "appreciate," "take," "salute," "activate," and "open" are all cue words that are used in Silvestre training. When training newcomers who may have not studied western dance forms, the instructor may say flex or bend knees, instead of saying plié. These cues have universal meanings that one does not need prior dance training to understand. Another example, instead of referring to posture, instructors emphasize verticality. "Seek your verticality with the universe." Posture could refer to any positioning of the body, which may involve copying others, slouching, or relaxing. When verticality is sought in alignment with the universe, the body structure lengthens from the earth to the skies.

Silvestre Technique instructors incorporate musicality and vocalizations during class. Participants sing the music since there is always rhythm in the body. Rosangela tells us, "Sing! Sing the counts and add rhythm, like the heart [beat]" (Williams, 2011–2014). She also informs us that sometimes counting rhythm in a 4/4 measure can be limiting for movement.

For example, a *développé* (extension of the leg) may stop on count eight because it is the last number, but it should continue until the very last possible second. For this reason, we sing and hum from within. For some, singing and humming relaxes my body while transitioning through movements. Teaching vocalization with movements provides students a tool for breathing while dancing; Rosangela advises teachers to watch their students to make sure they are breathing. Vocals are a part of the moving body. During the 2012 Silvestre Dance Technique Intensive, Rosangela taught the dancers that "the body must breathe each movement" (Williams, 2011–2014).

Rosangela insists, "When students have questions, allow them to discover to find out if they can find answers for themselves" (Williams, 2011–2014). This is the process of *discovery* that is deeply rooted within the methodology of Silvestre training. As Barbara Browning highlights in her interview with Rosangela, Silvestre Technique incorporates seven chakras and relating colors, four elements, and various Orixás (Browning, 2007). The complexity of its foundation, philosophies, and class structure demonstrates the richness and social construct of Silvestre Technique. The technique is multi-layered and complex, as life itself is. Within all of the layers, students are encouraged to experience and discover for themselves. In addition, the teachers of Silvestre Technique discover methods to go beyond students' restrictions and limitations. Teachers of this technique learn how to push students out of their comfort zone and limitations. It is imperative for teachers to discover how to go beyond blockages that exists in the minds of their students.

Deko Alves describes how the pedagogy of Silvestre Technique offers students a sense of ownership and leadership in the studio. The students are provided opportunities to demonstrate their understanding of the movement and the instructor is given the freedom to analyze the students' comprehension of the technique and symbology.

2018 Interview with Deko Alves

Pedagogy of Silvestre Technique

In the studio, when Vera gave regular classes, there was always a moment when she would gather the students who were with her for a long time. We could take our knowledge and share with our colleagues. There were moments that she called one student to start class. I think this was also a way of analyzing what the student learned and [the students] could give of themselves, too. This is an awakening from Vera; the students comprehend how to multiply the knowledge [Alves, 2018].[9]

---

9. See Appendix for original response in Portuguese

Each Silvestre Technique instructor has their own expressiveness in training others in the technique. Vera Passos describes the relationship that she and Rosangela have in teaching Silvestre Technique. Although there are differences in their teaching methodologies, the structure of the technique embraces their individual approaches.

2018 Interview with Vera Passos:

HARMONIZING

My form in the studio is very different from the form of Rosangela. Yet, the two forms add up and connect. Exactly, in that place that she has the most thirst.... I arrive; and also, in my place of dryness, she arrives to harmonize. Rosangela and I have connection and trust. In this space one completes the other. In this space we allow transformation. We do not transform because we want to transform, but, because life transforms.

The very place that the dance is … of change, it must be accompanied. We cannot be behind. This speaks to the world that the technique is alive; that it will not freeze. In this way, more people are interested in this process—where it is not closed [Passos, 2018].[10]

In efforts to deeper evaluate the pedagogical methods utilized by Silvestre Technique instructors, in addition to speaking with Deko Alves and Vera Passos, I interviewed professional dancer and choreographer, Jenifer Ferraro. Ferraro is a certified Silvestre Technique instructor who resides in Buenos Aires, Argentina. She began her training in Silvestre Technique in Salvador, BA in 2014 where I first met her. I was curious to know about her experiences and perceptions of Silvestre Technique in Argentina. My interview with her is as follows:

TAMARA: Who participates in Silvestre Technique? Who are your students and why do you think they come?

FERRARO: Young people and adults of different ages and interests participate. Some come for physical training and others because they consider it a way to reconnect with the physical and spiritual body.

TAMARA: What is necessary to be an effective teacher of Silvestre Technique?

FERRARO: I believe that the commitment to continue studying and practicing the technique beyond teaching is necessary. Keep studying, do not forget to be a student, know the anatomy of the body and the different dynamics with which the body can move. Being in touch with nature, with the essence of each element brought in class and how nature can inspire us is necessary. It is also vital to be connected to oneself at the time of class; there are physical and spiritual moments in our lives, and I think it is good to bring them into the classroom to be inspired and able to share with the students.

TAMARA: How important is music in Silvestre Technique?

10. See Appendix for original response in Portuguese

FERRARO: At first, I thought it was fundamental, but after several years of practice and now teaching, I think it can complement the physical work very well or it may not be there. Silent work is also interesting to notice the inner rhythms of self and how the body handles the sounds of the environment as well.

TAMARA: When or how did you decide to become a teacher of Silvestre Technique? Why did you make that decision?

FERRARO: When I finished my Silvestre Dance Technique Intensive certification in Salvador and seminars in Buenos Aires, I began to notice how many of the people attending the seminars wanted to continue training in art. It was then that I set up a schedule for two months to see how I felt teaching, and I realized that I wanted to give to them continuously. So, I opened a space in my house to a group, and then a new space became available where I am currently teaching. The truth is that it was not a very conscious decision at first–I let myself go, I flowed—and then I felt I wanted to work with this technique for a long time. Today, I choose to continue working until my body can no longer move.

TAMARA: How did the technique influence you, your dance, your life?

FERRARO: It totally changed my way of seeing the world, dance, and life. I allowed myself to feel and move in connection with my feelings and my doubts. I feel and believe that this technique has everything that the human being needs, not to leave the body aside, but without becoming mechanical to integrate the emotions and the spiritual connection that each one can have beyond religions. Working with the symbols of nature and universe brings us closer to all types of people and ages. It was a resounding change in my life.

TAMARA: How is teaching this technique different from teaching other dance styles?

FERRARO: It is different because it not only crosses the physical body, but it is also important to let go of what is perceived in the lesson, both as a student and as a teacher. Working the limits imposed on us by the mind and seeing how bodies evolve physically and emotionally is wonderful.

TAMARA: What do students receive through studying the technique?

FERRARO: As a student, I feel that every time I go to class, it's different; it's never the same; no matter how many times the sequences are the same. As a teacher, I try to have students also take a moment to connect with their body and to feel how the body changes in each encounter, exploring how this becomes more perceptive and receptive.

TAMARA: What is the significance of the vocabulary found in the Silvestre technique? What do terms such as Verticality, Four Elements, and Possibilities mean to you?

FERRARO: For me, the vocabulary was revealing because, being the basics of the Silvestre Technique, it differs from other techniques. Knowing what we mean by verticality, the correct position of the body, alignment with our energy centers and the connection we have with the earth and the universe seems so simple but is complex. The four elements allow me to inquire about the different qualities of movement, speeds, and rhythms. Besides being able to move with visualization and feel how nature surrounds us and how wonderful it is. I think this is what leads us to realize that there are possibilities, to move, to understand, to see, to think, to see the world, and to be able to include this all in one class. It makes us live in harmony with the environment and with ourselves [Ferraro, 2018].[11]

---

11. See Appendix for original response in Portuguese

Ferraro (right) participating in a class taught by Rosangela (left) in Argentina (photo by Diego Carrizo).

Silvestre Technique in Academia

In my Silvestre Technique course at the university, I teach the history of the technique, as well as the history of the culture from which the technique has developed. My students train in the physical practice of Silvestre Dance Technique, as well as investigate theoretical approaches of the technique. During our first semester together, students train heavily in practicing the codified movements and sequencing of the technique. The students are also required to write a research paper about the socio-economic conditions of Brazil during the 1970s to contextualize the influences of African-Brazilian history in Silvestre Technique. With the continuation of this training during the second semester, my students write papers detailing their experience of the *Body Universe* through the moving body. They detail how the concepts and practice of The *Body Universe* has deepened their overall physical practice and how this information influences their daily lives outside of technique class and dance performance. These type of research assignments allows the dancers to deepen their interpretations and contextualization of the physical training, and the integration of the principles of the technique.

It is important to have Silvestre Technique in academia for various reasons. As a scholar, it is vital that students are educated and understand how socio-economic occurrences affect the body through movement. In capitalist patriarchy societies, there is a stigma that cultivates the stereotype that women exist as unintellectual bodies in space.

The essay "The Dialectic of Women's Oppression Notes on the Relation Between Capitalism and Patriarchy," Val Burris examines "the subordination of women as an interaction between two relatively autonomous social structures: capitalism and patriarchy" (Burris, 1982, p. 52). In the essay, Burris explains that "capitalism and patriarchy are thus posited as two 'relatively autonomous' structures, neither of which can be subsumed under the other, but which interact to determine the concrete position of women in society" (Burris, 1982, p. 52). Although socio-economic inequalities for women are true in many junctures of society, the theories and practices of Silvestre Technique aim to eradicate these behaviors through training; by use of the philosophies, theories, and context of the Silvestre Technique, both observers and practitioners can understand that this technique is a full, mind-body-and-spirit experience. The mind is equally involved with the spirit and body discovering through movement in space. Through teaching and training in Silvestre Technique, one may discover that it offers, and is composed of, a "diverse cultural identity" (The Training, 2015).

My interviews with Passos, Alves, and Ferraro, as well as my observations of various other Silvestre Technique instructors have revealed important aspects of this training to me. The instructors of this codified form consider themselves lifetime learners of Silvestre Technique. They continue to study, explore and analyze through the technique. The instructors learn from Rosangela, Passos, each other, students, life and nature. Teaching, learning and practicing Silvestre Technique is an ongoing process that does not end with the intensive in Salvador, certification, Silvestre dance workshops, residencies, etc. The will to continue the vitality of Silvestre Technique comes directly from the very person who is discovering through its training.

Body-in-Nature Training

The Body-in-Nature training explores of the physical practice of Silvestre Technique as it is infused in nature. The practice of this dance technique outdoors, in varying natural settings, allows for participants from diverse backgrounds to appreciate the foundation of the work. Participants are able to make stronger connections between the symbology of the technique and the nature that surrounds them, whether it may be at an ocean, in a forest of trees, or at a park. This practice in nature allows the practitioner to connect to the essence of the earth felt beneath the feet as grass, gravel, or sand; the water of the ocean, waterfall, or river; the air from the breeze of the wind; and the fire of the sun above. These connections are significant as the body is forced to move differently than it is in artificial environments where the floor is made of marley, there may be air conditioning blowing from the vents, and the lighting source comes from electricity. Practicing this technique in nature allows people to understand how the elements of nature affect the body and are a part of the body. The internalization that occurs in the *Triangle of Inspiration* through this technique asks the participant to remove thoughts that may be influenced by society; instead, participants are directed to think clearly about the impetus of the moving body in time, space, and discovering with one's own abilities. Through the technique's foundation in nature, there is no discrimination of the physical body due to color, gender, or sex with the practice of Silvestre Technique. The mind is used as a source of power to transform thoughts into empowering conversations with the body. The practice of Silvestre Dance Technique outdoors also provides access for those who may not be able to afford to pay for studio space within an institutional structure. Practicing the technique through the Body-in-Nature training releases the limitations of accessibility in society.

The foundation of the Body-in-Nature training in Morro de São

Rosangela conducting Body in Nature training in Morro de São Paulo (author photo).

Paulo was developed many years ago when Kaley Isabella, another student of Rosangela and teacher of Silvestre Technique, and I engaged in a week of intensive training with Rosangela in Salvador. We studied the technique in detail each day for hours learning the messages, symbology, structure, alignment, and foundation of several movement sequences found in

Silvestre Technique. We danced movements inspired by the Orixás as well. We learned the mythology, the possibilities, more symbology and connections made from Orixás movements to Silvestre Technique.

The weeks were fulfilling as we were becoming stronger and more seasoned dancers. Kaley and I wanted to explore even more. Rosangela invited us to come with her to check on a property that she was having built in Morro de São Paulo as a dance compound. The following weekend, Rosangela, Kaley Isabella, and I ventured out to Morro de São Paulo to see the new dance compound that Rosangela was building on the island. Kaley and I, having studied under Rosangela for years, were excited to visit the new site. Since Rosangela's place was still being constructed, we stayed at a neighboring pousada (hotel), that was a beachfront property.

Once we arrived to the island we dropped off our bags, and Rosa took us on a tour of the island. The tour did not only consist of sightseeing. We experienced the island through movement. We engaged our body in several locations in nature throughout the island. We walked along a pathway and came across a forest full of ferns as well as banana, cashew, palm, cocoa and mango trees. Rosangela looked at Kaley and I and asked if we wanted to dance the essence of the hunter/gatherer in there. Without hesitation, we entered with our bags strapped to our back. We carefully crouched and peeled our way through the shrubbery, marking our territory. The more we danced, the more we discovered ourselves and were able to release our inhibitions through movement. It was the energy of the Orixá Oxóssi that we were exploring. As the day went along, several other dancing scenarios presented themselves. We passed by the roots of an ancient tree. The roots were exposed along the side of the cliff, intertwined, thick, and entering deep into the Earth. I looked up to see the green leaves reaching far into sky above. We stopped and discussed the ability of nature to cleanse and heal. Rosangela shared her views on the wisdom of nature. We discussed the body returning back to nature after this lifetime. We then danced the essence and messages of Orixá Omolú alongside the massive tree. From there, we continued our journey and walked pass a gate, which enclosed the cemetery. After Rosangela spoke with us about the importance of respect of this life and the afterlife, she invited us to dance. We had been working on movement symbols of Orixá Iansã and Nana in the studio. Here, we were able to embody the movement with a different intention and sensitivity. We continued walking until we reached a series of stairs; there were so many that it seemed as though they continued into the heavens. Combining the physical body with the Orixá mythology, we danced the symbology of Xangô carrying Oxalá on his back. We ended our practice for that day on a large wooden deck, overlooking the ocean. There were many people there waiting to view the sunset. Rosangela instructed Kaley and I to dance some sequences that we learned back in the studio in Salvador. As we started to dance, I could see people's focus shift and several making space for our movement. We danced and they observed as the sun disappeared beyond the waters. There was a strong applause as we finished and several compliments as well. We finished for the evening and made plans to continue our training the next day.

The next morning, we started early on the beach in front of the pousada where we stayed. With our feet in the sand we faced the water, saluting the nature surrounding us. Our Silvestre Technique training began as we witnessed the waves roll in and out to the sea. Afterwards, we began our journey to explore the island again. We headed down to the fort located in Morro de São Paulo (A Fortaleza de Tapirandú de Morro de São Paulo). There we were able to engage in several movement investigations: we came across an old canon where we examined the movement qualities and energies of Ogum; entered the fort and improvised Silvestre Technique symbology; and walked down to the ocean on the side of the fort and danced the essence of Iemanjá. Following our time at the fort, we hiked through the outer landscape of the island through forest and low tide ocean waters. We arrived at the streams of mud drizzling down from the high cliffs above. The mud in this area of Gamboa is considered to be medicinal and regenerative. We dived right in; covered from the top of our heads, down to our toes. Kaley and I started to revisit the movement sequences that we learned with Rosangela while studying with her in the studio. We danced the essence of Nana, using the yellow and red mud to mold our moving bodies. We wrapped up our afternoon session and headed back to Morro de São Paulo. That evening, we found ourselves on a wooden deck that surrounds a large tree; today, Rosangela refers to this tree as Irôko. Kaley and I danced several choreography phrases that we learned from Rosangela. Two young girls were playing on the deck when we arrived. As we began dancing they stopped to observe. Rosangela then invited the two girls to dance with us. Rosangela taught them some dance phrases, and we all began to dance together; this is the magic of Silvestre Technique and the Body-in-Nature Training. The natural encounters that occur and the discoveries within them. I was invigorated after seeing the eagerness, attention and passion of those young girls dancing.

Years later, I returned to Morro de São Paulo to delve deeper into the new course that Rosangela created. The *Body-in-Nature* training was developed out of our work years prior. Rosangela has streamlined the training of the *Body Universe* and has created a methodology of dance training that exists in the elements of nature. She says, "Body-in-Nature is utilizing the essence of nature in our reality" (Silvestre, 2018). Upon my return I realized that the Body-in-Nature training had developed into a full program with a concise structure and sequencing. Silvestre Technique always has new discoveries. The training in Morro maintains the physical challenge of dance, though in nature there is a different movement conditioning that is required.

The finished dance compound, named The *Templo* (The Temple), is majestic. The studio consists of three white walls, a wooden floor and an open side that looks out to a canopy of trees, plants, and animals. While dancing, you may see a few monkeys wrestling through the greenery or a small hummingbird hovering over a flower. The Body-in Nature program consists of a Monday through Friday schedule. Mondays and Wednesdays are dedicated to Silvestre Technique training at the Templo. The morning session is open to community members as well. The afternoon sessions are specifically designed for those who are part of the Body-in-Nature Training Program. Tuesday and Thursdays are spent in nature exploring the dynamics and inspiration of movement in various locations throughout the island. The Body-in-Nature explorations begin shortly after the break of dawn at around six in the morning. Throughout the week, participants engage in movement analyzations, reflections, movement composition, symbology and rehearsals. Friday reflections consist of discussions, studio work and a cumulative exploration of movement in a public space on the island if desired. In the Body-in-Nature training there is as much time dedicated to observation and reflection as there is to the movement practice.

2018 Interview with Rosangela

BODY-IN-NATURE TRAINING

> *The nature in Morro gives you a direct connection with the nature that we bring to [the symbology of] the Orixá training in Salvador. We bring nature in Salvador through the Orixás. You move, and you bring nature through the original source. It is another way for people to realize their connection to nature. For some people to realize, they need to go through that [training], and feel the connections* [Silvestre, 2018].

I interviewed dancer and Silvestre Technique student, Sandra Orellana Sears, to learn more about her personal experience in the Body-in-Nature training with Rosangela.

> TAMARA: What was your experience working with Rosangela during the Body-Nature training?
>
> SANDRA: My experience with Rosangela always involves tapping into the multi-dimensionality of dance. An extraordinary technician of dance, Rosangela also has a gift for making the more nuanced, spiritual and emotional aspects of movement accessible to all beings, regardless of their age, background, or skill level. The Body-Nature Training allows for a deepening of the subtler dimensions of her practice.... Rosangela always emphasizes nature as the driving force behind all movement, our physical bodies, our relationships, and space

itself. However, this is usually a theoretical concept because we practice indoors in a conventional dance studio with a ceiling, floor, and four walls.... We are asked to use our imagination, consciousness and intention to connect with the concept of nature theoretically. Body-Nature training is rooted in the foundation of relocating the practice and study of dance outside and into the wildness of nature. As a result, the surrounding elements of nature become inherent and immersed in the process, providing organic catalysts for transformation, alchemy, embodiment, and learning. The experience of dance in relationship to the elements of nature becomes empirical versus theoretical. From my experience, the physical, emotional and spiritual integration and learning process occur at an accelerated pace with the physical presence of nature incorporated into the training.

TAMARA: What were your experiences in nature for this training?

SANDRA: Interestingly, I felt that nature itself became the teacher and Rosangela became more of a witness to the dancers' honest relationship with nature. As a student who has studied with her extensively in a traditional classroom, she is constantly emphasizing and conjuring the presence of the natural world to inspire students to move towards their own natural, uninhibited, and wild nature. It is inherent in all of us, but we often become so disconnected from this wildness in the modern world. Dance has the potential to reunite us with this original essence if we connect with the natural, organic movement innate to our bodies. This can sometimes be confusing or tricky when a student is focusing on technical dance training, which is extremely precise, controlled, and structured. Dancing in nature was an invitation to release some of the rigid linearity of technique and explore the more primal, intuitive, non-linear aspects of movement. I also experienced the healing qualities of dance more deeply than ever while dancing in nature.... I understood the capacity of dance to heal on a cellular level—in the same way we intuitively know the healing power of immersing ourselves in nature.

TAMARA: How does the Body-Nature-Training relate to your development and studies of Silvestre Dance Technique?

SANDRA: This training has provided a more experiential, raw understanding of the foundational aspects of the technique—the four elements of nature, four directions, the symbology of the Orixá, the chakra system, and the Body Universe. These can be explored indefinitely in the studio—a lifetime is not enough.... However, I find that studying in nature has allowed for an accelerated learning of some of these qualities, systems, symbols, and archetypes. The immersive experiences I have had in nature exploring the raw elements of nature in nature have seeped into my way of being, which carries over into the studio. Now I no longer feel like I am only imagining what it is like to have water or mud in my hands–I have had the direct, intentional experience. Instead of a symbol for water, I truly identify with and experience the element itself, in my hands. I am able to embody the element because I've had the opportunity to experience it firsthand in its natural, original environment.

TAMARA: How does the Body-Nature-Training relate to your understanding of the Orixás?

SANDRA: Body-Nature training has only deepened and enriched my continuous study and relationship to the Orixás, the deities or divine forces of nature itself. Observing and exploring the relationship of my body among the elements of nature has taught me how the Orixás exist and manifest within my own being and my relationship to my ancestors. They are at once universal and highly personal, manifesting through our individual embodiment of the physical, spiritual, and ancestral, as well as through the expression of nature itself and the rhythms of the Earth. The Orixás emerged from this necessity to recognize, respect, and salute the sacred tie between nature's elements and human beings. This training has been a gift and great teacher in the deeper understanding of the necessity to honor my relationship to nature and my ancestors.

TAMARA: What impact has the training in nature had on your overall dance career including training, teaching and performance?

SANDRA: My journey as a dancer began somewhat recently in my late twenties, and has always been rooted in health, wellbeing, and healing. For as long as I can remember, I've been interested in movement, the physical body, and the healing of the subtle/emotional bodies. As an energy healing practitioner, dance was a wonderful way to explore some of these relationships and I naturally gravitated towards the Silvestre Technique because my mother is from Brazil and I felt connected, more than anything, to the symbols of the Orixás and dance as a spiritual and healing practice. The technical language of dance was unfamiliar to me, so I was challenged to assimilate the technique in order to deepen my spiritual connection to dance and the physical body—a journey that never ends! Training in nature gave me permission to focus less on technique and more on tuning and honing the instrument of my body as a conduit for the divinity of nature. Body-Nature training has reminded me of the importance of my individual expression and relationship to nature—no one else shares the connection that I do and that is the magic of my idiosyncratic movement and creativity. I have been fortunate to have the opportunity to perform several

Sandra Sears in performance with Moving Spirits, Inc., during 2016 intensive with Rosangela Silvestre (photo by Ace Murray).

times, but that was never the intention I had when beginning to study with Rosangela. The training has taught me the responsibility I have to honor this original essence within myself and share it with others in training, performance, and of course, in the arena of life! In witnessing others move through this process, I have realized the incredibly healing effect this training can have on one's life—essentially, we are learning to give ourselves permission and take full ownership of who we truly are.

TAMARA: How does the nature training impact your connection to nature overall?

SANDRA: Since childhood I have had a strong, spiritual connection with nature. The nature training has only fortified a connection that has always been there. I have received many healing benefits from connecting with the natural world of Brazil in particular. These experiences have allowed me to unearth and discover some of the deeper ancestral memories and connections that reside within me. The training has reminded me of nature's capacity to bridge present time with all dimensions of time—past, present, future.

TAMARA: What is one moment that resonated with you from the training?

SANDRA: One portion of the training involves gathering students at a local waterfall near Rosangela's home and exploring movement connected to the archetypal energy of fresh water. I had the honor of witnessing and photographing two different groups coming together to have this experience—what emerged was fascinating! Two completely different expressions of the healing power of water, nature, community, trust and movement. This demonstrated to me Rosangela's extraordinary capacity to hold neutral space and allow the energy of each group and individual to express itself freely and without interference. It is truly an art form to hold the container for self-discovery, trust, and exploration. It must be strong enough to contain and harness the collective energy, but also still fluid enough to allow for the mystery and magic of nature to penetrate and alchemize the group of individuals and inspire a natural unfolding of expression free of inhibition.

TAMARA: What discoveries did you make?

SANDRA: I discovered that my own range of expression—physical, emotional and spiritual—is far beyond what I believe I am capable of. This is something I always discover and rediscover with Rosangela: the limitlessness of my own potential.

TAMARA: What is something important to know about this work?

SANDRA: This work demands that you are present and courageous. In order to make discoveries, one has to be fearless and leave the ego at the door. Simply being in Rosangela's presence demands that you investigate the fears and self-limiting beliefs that hold you back not only in dance, but in your life. This work is not about comparison, but the discovery and embodiment of your original essence and limitless potential.

I believe this work is about the universality of nature, movement, creativity, and spirituality.

TAMARA: As a dancer, what is interesting or unique about Silvestre Dance Technique and the Body Nature Training for you?

SANDRA: The universality and inclusivity of the Silvestre Dance Technique are what make the practice so special and dear to me. I can honestly say that if it were not for the technique and Rosangela, I would never have embarked on the deeply enriching, empowering, and healing process that dance has become in my life. I would certainly never have identified as a dancer before beginning training in this particular technique…. I didn't believe that the world of dance and technique could belong to me, but Rosangela always emphasizes that dance and physical health is for everyone. The technique welcomes and warmly embraces anyone interested in exploring the physical body, ancestry, movement, nature, and/or the spiritual aspects of dance. Everyone is encouraged to bring all the knowledge they have, even if it is not necessarily related to the technical language of dance. I've never seen anyone turned away from the community because of inexperience or lack of skill. This ultimately makes for a more diverse, enriching community and environment of movement, creativity, and exchange while the technical skill and fluency of each student is developed and evolved. I am so grateful for the exquisite family I have acquired throughout the world on this incredible journey of the Silvestre Dance Technique. This has been the greatest and most unexpected gift of all! [Orellana Sears, 2018].

The Body-in-Nature training may be applied to the physical training of Silvestre Technique as well. Classes held outdoors allow the body to experience the sensations of dancing on the Earth's terrain. Dancers can discover how to manage the qualities of the outdoor air to breathe through the movements. Dancers learn how to navigate the landscapes of the Earth through movement investigations. Each semester, I take my university students outdoors to deepen their dance process. Training in nature provides the students with symbology, experiences, and images that can be applied to the *Body Universe* when dancing in any location. It is the understanding of nature in this capacity that inspires and influences movement. The Body-in-Nature training is always a ritualistic and sacred training for me. We arrive to these spaces, giving appreciation for the many offerings that nature provides for survival, inspiration, and support.

VIII

Self-Actualization

"Energy comes from everywhere."—*Rosangela Silvestre, 2013*
(Williams)

I must begin this chapter by defining self-actualization as I refer to it
in this text. Self-actualization is a state of enlightenment and self-empowerment. It is the state of existence in which individuals encompass their
full potential using their creativity through the application of wisdom integrated into Silvestre Technique. It is having faith in one's own abilities while
being open to various possibilities. Incorporating this sense of faith sub-
sequently affects body and mind. Abraham Maslow was a founding psychotherapist of the humanistic movement in psychology. His theory insists
that "self-actualization is the desire for self-fulfillment, and self-transcendence is the need to move beyond the self and connect to something higher
than ourselves-such as God" (DK Publishing, 2014, p. 139) In other words,
Maslow's theory proposes that a person may reach their full potential
through achieving self-actualization while self-transcendence releases personal desires and adheres to a greater connection; this higher connection
may be considered God, the Great Creator or a divine force. Scientists call
"energy" what many religions refer to as "God." Dancers are continuously
transferring energy through space, to each other and within the self. Every
space has energy and when a person enters the space, the energy of the person shifts in relation with the energy of the place. More so, when a person moves in a space with another body and with live music a new energy
is created. The quality of the energy depends on the reaction of the bodies moving, the interaction between the various bodies in space, and the
vibrations of the music. In science this phenomenon is known as energy. In
some spiritual practices, this energy may be referred to as a Divine Spirit.
In Yorùbá culture dance itself is a form of àṣẹ a powerful life force; this
force may also signify the power for things to transpire or to create change.
Through these transfers of energies lies the potentiality to connect to our
most divine, higher self; it is for this reason that I believe Rosangela says, *"I*

am not only a dancer, I am the dance" (Williams, 2011–2014). Through my years of dance training and performing, I have learned that all movement has the potential of àṣẹ (or axé as referred to in Brazil). When the dancer starts to realize this, the higher vibration of spiritual and dance consciousness begins. This axé awakens the divine-energy of a person and a space. Divine-energy awakens the divine self. I believe that Divine Spirits, such as the Orixás, give humans meaning, hope, and direction. In Silvestre Technique, through trial, error, and discovery participants can attain meaning, hope, and direction for themselves. It is the *Body Universe*, offering the concepts and theories of the triangles in connection with the symbology and physical practice which helps the individual to achieve self-actualization.

Barbara Browning describes the potent influence of movement in African-Brazilian spiritual ceremonies: "The mover, in a Candomblé ceremony, is instrumental to the manifestation of divine principles. It's through the motion of the person that Orixás make themselves present" (Browning, 2007, p. 174). Dance itself in any form, brings forth energy. The First Law of Thermodynamics states that energy is neither created nor destroyed, but rather transferred from one form to another (Wrigglesworth, 1997). In Silvestre Technique, the energy cultivated through movement can be transferred to achieve a higher state of being. From our own selves a higher power can be realized. Ecstasy in the movements of Silvestre Technique lives within this theory. The Divine Spirit can be unveiled from within; this is done by the conjuring of movement stimulated by nature, the Orixás, ancestral memories, live music, community and self-determination. In the following passage, Rosangela expounds upon this philosophy of the Divine Spirits as a source of empowerment.

2018 Interview with Rosangela

PERSONAL EMPOWERMENT

> One beautiful thing is that this technique gives you a gate to sense the power of your ancestral connections and how much power the ancestral connections give to you. People started to research the strength that they forgot. This technique gives you that. When you [Tamara] research Samba de Roda, it doesn't mean that you eliminate the technique, you empower your technique [Rosangela, 2018].

The following passages are from a collection of five interviews with Silvestre Technique Intensive participants after the final dance presentation held on February 1, 2014. The dancers address their overall experience in the training in Salvador over the summer.

Audrey Hailes:

Having to pass through each of the elements; having to go from being water to being quick and strong like fire, and then a different type of strength for water. This was really challenging my sense of discipline and my understanding of my capabilities, which is what Rosangela and Vera talk about all the time of how capable we are. So, I'm really finding once you decide that you are fully capable of going from [snaps fingers] sharp as a knife to cool as a creek, it becomes a whole new world [Hailes, 2014].

Hailes discusses the obstacles of overcoming self-imposed boundaries to arrive at a place, which allows more freedom in movement capabilities. Chief Yuya Assaan-ANU describes self-actualization by breaking down each word. On his November 7, 2014, Blogtalk radio show, *Enlightenment and Transformation*, he shared that "…self is a reflection of higher consciousness that you are endowed with" (Assaan-ANU H. Y., 2014). He continues by explaining that the word "actual" derives from the Latin word, energia, which is "energy." Therefore, in essence, self-actualization is "the process of energizing the reflection of the higher self" (Assaan-ANU H. Y., 2014). This is what Hailes explains above; understanding that each person is gifted, powerful and experienced enough to attain all that they desire. Hailes speaks of this in reference to the energies of sharpness and coolness, but this can be activated in all aspects of movement including both physical and mental movement. Movement of the mind is to take action and *do* something, bringing thoughts to realization, as the Blocos Afros accomplished in the 1970s.

Like Hailes, Carissa Matsushima provided me with her account of experiencing Silvestre Technique:

I feel strong when I practice Silvestre Technique. I see the lines that my body makes and how clear my body can be. I feel like Vera and Rosangela have opened these doors for me to discover just how capable I am. It's a challenge every day to realize that, and to realize that it's okay to realize that, because it's easy to hold back. It's easy to hold your strength back, especially in this crazy world of dancers. [We tell ourselves] "Oh, I'm not good enough." Or "I'm not a dancer," things like that. But, after a couple weeks of the training I forgot about all of that and it was just all about keeping going and how far can I go through … through the struggle [Matsushima, 2014].

Matsushima describes Silvestre Technique as giving her power and strength to overcome insecurities, self-doubt and apprehension. It reveals adequacy, proficiency, capacity, and potentiality to her. These are all aspects of her self-actualization. There are many challenges in the technique; physically with movement, musicality, phrasing, the embodiment of the movement, etc. There are even more challenges with each individual body. Nonetheless, the physical challenges of Silvestre dance training push the mind and body to decide in the spur of the movement to do what is being asked. When practicing Silvestre Technique, practitioners do not have to think about the technique, but instead focus on one's own capacities and discoveries. People can express their own story inside of the training.

Matsushima and Hailes articulate how the technique provided a lens to discover their capabilities. Knowing one's own capabilities gives power to the individual; this is an integral component to one's personal development. Chief Yuya Assaan-ANU explains that self-actualization is "the process of being Self-Determined and Self-Defining" and that is exactly what Silvestre Technique offers its participants (Assaan-ANU H. Y., 2014). Through understanding and connecting to the strength of the Ori and the symbols of the Orixás, with the support of the ancestral memories, Silvestre Technique students may be able to eliminate fears, and self-imposed limitations, and undesired energies of others in a room through dance. Harmony within self is also required to release limitations and fear. Balance is needed; Silvestre Technique does not provide a space where participants look to others with intimidation or anger. Instead, harmony within oneself and focus on internalization prepares the dancer to overcome obstacles and ego. Silvestre Technique provides the tools, and it is up to the participant or student to use them.

Working with Rosangela and Passos in this technique has inspired me to make life changing decisions each year. I am empowered. I have reoccurring experiences of self-actualization in dance and my personal life. My experiences led me to create my dance company, Moving Spirits, Inc. The

Rosangela teaching Silvestre Technique in Trinidad (photo by Brooks Anderson).

difficult choice was made to leave my full-time job to focus on my dance company and career. Later, graduate school became my priority. I made a conscious decision to focus on studying dances of the African Diaspora and movements of the Òrìṣàs (Orixás, Orishas) in Brazil, Trinidad and Nigeria. A significant portion of my research has always been devoted to Silvestre Technique, which led me to the writing of this book. All of these accomplishments have brought me closer to my destiny in life, empowering me to continue on my path towards self-actualizing as a daily practice. After reflecting over my experience in Silvestre training while studying with Rosangela in Trinidad, I wrote the following passage in my journal:

> *October 2013* (Journal Entry)
> It is in the ENERGY: the movements, music, and gathering of people that summons higher beings. Whether it is the Holy Ghost, the Orixás, or the Divine Self, transcendence is a result of these three key elements. I believe this is true in dance as well. The higher self is achieved through intention, which guides movement, music that also expresses, the beat of the drum [correlating to the heartbeat], and the dancing family or community [Williams, 2011–2014].

2018 Interview with Rosangela

DISCOVERY

> Everyone that chose to discover through this work, has never been disappointed. They always went forward in their own way. Tamara, you are one example. Look at how far you went, when you decided to go to the intensive, at that time. So, from there to now everything that you have been doing has created that link with the foundation of this technique. For me, it's not only based on training the body in terms of the muscles, the physical, it's something in there, in my opinion, that allowed you to find your own way. Allowed you to find the dancer that you are. And then you used your body's ability and physicality in that. You're never empty, nor made yourself like the kind of model of dance, but You are the Dance. You discover that you can keep diving in and you're never going to feel that you cannot create and develop and go forward. Because this is a work that is alive. Since it is alive, it's in the hands of everyone who also lives the life. It is not my property. I don't own this.... I just develop, and more people come and find that they can develop inside of this development [Silvestre, 2018].

In 2013, following my attendance at several religious Shango/Orisha ceremonies in Trinidad (a religion that also stems from traditional West African origins) and taking classes with Rosangela, I had a deeper understanding of how the movement, live music, community and self-absorption in this technique creates an almost trance-like state of being. By trance, I mean a suspension of my walking consciousness; I find myself moving from a higher vibration—the subconscious self. This trance-like state is my self-actualization. It resonates with me long after leaving the studio and as a result my life has changed, transcended. My connection to nature has changed. My connection to people has changed. My dancing has changed.

In his definition, Abraham Mosley claimed that self-actualized people are "without one single exception, involved in a cause outside their own skin, in something outside of themselves. They are working at something which fate has called them to somehow...." (Maslow, 1972, p. 43). This cause is the higher self that I have described above and the Divine Self that I mention throughout this section. Mosley describes self-actualization as "experiencing fully, vividly, selflessly, with full concentration and total absorption" (Maslow, 1972, p. 45). Silvestre Technique is designed for students to aspire to and reach their full potentiality in any given moment while dancing. Mosley defines these moments as "peak experiences" and as "moments of ecstasy which you cannot buy, cannot guarantee..." (Maslow, 1972, p. 48). In dancing Silvestre Technique, the peak experiences are periods of feeling enlightened and are driven by movement and the Body Universe.

In the *EdITS Manual for the Personal Orientation Inventory, POI*, Everett L. Shostrom deciphers that self-actualized people seem to have liberated themselves from social pressures, expectations and goals (Shostrom, 1974). The aforementioned idea is what Hailes and Matsushima express in their experiences of Silvestre Technique, their liberation. Realizing capabilities in their dancing could possibly synthesize and reveal itself into their daily lives. Shostrom continues by stating, "The self-actualized person appears to live in the here and now more fully and is able to tie the past and the future to the present in meaningful continuity" (Shostrom, 1974). Silvestre draws the connection to the students' past experiences and their ancestry into their dancing. The technique also encourages dancers to bring their "truth" to their movement. Dancers should not "leave their problems at the door" as I have heard countless times in my dance career. Silvestre Technique invites dancers to move through their pain, anger, happiness, fear, and shame; these sensations are the expression. This is the training space to find balance and be inspired. Silvestre Training challenges its students to dance through life experiences. In the documentary, *A Litany for Survival: The Life and Work of Audre Lorde,* the inspirational poet Audrey Lorde proclaimed, "Don't wait for inspiration. You don't need to be inspired.... You need to reach down and touch the thing that's boiling inside of you and make it somehow useful" (Griffin & Parkerson, 1996). Rosangela's pedagogy includes the concept of searching for inspiration within. The principles of Silvestre Technique teach participants how to discover through dancing the wisdom of the ancestors, knowledge of the Orixás, and dancing one's life story. Students are encouraged to dance in the here and now moment with the guidance of their intuition and perception to express the movements; this process occurs while visualizing and being conscious of what may occur in the future. This complex analysis should continuously occur within the inner dialogue of the *Body Universe*. When walking into a Silvestre Technique class, if I am not open, then I may not have compassion for myself, and I conjure my own prejudices. Our Divine Spirit is essence and existence; we do not create this higher spirit, but through training we discover it for ourselves. In Rosangela's interview with Barbara Browning she offers that in Candomblé initiates are

> not merely learning the choreographies of the Orixás, but learn the mythology, the songs, even washing the garments and prepare the food necessary for the ceremonies and all these processes of training prepare the body to "let itself be carried away." In that moment in which you let yourself be carried away, how does it happen? You connect this being carried away to a structure. This way, you can respond to an incentive which comes to you, to carry you [Browning, 2007].

Silvestre Technique is a training that teaches participants how they may let go and dance. The structure of the technique training sustains the body. The Body Universe trains the body to allow freedom for self. Curiosity and wisdom allow discovery, and through discovery expression can occur. Knowledge provides physical material, but wisdom offers expression. "You must involve yourself in wisdom, not only knowledge. Your body only needs TWO things: to eat and to sleep, but life offers so much more for you to do. You can connect your body to your spiritual," Rosangela made this statement while facilitating a theory class during the 2013 intensive (Williams, 2011–2014). Rosangela explains that one's true potentiality can be reached if the person learns to unblock predetermined limitations of the mind "if you think little of the body (in limitations), you will dance little. When you think minimal, you dance minimal" (Williams, 2011–2014). The physical body responds to the systems of the brain and mental stimulation; for this reason, the Internalization portion of the Silvestre technique class occurs first. A personal conversation (or some refer to as meditation) within the mind to open oneself to all possibilities, known and unknown, of the body and spirit is advantageous in dance training.

How Are Silvestre Technique and Life Inseparable?

The *Body Universe* in Silvestre Technique is an outlet for participants to connect with their own Divine Spirit, nature, ancestors, music, other participants, and the open space. As I have mentioned throughout this text, Silvestre training is for the body, mind and spirit. It offers tools to use in life situations whether it is in dance, connection or relation to space, time, natural resources, or other people. In the book *Thought in the Act,* Eric

Manning and Brian Massumi describe the act of intertwining practice and philosophy:

> Every practice is a mode of thought, already in the act. To dance: a thinking in movement. To paint: a thinking through color. To perceive in the everyday: a thinking of the world's varied ways of affording itself [Manning & Massumi, 2014, Preface].

Silvestre Technique encourages its participants to perceive and discover in the manner in which *Thought in the Act* suggests. This method of practice, *thinking in movement,* opens the possibility of Self-Actualization. In the journey to Self-Actualization in Silvestre Dance Technique, the dancer may come to acknowledge:

I am the *Body Universe*
I am my Inspiration
I am Expression
I am Balance
I am open to all Possibilities

Silvestre Technique not only offers the physical training practice of the body; it offers a philosophy for living. Dance educator and contemporary ballet pioneer, Alonzo King, declares that *"dance training can't be separate from life training"* (Lynch, 2016). King, a prominent figure in the development and training of diverse artists states that:

> Everything that comes into our lives is training. The qualities we admire in great dancing are the same qualities we admire in honesty, courage, fearlessness, generosity, wisdom, depth, compassion and humanity [Lynch, 2016].

The aforementioned admirable qualities have all been offered to me through my studies of Silvestre Technique. The three triangles, concepts of nature, understanding of the Orixás and the ancestors, self-reflection, and connections within community can all be applied as principles for life. Rosangela often asks dancers to "bring your life to your dance" (Williams, 2011–2014). In other words, when entering the dance class to train the body, dancers should bring all of their life experiences with them. Life situations should be used to empower the dance; this gives life to movement. Silvestre Technique has provided me with these perceptions and philosophies, and my own self-actualization in addition to the physical training. I encourage anyone with interest or curiosity in dance training, personal growth, and sustenance to discover what Silvestre Technique can do for you.

My body is an instrument that plays
Rhythms of movement into vibration
And the dance of the universe
I embody nature to express the voice
Of the invisible, that brings me
The messages of intuition,

Opening the way to the forest
Where I gaze towards the sky
Which reflects the colors of the rainbow.

My feet on the ground
Feel the power of the land
That is hot like fire,
And strong, like the voice of thunder.
Calmly, the land connects me
To the river and refreshes my whole body
With the wind that sets me free

To walk in the mud
To dive into the arms of the ocean
Embracing me with the wings of a bird
Guiding me to live in harmony and wisdom!

—Rosangela Silvestre, *Faces of Nature*

Afterword

It has taken me several years to fully understand why I dance. As a whole, I think most performing artists, especially dancers, involve themselves in this form so that we can share our thoughts, emotions and expressions with our audience in a manner that is comfortable to us. Movement is undeniably a familiar language and most people outside of dance understand bodily gestures at least. For dancers, movement is the ultimate mode of expression.

I have learned that I dance because it is a part of my spiritual journey. I view my dancing as a gift from the creator in which I must use to articulate issues within society and our culture; it is also used to express my reflections of my own journey. All of these ideas in which I endeavor to express through movement, hopefully, inspires the spectators of this phenomenon.

Dancing matters as all forms of language and expression matter; we articulate our concerns or feelings through verbal language and this is also done through movement. Silvestre Technique has provided me with efficient tools to deepen my physical articulation. In expressing ourselves in dance, we create critical seeds of thought for conscious minds to perceive and reflect upon long after the movement has ended.

Appendix

Page 33

2020 Interview with Luanda Mori in Portuguese

Linguagem é para mim uma master pièce no sentido que ela contém a essência da técnica silvestre como proposta artística espiritual.Neste trabalho a gestual sagrada , preservada e guardada no contexto religioso busca o universal, o que pode ser comunicado à través do corpo. Este para mim é o corpo universo, aquele que decodifica e codifica para comunicar, busca do comum em nos. Linguagem para mim representa a busca para entrar nesse templo que é comum a todos, o corpo. A coreografia começa com esa preparação e a saudação ao sagrado, e revela no final e para mim, o estágio de pureza que mantém a vida, (gesto de limpeza, água que lava, que representa a vida mesma). Linguagem foi dançada pela primera vez em 1999 em Salvador. Varias versões foram feitas, uma mais longa Temple in Motion dançada pela Cleo Parker Robinson Company em COlorado. Linguagem começou como uma célula de workshop, nessa época éramos poucos no processo. Rosangela tendo compromisso no exterior nós mesmas Noemia Reis, Fabiana Guirar, Kênia Sampaio e Luanda Mori, ensaiamos e nos preparamos juntas. Rosangela veio assistir diretamente o trabalho no palco. O processo foi intenso, nesse momento sem muitas reflexões mais com uma intuição: a mensagem era profunda. Linguagem contendo o essencial pode sempre ser revisitada e recriada pois a mensagem está intrínseca na motivação inspiradora, por isso cada vez que a recriamos ela nos proporciona mais conhecimento deste corpo símbolo da energia sagrada.

Page 33

2018 Interview with Vera Passos in Portuguese

HOW HAS THE TECHNIQUE CHANGED, EVOLVED AND
DEVELOPED OVER TIME?

Por mim, a técnica e como uma borboleta, ela está sempre em mudança e trocando. Ela está andando em espaços diferentes, tem cores diferentesestá transitando em lugares especiais, e importante para o ser humano reconhecer este lugar, onde eles não estão presos. Onde a individualidade é respeitada. Talvez, esse seja uns dos motivos que me prendeu.

Page 45

2018 Interview with Vera Passos in Portuguese

PASSION OF SILVESTRE TECHNIQUE

Antigamente, muitas pessoas me perguntavam por que você não faz uma coisa que é sua? Com seu nome? As pessoas achavam que era um absurdo que eu estou trabalhando por muito tempo com o nome de Técnica Silvestre. Já que eu tinha um trabalho que era diferenciado. E ate mesmo, por já ser professora antes de trabalha com Técnica Silvestre. Já tinha um grupo de pessoas que me seguia. Tanto como meu talento como bailarina e também como professora. Mas a técnica, ela acabou, me roubando. Não me escondendo, mas silenciando este lugar que poderia trazer uma coisa que era minha.

Page 45

Interview with Deko Alves in Portuguese

HOW DOES SILVESTRE TECHNIQUE INFLUENCE YOUR LIFE?

Eu comecei fazer dança moderna com Mestre King, foi a primeira técnica que eu fiz. Mas, eu não conseguia me encontrar em um lugar. Então, a partir do momento que eu encontrei a Técnica Silvestre, eu percebi que havia um lugar que respeitava o meu lugar, onde eu me encontrava. Isso vem influenciando de forma que hoje eu vejo a Técnica Silvestre como uma filosofia de vida. É um momento que eu busco me equilibrar enquanto pessoa, enquanto bailarino ... é o lugar que me inspira. Eu sempre falo com Rosangela e Vera que eu preciso está nos intensivos janeiro e agosto. Porque, é o momento que eu me renovo. É o momento que eu busco dentro de mim, uma coisa que o dia a dia não vai me permitindo. Porque eu tenho ferramentas para pensar. Isso influencia todos os dias na sala de aula … com uma duvida, com uma troca com elas, trocando com um aluno, trocando com alguém que está na porta, ou trocando com as crianças dos preparatórios que assistir a aula. E depois se encanta com esta aula e vem te dar um abraço. Isso mudou completamente minha vida. Influencia na minha essência como pessoa, como professional, como professor, como filho, com a minha relação com as pessoas … a forma de ver o mundo, é completamente diferente. Me perceber como parte de um todo. Eu não estou sozinho. O que eu sou, depende do que você é, do que todo mundo é. Isso faz toda diferença.

Page 47

2018 Interview with Vera Passos in Portuguese

ANCESTRAL CONNECTIONS

Eu fico reflexiva muito, e tentando entender porque não aconteceu dessa forma antes de fazer técnica Silvestre. Sempre tinha uma preocupação grande quando estava dançando para me expressar. Tanto que eu carrego esse discurso forte dentro das minhas aulas como professora. Sempre carrego isso antes de trabalhar com Silvestre. Mas, os meus mestres, com exceção de Jorge Silva ele realmente foi fantástico no processo dele de formação. Gal Mascarenhas também, que é a minha mãe da dança que era meu primeiro contato com a dança. Mas eu encontrei muitos mestres que me pediam pra que eu tivesse essa dedicação da expressividade, mas não me falavam *como*. Eles não me falavam que eu podia encontrar esse caminho dentro da minha cultura. Que isso estava em mim, que fazia parte da minha essência, da minha origem. Ninguém nunca me falou dessa ancestralidade que me cerca. Eu nunca nem ouvir essa palavra, ancestralidade, quando eu comecei a dançar. Eu se eu tivesse escutado teria sido, mais fácil, saber que meus ancestrais estavam dançando comigo. Que eles eram meus reis, minhas rainhas. Que eles estavam ali me guiando. O caminho teria sido mais interessante para mim porque eu estaria trazendo uma coisa mais palpável. O caminho e muito mais fácil quando você entende quem você é … e a força que você busca, é nos que te representaram no passado. Sabe que essa estrela, que essa princesa, essas rainhas, esses guerreiros, eles tiveram seu sangue. Eles lutaram por você, eles fizeram por você, eles sofreram por você. Agora você traz eles através dos símbolos.

Page 58

2018 Interview with Vera Passos in Portuguese

HOW DID YOU BECOME A TEACHER OF SILVESTRE TECHNIQUE?

Eu já estava durante muito tempo, estudando a técnica. Muito antes de conhecer Rosangela, quando eu entendo que queria trabalhar com dança, realmente, eu queria ser professora, a verdade eu fiz o caminho inverso. Primeiro foi professora, depois eu fui estudar dança. Já tinha um grupo de dança de minha rua onde eu dançava, já coreografa, mesmo, sem saber o que era um pilé.

Quando eu entrei a FUNCEB, a realmente FUNCEB não era minha primeira escola de dançar. Era uma escola de meu bairro do Bar Balho chamada, Arte Viva, tenha três recém-formadas da UFBA. Eu entre para essa escola de lá eu fui pra FUNCEB com Jorge Silva, que me levo pra FUNCEB, quando era no Campo Grande no Teatro Castro Alves. La eu comecei a ver Rosangela, e seguir ela. Comecei a fazer aula, aconteceu uma conferencia de dança contemporânea, ou uma coisa assim, que Rosangela chegar e dar aula. E como estudante da FUNCEB eu tinha uma bolsa de estudo, e eu fazia as aulas com ela. I aí passei a ser seguidora dela. Então, em todos lugares que ela ia eu estava grudada como aqueles agarradinho como aqueles bichinhos, que ficar difícil para você larga. Eu ficava com ela o tempo inteiro.

Dez anos depois, que eu dancei no Bale Folclórico, e sai da compan-hia, eu estava mais uma vez no Villa Velha fazendo o curso dela. No verão em janeiro, e em fevereiro ela vem aqui pra FUNCEB para dar continui-dade para algumas alunas que iriam ficar na cidade. Eu fiz, esses dois meses Janeiro e fevereiro. E no penúltimo dia da aula, ela me falou que os estu-dantes estavam perguntando para ela se eu não poderia dar continuidade para turma. Já que algumas iria ficar na cidade para mais um mês. Ai, eu topei. Tá bom então, eu vou dar aula. Eu estava sem dar aula, já que tinha acabado de sair da companhia. Safira era muito pequena. E assim, eu fiz, convidei Nei [Sacramento]—estava mais próximo de mim, como musico, e as aulas era com musica a vivo. Nei chamou Felipe [Alexandro] e Luciano [da Silva], e agente começou assim aqui no FUNCEB. Na época minha turma tinha 30 alunas, todos estrangeiros dentro da escola, a proposta foi de ter mais um mês de aula, então eu fiz pedido de sala para um mês. Depois um mês, ninguém queria ir embora, eles me pediram mais um mês, eu renove para um mês, e fiquei renovando, renovando, renovando—isso perdurando para anos aqui em Salvador. Pessoas iram, pessoas voltaram. E teve uma coisa muito curiosa que, por ter ficado por muitos anos no mesmo horário, tinham pessoas que veneram no primeiro ano e voltaram cinco anos depois e no mesmo horário veio aqui no FUNCEB, e eu estava lá—ainda dando aula de Técnica Silvestre.

Então, foi uma aula que marcou, a época. Pessoas iam e voltavam porque sabiam que estava acontecendo Salvador inteiro, sabia oque estava acontecendo. Que era nesse horário não comum, era um horário de almoço. Ingressado que eu tenho esse habito ate hoje. Eu não sinto fome no horário de almoço. Se tiver dançando, não me importa.

Então, foi assim, na verdade não escolher da aula de Silvestre. Ela não foi aquela pessoa que disse, "eu quero estudar para ser professora." Não, eu queria estudar a técnica. Mais não tinha nenhum intensão em ser professora da Técnica Silvestre. Depois da técnica me escolher.

Page 59

2018 Interview with Deko Alves in Portuguese

How Did You Become a Teacher of Silvestre Technique?

Vera foi falando e eu fui pensando fazendo uma reflexão sobre isso. Eu nunca quis ser professor, eu sempre quis ser bailarino. E ser professor, era uma coisa muito distante, eu dizia a eu vou ser professor quando eu já não poder mais dançar.

E aí eu dentro do processo, eu estava muito próximo de Vera e muito próximo de Rosangela, sempre. Na sala de aula, sempre dando assistência, sempre tive uma memoria muito boa, dos exercícios, e tinha uma facilidade para ter um entendimento da fisicalidade do exercício. Isso era um ponto positivo para mim, sem pretensão nenhuma, mesmo, de ensinar isso porque eu achava que estava muito além. Quando eu via Vera e via Rosangela, eu achava que uma coisa que é transcendente. Estava além de você ser professor. Uma coisa que para mim era muito difícil de alcançar.

Dentro do processo da Técnica Silvestre, eu estava muito próximo dela e Rosangela Silvestre. E por esta sempre próximo delas, e por algum motivo elas me traziam. Quando foi no intensivo que a gente estava com Lucimar, elas colocaram eu e Lucimar juntos no processo. As vezes eu dava aula, as vezes Lucimar. E sempre achava que era um lugar meio sagrado … aquele lugar que eu pensava que nunca estava preparado. Teve um momento que elas decidiram, "O momento é esse! Se você for esperar o momento, você nunca vai estar pronto." A descoberta, ela vai acontecendo todos os dias, como aluno, você vai em busca da descoberta sempre dessa forma.

Nos intensivos, eu fiquei responsável pelo Grupo 1. Eu só estava multiplicador de Técnica Silvestre no período do intensivo. Vera chegou para mim e disse, "Deko, as pessoas vem para Salvador, não tem uma referencia.

Você já esta aí, você está descobrindo as coisas, está fazendo coisas que são legais, agente tem trocado informações. Por que você não multiplicar isso?"

Foi neste momento que eu entendo o chamado. Ate então, eu não tinha entendido o chamado. Eu estava como professor em técnica no intensivo e isso para mim era confortável, e tinha o suporte delas, se tivesse algum problema eu tinha um suporte. Se tem alguma duvida, se tem alguma coisa, eu descobrir, eu estou perguntando, e a gente está sempre em comunicação.

Elas estavam ali. E mesmo de longe elas estão perto. Entender a necessidade do universo.

Page 61

2018 Interview with Rosangela in Portuguese

Music in Silvestre Technique

Existe um casamento do instrumento da pessoa que está tocando, com o corpo do bailarino que transmite uma sonorização no movimento. Movimento vem musical. Esse movimento musical faz o que o musico perceba essa musicalidade e dance esta musicalidade com instrumento. Então, as composições som também descobertas naquele momento cada um vai ter um processo. Eu trabalhei por alguns anos em universidades que eles têm cursos que preparam músicos para dança. E o que interessante, que esses músicos para a dança, eles não tocam são um instrumento só. Eles tocam alguns instrumentos. Eles também usam uma voz. E uma universidade que eu trabalhei muito, foi uma universidade em Boulder, Colorado, e lá tem músicos que são trainados para isso. Então para a Técnica Silvestre eles entendem o que trazer na musicalidade. Como agente tem também, Nei Sacramento, e varias músicos que passam por esse processo. Acaba, em que cada aula e uma musica. Uma musica que vem do comportamento do movimento e comportamento do bailarino com o movimento. E a muito tempo antes eu lembro que meu irmão, Marivaldo e meu irmão Paulo Cesar, criou um tema, e que o tema em que toda vez que agente fazia a conversas do corpo, os exercícios que chamamos de conversas é o diálogo. Então, tinha uma musicalidade de inicio, e depois ela variava. Essa coisa musical, nesse trabalho, ela é permitida ser descobertas. Ela abraça as expressões diversas de instrumentos. Pode ser, saxofone, percussão, flauta, bateria, congas ... o instrumento que te ver ali, vai ser o instrumento da musicalidade daquele dia. E a musicalidade, do próprio silencio. Porque o corpo movendo nos fazemos ate este tipo de prática, quando todo mundo parar, os músicos param de tocar, mas o musica não sumiu.

Page 63

2018 Interview with Vera Passos in Portuguese

MUSIC IN SILVESTRE TECHNIQUE

Eu comecei as aulas de técnica com Nei. Quando agente começou, ingressado quando Nei começou esse processo da musica primaria de som e movimento, muito antes de mim conhecer. Ele vem de uma família de artistas. Paco é coreografo, é pai delepraticamente quem crio Nei. A Técnica Silvestre em se, ela não tem uma ligação direto com um estilo musical. Ela é livre para trabalhar com qualquer estilo. E, não é todo mundo que tem esse presente para trabalhar com Nei. Eu fui presenteada com isso, porque ele veio para trabalhar comigo e nos desenvolvemos exercício por exercício dentro de uma musicadentro de uma qualidade musical, que é diferenciada. E por muitos anos, para cada exercício era uma musica diferente. Quando agente começou reconhecer aquela musica dentro do exercício, ele já estava afrente da gente. Ele já estava descobrindo outras coisas e ele começou a mudar a cada dia, para cada exercício era uma musicalidade diferente. Pra mim, esse era o melhor lugar para viver com musica. Nei ele é especialista em dançar o movimento com a musica.

Em janeiro, aconteceu uma aula que eu deixe um celular filmando, e Nei resolveu ficar exatamente na frente do celular. Então, eu capitei uma imagem muito linda. Porque, ele ficou na frente, e a imagem ficou entre as pernas de Nei. E todos dançando ali no mesmo lugar. Ele, a tempo inteiro dançando com agente! O sax faz "PAN!," ele faz "PAN!" com o corpo. Ele faz plié, ele salta. Ele fica dançando.

Eu estou trazendo esta musica primaria para toda minha pratica. Eu gosto muito deste lugar, é um lugar que não é certinho. Este lugar que é quadrado, onde os estudantes já esperam. Eu nunca gostei esse lugar da dança que o musico fala tudo que o bailarino tem que fazer. E quando ele não dar, o bailarino quer brigar. Eu acho que tem nuances, rítmicas, que estão são lindas—necessárias para os bailarinos desenvolver sua dança. Esse casamento da musica ia dança, onde um puxa o outro. E não somente a musica fica em cima do bailarino.

Para mim, hoje, é muito importante trabalhar com musica ao vivo, porque o corpo responde diferente e nos dar mais possibilidades dentro do processo. Não me importa o quanto eu irei ganhar, eu sempre vou levar um musico onde quer que eu vá. Para aula do Movimentos dos Orixás, para técnica, para composição, é muito importante ter musica ao vivo. Principalmente, musico da terra que entenda da musica, da dança, da cultura. Não é o mesmo para ter alguém que ainda está estudando. Musica é especial, e tem que ter confiança na musica.

Page 83

2018 Interview with Vera Passos in Portuguese

SILVESTRE TECHNIQUE AND CHOREOGRAPHY

As vezes pessoas perguntam se quando estou coreografando se vão ver a Técnica Silvestre. Eu respondo, o que é feito em sala de aula você não vai encontrar. Pessoas não podem pensar que eu vou colocar elemento água, terra ou fogo ... porque não vai encontrar. A técnica vai funcionando como o meio da coisa. Mas o que eu vou mostrar no show é a dança. E as vezes não tem nenhum elemento que apareça. Mas a técnica está ali semeando aquele processo.

Page 234

2018 Interview with Deko Alves in Portuguese

PEDAGOGY OF SILVESTRE TECHNIQUE

Nas aulas, quando Vera dava cursos regulares, tinha sempre um momento que ela pegava os alunos que estavam com ela para muito tempo, e sempre tinha um momento que agente podia pegar aquele entendimento e partilhar com os nossos colegas. Existe o momento que ela chamava um para começar a aula. Acho que também era uma forma de analisar o que o aluno também tem aprendido, e se doar também. Isso já era um despertar de Vera, para essa coisa do aluno; o olhar do aluno em multiplicar o saber.

Page 235

2018 Interview with Vera Passos in Portuguese

HARMONIZING

A minha forma de sala de aula e bem diferente da forma de Rosangela. E que as duas formas se somam e se conectam. Exatamente, naquele lugar que ela tem mais sede, que eu chego, e também, nesse meu lugar de resseca-mento que ela chega para harmonizar. Eu e Rosangela temos conexão e confiança. Neste espaço uma completa a outra. Neste espaço que per-mitimos transformação. Não transformar porque quer transformar, mas, porque a vida transforma.

O próprio lugar que a dança esta, de mudança, e preciso acompan-har. Agente não pode ficar por traz. E esse lugar que fala por mundo que a técnica está viva. Que ela não vai congelar. Dessa forma, mais pessoas estão interessadas nesse processoonde não está fechado.

Page 235

2018 Interview with Jenifer Ferraro in Portuguese

PEDAGOGY

1. Quem participa desta técnica? Quem são seus alunos e por que acham que eles vêm?

Jovens e adultos de diferentes idades e interesses participam. Alguns chegam pelo treinamento físico e outros, porque consideram uma forma de se reconectar com o corpo físico e espiritual.

2. O que você acha que é necessário para ser um professor eficaz da técnica silvestre?

Acredito que o compromisso de continuar estudando e praticando a técnica além do ensino é necessário. Continue cursando a aula, não deixe de ser estudante, conheça a anatomia do corpo e as diferentes dinâmicas com as quais o corpo pode se mover. Estar em contato com a natureza, com a essência de cada elemento trazido em aula e como a natureza pode nos inspirar. Também esteja conectado consigo mesmo na hora de dar a aula. Há mais momentos físicos e outros mais espirituais em nossa vida e eu acho que é bom trazê-los para a sala de aula para serem inspirados e capazes de compartilhar com os alunos.

3. Qual é a importância da música na técnica?

No começo eu achei que era fundamental, mas depois de vários anos de prática e agora ensinando, acho que pode complementar muito bem o trabalho físico ou pode não estar lá. O trabalho em silêncio também é interessante para perceber os ritmos internos e como o corpo lida com os sons do ambiente também.

4. Quando ou como você decidiu se tornar um professor de técnica silvestre? Por que você tomou essa decisão?

Quando eu terminei a minha certificação em Salvador intensivo e seminários que tirei em Buenos Aires, comecei a notar como muitas das pessoas que frequentam os seminários que eles queriam continuar a formação na arte e foi lá que eu abri um cronograma para dois meses para ver como eu me sentia ensinando, e percebi que queria dar a eles continuamente. Então eu abri um grupo em minha casa, eu tenho um espaço e então um novo lugar chegou onde eu estou ensinando atualmente. A verdade é que não foi uma decisão muito consciente no começo, eu me deixei ir, eu fluía e então senti que queria trabalhar com essa técnica por um longo tempo. Hoje escolho continuar trabalhando até que meu corpo não possa mais se mexer.

5. Como a técnica influenciou você, em sua dança, em sua vida?

Isso mudou totalmente a minha maneira de ver o mundo, da dança e da vida. Eu me permiti sentir e me mover em conexão com meus sentimentos e minhas dúvidas. Eu sinto e acredito que esta técnica tem tudo que o ser humano precisa, não deixar o corpo de lado, mas sem se tornar mecânico, integrar as emoções e a conexão espiritual que cada um pode ter além das religiões. E trabalhar com símbolos da natureza e universais nos aproxima de todos os tipos de pessoas e idades. Foi uma mudança retumbante na minha vida.

6. Como ensinar esta técnica é diferente de ensinar outros estilos de dança?

É diferente porque não só atravessa o corpo físico, mas também é importante se deixar passar pelo que é percebido na aula, tanto como aluno quanto como professor. Trabalhar os limites impostos a nós pela mente e ver como os corpos evoluem física e emocionalmente é maravilhoso.

7. O que os alunos recebem através do estudo da técnica?

Como estudante, sinto que toda vez que vou para a aula é diferente, nunca é o mesmo, não importa quantas vezes os exercícios sejam os mesmos. E como professora, tento que os alunos também reservem um momento para se conectarem com seu corpo e possam sentir como o corpo muda em cada encontro. Como isso se torna mais perceptivo e receptivo.

8. Qual é o significado do vocabulário encontrado na técnica silvestre? Verticalidade, Quatro Eelementos, & Possibilidades:

Para mim, o vocabulário foi revelador porque, sendo os fundamentos da técnica selvagem, eles diferem de outras técnicas. Saber o que queremos dizer com verticalidade, a posição correta do corpo, alinhamento com os nossos centros de energia ea ligação que temos com a terra eo universo parece tão simples, mas mantê-lo é complexo. Os quatro elementos permitem-me indagar sobre as diferentes qualidades e qualidades de movimento, velocidades e ritmos. Além de poder viajar com visualização e sentir como a natureza nos rodeia e como isso é maravilhoso. Acho que é isso que nos leva a perceber que existem possibilidades, mover, entender, ver, pensar, enxergar o mundo e poder incluí-los todos em uma aula. Nos faz viver em harmonia com o meio ambiente e com nós mesmos.

Bibliography

Alves, D. (2018, August 10). Interview: Silvestre Technique. (T. Williams, Interviewer).

Armstrong, P. (1999). The Aesthetic Escape Hatch: Carnaval, Blocos Afros, and the Mutations of Baianidade Under the Signs of Globalisation and Re-Africanisation. *Journal of Iberian and Latin American Research*, 65–98.

Assaan-ANU, H. Y. (2010). *Grasping the Root of Divine Power: A Spiritual Healer's Guide to African Culture, Orisha Religion, OBI Divination, Spiritual Cleanses, Spiritual Growth and Development, Ancient Wisdom, and Mind Power.* Scotts Valley: Create Space Publishing.

Assaan-ANU, H. Y. (2014, November 7). Witches, Manhood, Family Relationships, Orisha- Foundational Friday. *Enlightenment and Transformation.* New York City, New York: Blogtalk Radio.

Bagwell, O. (Director). (1999). *Great Performances: Dance in America: A Hymn for Alvin Ailey* [Motion Picture].

Browning, B. (2007). Conversations with Rosangela Silvestre and Steve Coleman. *Women & Performance: A Journal of Feminist Theory*, 171–184.

Burris, V. (1982). The Dialectic of Women's Opression: Notes on the Relation Between Capitalism and Patriarchy. *Berkeley Journal of Sociology, 27*, 51–74. Retrieved January 20, 2020, from www.jstor.org/stable/41035317.

Cabiao, H. (2011, April 21). *Movimento Negro Unificado.* Retrieved from Online Encyclopedia of Significant People and Places in Global African History: BlackPast: https://www.blackpast.org/global-african-history/movimento-negro-unificado-founded-1978/.

Chu, L. (2018, January 19). You Are What You (And Your Microbiome) Eat, Scientists Say. *Chicago Tribune.*

Crook, L. (1993). *Black Consciousness, Samba Reggae, and the Re-Africanization of Bahian Carnival Music in Brazil.* New York City: World of Music.

Csordas, T. (1995). *Embodiment and Experience: The Existential Ground of Culture and Self (Cambridge Studies in Medical Anthropology).* Cambridge: Cambridge University Press.

Daniel, Y. (2005). *Dancing Wisdom: Embodied Knowledge in Haitian Vodou, Cuban Yorùbá, and Bahian Candomblé.* Champaign: University of Illinois Press.

DK Publishing. (2014). *The Psychology Book.* London: Penguin.

Erkert, J. K. (2003). *Harnessing the Wind: The Art of Teaching Modern Dance.* Champaign: Human Kinetics, Inc.

Ferraro, J. (2018, November 27). Interview on Being a Silvestre Technique Instructor. (T. Williams, Interviewer)

Gottschild, B. (2018, February 9). Pew Fellow of the Week: An Interview with Writer and Cultural Scholar Brenda Dixon Gottschild. (T. P. Heritage, Interviewer).

Gottschild, B. D. (2017, October 2). Reclamations! Lecture on Black Feminist Performance with Brenda Dixon Gottschild. (J. O. Kosoko, Interviewer).

Graden, D. T. (2006). *From Slavery to Freedom in Brazil: Bahia, 1835–1900.* Alburquerque: University of New Mexico.

Griffin, A., & Parkerson, M. (Directors). (1996). *A Litany for Survival: The Life and Work of Audre Lorde* [Motion Picture]. New York City: Third World Newsreel.

Grimassi, R. (2009). *The Cauldron of Memory: Retrieving Ancestral Knowledge & Wisdom.* Woodbury: Llewellyn Publications.

Hailes, A. (2014, February 1). Hailes Reflection on Studying Silvestre Technique. (T. Williams, Interviewer).

Hazzard-Donald, K. (2011). Hoodoo Religion and American Dance Traditions: Rethinking the Ring Shout. *The Journal of Pan African Studies,* 194–212.

Hoffman-Carter, S. (2014, February 1). Interview of Practice & Reflection. (T. Williams, Interviewer).

Hudson, R. A., & Library of Congress. (1998). *Brazil: A Coutnry Study.* Washington, D.C.: Federal Reserach Division, Library of Congress.

Ito, T. (1999, January). *Brazil: A History of Political and Economic Turmoil.* Retrieved from Washington Post: https://www.washingtonpost.com/wp-srv/inatl/longterm/brazil/overview.htm.

Judith, A. (2012). *Wheels of Life: A User's Guide to the Chakra System.* Woodbury: Llewellyn Publications.

Kowal, R. J., Siegmund, G., & Martin, R. (2017). *The Oxford Handbook of Dance and Politics.* New York City: Oxford University Press.

Kraay, H. (1998). *Afro-Brazilian Culture and Politics: Bahia, 1970s-1990s.* Abingdon: Routledge.

Lynch, G. (2016, September 12). *Dance and Spiritual Expression: Rhythmic Bodily Movement and the Religious Life.* Retrieved from HeadLINES: The Official Blog of Alonzo King LINES Ballet: https://blog.linesballet.org/2016/09/12/lines-ballet-bfa-program-celebrates-its-10th-anniversary-speaking-with-faculty-and-alumni/.

Manning, E., & Massumi, B. (2014). *Thought in the Act: Passages in the Ecology of Experience.* Minneapolis: University of Minnesota Press.

Martin, R. (1998). *Critical Moves: Dance Studies in Theory and Politics.* Durham: Duke University Press.

Maslow, A. H. (1972). *The Farther Reaches of Human Nature.* New York City: Viking Press.

Matsushima, C. (2014, February 1). Matsushima Reflection on Studying Silvestre Technique. (T. Williams, Interviewer).

Meade, L., Symington, A., & Oliver, E. (1895–1896). Ancestral Memory. *Atalanta: The Victorian Magazine, Volume IX,* p. 114.

Mier, B. (2015, May 21). *A Brief Look at Brazilian Social Movements.* Retrieved from Center for Economic and Policy Research: http://cepr.net/blogs/the-americas-blog/a-brief-look-at-brazilian-social-movements.

Mori, L. (2020, January 16). Linguagem Interview. (T.Williams, Interviewer).

Mosston, M., & Ashworth, S. (2001). *Teaching Physical Education (5th Edition).* San Francisco: Benjamin Cummings.

MST, F. o. (2003, February 12). *History of the MST.* Retrieved from Movimentos dos Trabalhadores Rurais Sem Terra: Friends of the MST: https://www.mstbrazil.org/content/history-mst.

Parés, L. L. (2013). *The Formation of Candomblé: Vodun History and Ritual in Brazil (Latin America in Translation).* Chapel Hill: The University of North Carolina Press.

Passos, V. (2018, August 10). Silvestre Technique Interview. (T. Williams, Interviewer).

Prandi, Reginaldo. *Mitologia Dos Orixás.* Illustrations by Pedro Rafael. São Paulo, BA: Companhia Das Lettas, 2001., n.d.

Price, L. (July 10, 1962). Lucien Price to Ted Shawn. *Shawn Collection, Folder 39. NYPL.*

Reclamations! Lectures on Black Feminist Performance, c. b. (2017, October 2). *The Black Dancing Body As A Measure of Culture.* (B. D. Gottschild, Performer) Princeton University's Lewis Center for the Arts, Princeton, NJ, USA.

Reiter, B. (2009). A Genealogy of Black Organizing in Brazil. *Revista Nera*, 49–62.

Schneider, M. S. (1995). *A Beginner's Guide to Constructing the Universe: Mathematical Archetypes of Nature, Art, and Science.* New York City: HarperPerennial.

Sears, S. O. (2018, July 9). Body-in-Nature Training Interview. (T. Williams, Interviewer).

Sharma, S. N. (2013). *Best Thoughts and Quotes of the World.* Scotts Valley: CreateSpace Publishing.

Shostrom, E. L. (1974). *EdITS Manual for the Personal Orientation Inventory, POI.* San Diego: Educational and Industrial Testing Service.

Silvestre, R. (2018, November 3). Interview in Toronto. (T. Williams, Interviewer).

Silvestre Technique Summer Intensive Performance. January 28, 2011. Escola Da Danca. Salvador, BA.

Silvestre Summer Intensive. Silvestre Technique Summer Intensive Performance. February 2, 2013. Espaco Xisto Bahia. Salvador, BA.

Skidmore, T. E. (2010). *Brazil: Five Centuries of Change.* Oxford: Oxford University Press.

Stewart, V., Wigman, M., Graham, M., & Weidman, C. (1935). *Modern Dance.* New York City: New York, E. Weyhe.

Tamura, Y. (2014, February 19). Interview & Reflections Via Email. (T. Williams, Interviewer).

Tamura, Y. (2018, November 15). Scheduled Interview Via Email. (T. Williams, Interviewer).

The Training. (2015, June 25). Retrieved from Silvestre Technique Training: www.silvestretraining.com/thetraining.

Thompson, K. D. (2014). *Ring Shout, Wheel About: The Racial Politics of Music and Dance in North American Slavery.* Champaign: University of Illinois Press.

Warburton, E. C. (2011). Of Meanings and Movements: Re-Languaging Embodiment in Dance Phenomenology and Cognition. *Dance Research Journal*, 65–84.

Wilde, O., & Pearson, H. (1950). *Essays.* London: Methuen Publishing Ltd.

Williams, Tamara. "Personal Journal Notes Including Quotes from Rosangela During Intensives and Workshops." 2011–2014 in Salvador, BA. October 23–26, 2013 in Port of Spain Trinidad. November 23–25, 2014 in Morro De São Paulo, BA.

Wrigglesworth, J. (1997). *Energy and Life (Modules in Life Sciences).* Boca Raton: CRC Press.

Index